1924

THE YEAR THAT MADE HITLER

1924

PETER ROSS RANGE

LITTLE, BROWN AND COMPANY

New York   Boston   London

Little, Brown and Company
Hachette Book Group
1290 Avenue of the Americas, New York, NY 10104
littlebrown.com

First Edition: January 2016

Little, Brown and Company is a division of Hachette Book Group, Inc. The Little, Brown name and logo are trademarks of Hachette Book Group, Inc.

The publisher is not responsible for websites (or their content) that are not owned by the publisher.

The Hachette Speakers Bureau provides a wide range of authors for speaking events. To find out more, go to hachettespeakersbureau.com or call (866) 376-6591.

The photograph on the jacket, which shows Hitler practicing rhetorical poses in 1926 or 1927, captures the bombastic speaking style he had developed by 1923.

ISBN 978-0-316-38403-2
LCCN 2015952383

10 9 8 7 6 5 4 3 2 1

RRD-C

Printed in the United States of America

For
Christopher and Shannon

The Germans have been liberated from Hitler but they will never be able to get rid of him.

— EBERHARD JÄCKEL, HISTORIAN, 1979

How it happened that Hitler came to power is still the most important question of nineteenth- and twentieth-century German history, if not of all German history.

— HEINRICH AUGUST WINKLER, HISTORIAN, 2000

Auschwitz is a German wound that never heals.

— GABOR STEINGART, JOURNALIST AND PUBLISHER, 2015

Contents

1924

The Unfathomable Ascent

*"The failure of the putsch was perhaps the greatest good
fortune of my life."*[1]

—ADOLF HITLER

On the evening of November 8, 1923, with a coming snowfall in
the air, Adolf Hitler, a thirty-four-year-old politician known for his
hot rhetoric, forced his way into a crowded beer hall on the south-
east side of Munich. Surrounded by three bodyguards, two of them
in military gear, Hitler held a pistol in one hand. With "his eyes
opened wide and looking like a drunken fanatic," the unimposing,
five-foot nine-inch Hitler tried to interrupt a speech by the head of
the Bavarian government.[2] But he could not make himself heard.
Climbing onto a chair, he raised his arm and fired a shot into the
high coffered ceiling. "Silence!" he shouted. The three thousand
audience members fell "dead still," one witness recalled. Then the
man on the chair made a shocking announcement.

"The national revolution has begun! The building is surrounded by six hundred heavily armed men! No one is allowed to leave." Behind Hitler, a platoon of steel-helmeted men under the command of Captain Hermann Göring dragged a heavy machine gun into the beer hall entrance.

Thus began Adolf Hitler's infamous beer hall coup d'état of 1923. Called a *putsch* in German, the attempted overthrow had crumbled within seventeen hours. Fifteen of Hitler's men, four police troops, and one bystander had been killed. Two days later, Hitler was caught and carried off to Landsberg Prison, thirty-eight miles west of Munich. He was imprisoned for the next thirteen months, from November 11, 1923, to December 20, 1924.

The failed putsch—an effort to unseat both the Bavarian and German governments—was a high-profile defeat for the budding Nazi leader and his small but radical movement. Hitler's year in prison—virtually all of 1924—was the price he paid for his premature lunge for power. He not only had botched the biggest gamble a politician can make, but also had lost face: he was dismissed by some as an extremist clown who had led his followers into disaster and death.

Yet, by the time he was released from prison, Hitler had converted his plunge into disgrace and obscurity into a springboard for success. The aborted coup d'état, it turned out, was the best thing that could have happened to him, and to his undisguised plans to become Germany's dictator. Had Hitler not spent 1924 in Landsberg Prison, he might never have emerged as the redefined and recharged politician who ultimately gained control of Germany, inflicted war on the world, and perpetrated the Holocaust. The year that brought Hitler down—late 1923 through late 1924—and that by rights should have ended his career, was in fact the hinge moment in Hitler's transformation from impetuous revolutionary to patient political player with a long view of gaining power.

How did this transformation occur? How did Hitler make strategic use of his failure? For one thing, the man knew a good publicity opportunity when he saw it; he brazenly turned his monthlong, widely watched trial for treason into a political soapbox, catapulting himself from Munich beer-hall rabble-rouser to nationally known political figure. A prosecution for high treason that could have put Hitler out of political circulation long enough for his movement and his charisma to disappear instead became what many jurists regarded as an embarrassment to the German justice system—and that historians see as a turnaround moment in Hitler's climb to power.

Soon after recovering from his initial dark moments in Landsberg, Hitler turned his long months out of the political fray into a time of learning, self-reflection, and clarification of his views. In prison, he had a captive audience of forty men, his fellow culprits in the unsuccessful putsch, and he often treated them to long lectures from his writings and busy mind. But he needed to speak to the world. He was bursting with the urge to write, to capture his political philosophy for his followers, to cast into the permanence of print his beliefs and increasingly certain dogmas. For long days and late into the night, he banged away on a small portable typewriter to produce what became the bible of Nazism, an autobiographical and political manifesto called *Mein Kampf*. Published after his release from prison, the book soon became Hitler's ticket to intellectual respectability within his own movement. He called his time in prison "my university education at state expense."[3]

His year of "education" changed Hitler's strategic vision, and it changed him. From a frustrated and depressed man stricken with self-doubt (suicide and death were repeated refrains during and after the putsch attempt), Hitler became, during his time behind bars, a man of overweening self-assurance and radically fixed beliefs on how to save Germany from its assorted ills. He recast the fatal march he had led on November 9, 1923, into heroic martyrdom. At a safe remove from everyday politics, Hitler cunningly allowed the Nazi Party to squabble and self-destruct so he could later call it back to life on his own terms, remade in his own image and decisively under his thumb. Reenergized and obsessively messianic, the post-prison Hitler was ready for the march to high office. The brutal ideologue Alfred Rosenberg, one of Hitler's closest cronies at the time of the putsch who later became Hitler's state minister for the occupied eastern territories, said simply: "November ninth, 1923, gave birth to January thirtieth, 1933" — the day Hitler became chancellor of Germany.[4]

In the voluminous study of Adolf Hitler, the emphasis has understandably been on the twelve harrowing years of the Third Reich, 1933 to 1945. Yet the preceding fourteen years, 1919 to 1933, are critical for comprehending Hitler's political rise and the Nazi nightmare. "How it happened that Hitler came to power is still the most important question of nineteenth- and twentieth-century German history, if not of all German history," wrote historian Heinrich August Winkler.[5] It's a question that continues to baffle and haunt the world. Even Hans Frank, one of Hitler's closest confidants, writing his mea culpa memoir during the Nuremberg trial in 1946, called Hitler's climb "the unfathomable ascent."[6] But we keep trying to fathom it. How did the unschooled former army private, with only a coruscating voice and an extraordinary belief in his calling as Germany's savior, turn himself into the leader of millions? And what did the millions find so compelling about the loud little man with the quick mind and convenient certainties regarding history and destiny? How did Hitler, fairly driven from the field in 1923 by his delusions of grandeur and overreach, reinvent himself in a prison cell as fated for greatness and leadership? For answers, we continue to turn the Rubik's Cube of history, looking again for clues and insights.

Hitler's fourteen developmental years fall into two main periods. The first is Hitler's "apprentice" years, 1919 to 1923, when the newly self-discovered politician was finding his feet and learning the polemical game, using fists, elbows, and words to reach for power through incendiary rhetoric and violent revolution. "From 1919 to 1923, I thought of nothing else but revolution," said Hitler.[7]

The second period, 1925 to 1933, often called the "fighting" years, begins with Hitler's relaunch of the Nazi Party in the same beer hall where his putsch had failed. It ends after eight years of fierce political combat, with Hitler's 1933 takeover of the chancellery in Berlin.

Between those two key developmental periods lies 1924, Hitler's year in prison. Despite its obvious historical significance, this is one of the least written about and least understood moments in Nazi history. It's also the point when the arc of Hitler's political trajectory bends, the pivotal moment that forms the connective tissue between two distinctly different phases, the revolutionary and the electoral. Nineteen twenty-four shifted Hitler's focus, hardened his beliefs, and set the stage for his remarkable comeback after a seemingly insurmountable defeat. That period is the subject of this book.

To make sense of Hitler's transformational year in prison, we must first understand the putsch that put him there. To understand the putsch requires a look at the crazed Bavarian political scene in the first ten feverish months of 1923. To grasp Bavarian politics means pulling back the curtain on the strange political carnival of the 1920s Weimar Republic.

These forces set the scene for the year that made Hitler.

CHAPTER ONE

Discovering the Mission

"The First World War made Hitler possible."
— SIR IAN KERSHAW, 1998[1]

For months, Munich had swirled with rumors of a coming putsch. In autumn 1923, the magic word in the crowded beer halls and leafy outdoor cafés of the Bavarian capital was *losschlagen*.[2] In German, *losschlagen* means to attack, to strike out, to let loose—to make it happen. When, everyone wanted to know, would Adolf Hitler and his Nazis *losschlagen*? Or, for that matter, when would the established powers in Bavaria—a strange mix of civilian-military leadership embodied in an unofficial ruling triumvirate—*losschlagen*? Somebody had to do something. Hitler's hope was to stage a march on "that den of iniquity," Berlin, to unseat the government of the Weimar Republic; it seemed like a fine idea to most Bavarians at the time, reported Wilhelm Hoegner, a Social Democratic member of the Bavarian parliament. In a time of turmoil and uncertainty, the probability of a putsch had "become an idée fixe" in the Bavarian capital, he wrote.[3] Hitler noted: "People were shouting it from the rooftops."[4]

Five years after the end of World War I, Germany was experiencing upheaval, social disorder, and steady descent. The war had shifted the political planet on its axis. Centuries-old monarchies had fallen. A world not significantly altered since the 1815 Congress of Vienna had split and fissured. Boundaries were redrawn, populations shifted under new sovereignty. Germany had lost its overseas possessions and was thrown out of the great game of colonization. In Russia, a Communist revolution had seized the country. And the Weimar Republic—Germany's first attempt at full democracy—was on constantly shaky legs. It had already gone through seven chancellors (prime ministers) and nine government cabinets.[5] The sudden 1918 postwar shift from Berlin's four-hundred-year-old Hohenzollern monarchy to an untried parliamentary system—a revolution from the top—had never been fully accepted by the far-right nationalists, by many in the military, and by parts of the political elite. Even the republic's first head of state, President Friedrich Ebert, had been ambivalent: the Social Democratic Party leader had wanted a constitutional monarchy in the British style to follow Kaiser Wilhelm II's abdication in November 1918; he opposed a simple republic with no unifying hereditary figure at the top. "You have no right to proclaim the republic!" he raged at Philipp Scheidemann, the politician who did just that from a window of the Reichstag (the German parliament) on November 9, 1918.[6]

In the early 1920s, a crashing economy drove the longing among some groups for the return of a strongman—maybe even of the monarchy itself. Nineteen twenty-three was Germany's worst year since the crushing 1918 defeat in war. The country's hyperinflated currency reached 4.2 *trillion* marks per dollar—a loaf of bread cost 200 billion marks, one egg about 80 billion marks;[7] a theater ticket sometimes could be had not for money but for two eggs. Worse, people's savings were destroyed, and farmers, despite a bumper crop, refused to release their produce for prices that were nearly meaningless by the next day. The food shortages sparked food riots. The German government reacted to the inflationary spiral by simply printing more and more money; people sometimes carried it in wheelbarrows to go shopping.

Internally, Germany was riven by deep and bitter political antagonisms. Extremists on the left (Communists) and on the right (nationalists and race-based parties called *völkisch*) competed for space with numerous parties in between. In 1920, a right-wing coup d'état led by Walther von Lüttwitz and Wolfgang Kapp—it became known as the Kapp Putsch—had taken Berlin for four days, chasing the government from town before falling apart. Political violence was rampant, beginning with the 1919 assassinations of the Communist leaders (then called Spartacists) Karl Liebknecht and Rosa Luxemburg. Between 1919 and 1922, right-wing groups committed more than three hundred fifty political murders, adding to a mood of "moral indifference to violence" that characterized the early years of the Weimar Republic.[8] A right-wing hit squad called Organisation Consul took credit for the assassinations of Matthias Erzberger, the German politician who signed the 1918 World War I armistice, and Walther Rathenau, Germany's foreign minister and a Jew.

Discontent was also fueled by Germany's uncertain place in the world. The loss of Alsace-Lorraine to France and key parts of Upper Silesia to Poland through the 1919 Treaty of Versailles rankled most Germans. Still more, they were enraged by the occupation by mainly French forces of the Rhineland beginning in 1918 and, more recently, in Germany's industrial heartland, the Ruhr region. In

January 1923, Belgian and French troops—six full divisions,[9] some of them Senegalese soldiers from the French African colonies—occupied the coal-and-steel-producing Ruhr area, which included the key cities of Düsseldorf, Duisburg, and Essen. The incursion was officially a reprisal for Germany's failure to meet postwar reparations payments, but many believed that French prime minister Raymond Poincaré was mainly looking for a convenient excuse to carve out a buffer zone along Germany's western border with France, Belgium, and the Netherlands, while gaining access to German coal fields. This aggressive rearrangement of territory was opposed by the British. Since a large part of the overdue reparations payment was supposed to be made in coal and wooden telegraph poles, one British politician groused: "No more damaging use of wood has occurred since the Trojan Horse."[10]

Either way, the upheavals and uncertainties generated an atmosphere ripe for revolution, putsch, and violence. The Berlin government called for passive resistance to the French invaders; workers walked off their jobs. Some Germans mounted active resistance and sabotage; some were caught, tried, and executed by French firing squads. A right-wing saboteur named Albert Leo Schlageter, captured and shot, became a national martyr and a Nazi hero. The political defiance felt good to the Germans but had disastrous economic results: all-important industrial production came nearly to a standstill and unemployment was rampant. To cover lost salaries and benefits, the government resorted to printing even more money, further weakening the hyperinflated currency. Hunger strikes broke out in Berlin, Hamburg, Cologne, and other cities, forcing German police and troops to fire on starving Germans.

The rapid post–World War I demobilization had flooded the labor market with more than five million men, many without jobs or prospects, but all trained in one skill: fighting. And they had plenty to fight about. People felt their culture, politics, and social structures were at risk, driven by centrifugal forces they could not control. The Weimar Republic's "normal state was crisis," wrote historian Gordon Craig.[11] Insulted and humiliated by the "sole war guilt" clause of the 1919 Treaty of Versailles, Germans were saddled with a $12.5 billion reparations obligation they felt was ruinous. Even the onset of the Golden Twenties—a flowering of avant-garde culture, mainly in Berlin—was seen in many parts of Germany, especially Bavaria, as proof of decadence and disintegration in the capital.

Nowhere were these issues more hotly debated than in Bavaria. Home to Hitler's Nazis and numerous other bitterly nationalistic parties and groups, Bavaria was the unruly renegade in the German federation, constantly making special demands, refusing to accept national rulings, and threatening separation or partial secession by establishing its own currency, postal system, or railroad network. The second-largest state after Prussia, Bavaria was the Weimar Republic's bête noire, the putsch capital of Germany. The Free State, as it called itself, had suffered through uprising and turmoil since 1918, when a left-wing march led by a shaggy-bearded intellectual named Kurt Eisner had successfully chased the Bavarian king out of his palace overnight. Within three months, after a failed attempt at socialist government, Eisner had been assassinated on a Munich sidewalk. More mayhem followed. To the horror of middle-class Munichers, a Bavarian Soviet Republic held power for three weeks, only to be ousted in another spasm of violence involving right-wing Freikorps troops sent from outside Bavaria. Atrocities were committed on both sides.

Ever since, Bavaria had been leaning hard to the right, attracting more and more militant nationalists and potential revolutionaries like Hitler and his anti-democratic Nazi Party. The revolutionaries were also anti-revolutionary; they refused to accept the legitimacy of the November 1918 republican revolution. "If I stand here as a revolutionary," Hitler would later remark, "I also stand against revolution and [political] crime."[12] Hitler, along with many others on the radical right, called the revolutionaries of 1918 "the November criminals." To riled-up members of the *Frontgemeinschaft*—the frontline brotherhood that had fought so long in the World War I trenches—it was the Berlin civilians who had stabbed them in the back. "Unbeaten on the battlefield" was their motto. One of their chief heroes, General Erich Ludendorff, the great strategist of World War I, had also moved from Berlin to Bavaria, where he drifted into hard-core, race-based politics. Bavaria even gave sanctuary to Captain Hermann Ehrhardt, a leader of the Kapp Putsch who was wanted for arrest by the national government in Berlin. With the Berlin governments often dominated by Social Democrats—considered Marxists by the conservative Bavarians—Munich became the favored stomping grounds of the *völkisch* parties, a movement based on pro-German, anti-Semitic racism.* Pushing a hard line, a new conservative government in 1920 announced that Bavaria would become "a bastion of order"—an enclave of peace and respectability, especially for right-wing parties, in the morass of leftism that seemed to dominate the rest of Germany. Bavaria was, as always, a land apart.

---

* *Völkisch* is very hard to define and almost untranslatable into English. The word has been rendered as popular, populist, people's, racial, racist, ethnic-chauvinist, nationalistic, communitarian (for Germans only), conservative, traditional, Nordic, romantic—and it means, in fact, all of those. The *völkisch* political ideology ranged from a sense of German superiority to a spiritual resistance to "the evils of industrialization and the atomization of modern man," wrote scholar David Jablonsky. But its central component, as Harold J. Gordon, Jr., noted, was always racism.

*   *   *

For Hitler, Bavaria was a kind of heaven. A born Austrian, Hitler had grown up in the provincial town of Linz. But he spent five formative years, from age eighteen to twenty-four, in Vienna, the Austrian capital. There, he lived as a failed artist and drifter. Rejected twice by the Austrian Academy of the Fine Arts and lacking a high school diploma, Hitler was from 1908 to 1913 reduced to scratching out a living by drawing or painting postcard-style scenes for tourists, selling his wares on the Viennese streets or to small art dealers, mainly Jews.[13] He was downwardly mobile, moving from a cheap shared room to a shabby single room to two different men's shelters (one of them partially funded by well-off Jewish families). In autumn 1909, he apparently became a vagrant, spending at least a few miserable nights in twenty-four-hour cafés and on park benches, later claiming "frostbite on fingers, hands and feet" as a result.[14] Partly because of these privations, Hitler called Vienna "the hardest but most thorough school of my life."[15]

Politically, Hitler became steeped in the frothing nationalist and anti-Semitic politics of prewar Vienna—a city with a prosperous, well-established Jewish elite, plus a more recent torrent of poor Jewish immigrants fleeing pogroms in the East. Impressed by the political style of Vienna's radically anti-Jewish mayor, Karl Lueger, Hitler also became an adherent of the Pan-German movement promoted years earlier by Austrian Georg Ritter von Schönerer. Schönerer was a rabid nationalist and anti-Semite who believed all German-speaking peoples belonged together in a single Greater Germany. Schönerer felt that German speakers, although they were the ruling class in the Austro-Hungarian empire, were being marginalized because they were outnumbered by non-Germans—Czechs, Slavs, and Magyars. In that same spirit, Hitler deplored what he called "Austria's Slavization" by the Hapsburg royalty.[16]

Young Hitler, now twenty, was horrified by the sight of

incomprehensible, multilingual debates, with occasional cross-cultural screaming, in the polyglot parliament in Vienna.[17] He immersed himself in the teeming city's German-nationalist newspapers, proselytizing pamphlets and extremist pulp like *Ostara,* a racist periodical, that Hitler almost certainly bought or picked up free in the "cheap people's café" that he said he frequented. He developed a militant aversion to Marxism—"a tool for the destruction of the nation state and the creation of Jewish world tyranny,"[18] Hitler called it—and to Austria's Social Democratic Party. He rejected the party's focus on organized labor and international working-class solidarity rather than on race-based nationalism, though he later claimed to have learned his own successful combination of propaganda and force ("terror") from the Socialists.[19] After a year of what he called "tranquil observation," Hitler rejected parliamentary democracy as a fatally flawed form of government that could only lead to mob rule from the left. "Today's Western democracy is the forerunner of Marxism," he wrote.

Hitler began to regard as anathema all forces on the left, and to associate Jews with the power and growth of these forces. His first truly anti-Semitic feelings, he claimed, were aroused by the sudden notice of an Eastern Jew on a Vienna street—"an apparition in a black caftan and black hair locks."[20] Since only a blind person could not have noticed Orthodox Jews all over Vienna at the time, this smacks of a stylized eureka moment to dramatize Hitler's developmental tale. Yet while most historians believe this anecdote is made up or drawn from numerous experiences, many accept Hitler's general assertion that his obsessive, political anti-Semitism began in Vienna[21]—the view he would put forth in *Mein Kampf* and during his 1924 treason trial. Yet others argue that, for lack of corroborating evidence to support his version of events, Hitler's anti-Semitism only became "manifest, radical and active," as historian Othmar

Plöckinger put it, after World War I in Munich. In their view, Hitler's elaborate description of his politicization during his Vienna period was fabricated to fit the invented image of a naive young man reacting to real conditions, not the reality of an aimless war veteran looking for work as a politician. In this interpretation, Hitler only seized on anti-Semitism "as the winning horse in the existing political environment," notes historian Roman Töppel.[22] But that gets ahead of the story.

In May 1913, after five hard years in the Austrian capital and after receiving a small inheritance on his twenty-fourth birthday, Hitler left Vienna for Munich—the fulfillment of his dream to live in an all-German environment surrounded by monumental architecture and a spirit of artistic creativity. Munich became the place to which Hitler was "more attached...than any other spot in the world," he claimed.[23] "This time before [World War I] was by far the happiest and most contented period of my life."[24] Hitler later claimed to have moved to Germany "mainly for political reasons"—his dislike of the Austro-Hungarian hybrid state. But relocating to Munich appealed to Hitler for another reason: he was trying to stay one step ahead of Austrian authorities who wanted to draft him into their army, where he would have to serve three years on active duty followed by seven years in the reserves and two more in the national guard.

In Munich, the city he would now consider his true home for the rest of his life, the poorly educated Hitler was again without real work. Again, he sketched and painted postcards and tourist scenes for sale on the streets and in Munich's raucous beer halls. Again, he lived alone in a simple, cheap sublet room. Again, he was a marginal figure without personal or professional prospects. Then Hitler's fortunes took an even worse turn. In January 1914, the Austrian draft board caught up with Hitler and demanded his appearance in Linz for military induction. He was even arrested for one night. Hitler dodged around with pleas and letters. Finally, he arranged to report just across the Austrian border in Salzburg. There, to his immense relief, he failed the physical examination. The pallid and puny Adolf Hitler, future war maker and mass murderer, was pronounced "too weak" to be a medic and "unfit to handle weapons."[25] Hitler had, as so often happened during his developmental years, barely escaped a fate that might have kept him unknown and unfeared for life.

Ironically, it was another chance to join an army that changed Hitler's life in the opposite way. In June 1914, the assassination of Archduke Franz Ferdinand on the streets of Sarajevo, Bosnia, set the stage for war. In August 2014,[26] Hitler appears to have joined the war-fevered crowd of thousands gathered on Munich's Odeon Square—his joyful face was later identified in a mass photograph of the scene, though some believe his visage may have been doctored into the picture after the fact for political and propaganda purposes.[27] In any case, Hitler followed millions of young Germans into the military, leaving behind his life as a penniless drifter for that of a soldier. Hitler's enlistment took an extra day because, as an Austrian, he needed special permission from the Bavarian royal house to enlist. He said he wrote the king a letter and had a positive response from the royal chancellery within twenty-four hours. "His Majesty's cabinet office works fast," Hitler noted.[28] Doubts have been cast on this anecdote, too, but in any case, Hitler was quickly enlisted in the Bavarian army, part of the German armed forces then girding for war. This time, no one found him unfit for service. Once again, Hitler's life was changed by a single event, and a single letter, that would shape the course of history. "The First World War made Hitler possible," wrote historian Ian Kershaw.[29]

As part of the 16th Bavarian Reserve Infantry Regiment, Hitler spent four harsh years in the muddy trenches of the western front as a foot messenger, running orders from headquarters to the front lines, participating in numerous engagements, including the brutal battles at Ypres, Belgium, and on the Marne in France. Running to and from the trenches was extremely dangerous duty punctuated by relaxed moments at the rear headquarters units (frontline soldiers cursed the messengers as "rear area pigs"). During those lulls, Hitler read voraciously—he said he kept a small copy of Arthur Schopenhauer's *The World as Will and Representation* in his knapsack—and was often seen perusing books on history or memorizing historical dates.[30] He also occasionally sketched nearby farmhouses; his fellow messengers sometimes called him "the artist," said his sergeant, Max Amann (later Hitler's publisher). He also was considered a bit of a klutz; one fellow soldier joked that Hitler would starve to death in a food-canning factory because he, alone among the messengers, never figured out how to open a can of army rations with his bayonet.[31] Photographs from the war show Hitler as a nice-looking but unsmiling young man; he sported a full, sometimes twirled mustache, not the stubby and easily mocked Charlie Chaplin smudge of later years.[32] But, as historian Thomas Weber has noted, in all six extant wartime group pictures, Hitler is standing or sitting at the edge of the group—a metaphor for his self-imposed outsider status. Except for a pet dog named Foxl that he had caught and adopted when it jumped into a trench chasing a rat, Hitler had few close comrades.[33] Other soldiers recalled him as a loner and "an oddball" who sent and received very little mail. "He had no one who would send him a care package," said Amann.[34]

Yet Hitler was considered a brave and willing soldier. He was twice wounded and twice decorated with the Iron Cross First and Second Class. Still, he was never promoted beyond private first class—partly because he did not want to leave the cocoon of his dispatch unit, one comrade claimed, and partly because he displayed none of the leadership qualities that would be required of a non-commissioned officer.[35] (After an early battle, with huge losses, many soldiers were promoted; Hitler was made a *Gefreiter,* which has been erroneously translated for decades as corporal. Yet *Gefreiter* includes none of the command responsibilities of a noncommissioned officer like a corporal. It was only a step up within the rank of private — from "buck" private to private first class, just as in the American military.)[36]

According to army records, Private Hitler spent the last days of the war, October to November 1918, in an army hospital for "gas sickness" after a British mustard gas attack. He later reported that he suffered temporary blindness but bawled openly ("for the first time since my mother died"[37]) when news of Germany's capitulation reached the infirmary. "So it was all in vain!" he howled.[38] Less credibly, Hitler also purported to have made the decision, as he still lay wounded and filled with hatred for "the gang of miserable criminals" who caused the war's loss, to "become a politician."[39] Though doubted by some historians, this claim sounded good and later became part of Hitler's carefully constructed leadership legend. In late November 1918, Hitler ended up back in Munich, still in the army,[40] and still without much purpose. He had no outside job and no marketable skills. He was not even a pretend artist or postcard sketcher. Hitler opted to stay in the secure embrace of the military, the only real home he had known since he was eighteen, a place that guaranteed him a roof and his meals, even as millions of other soldiers were demobilized. He lingered at the barracks, pulled guard duty at the main train station, and went on temporary assignment to a fast-emptying prisoner-of-war camp at Traunstein, near the Austrian border. Back in his Munich garrison, Hitler was elected in spring 1919 as an alternate representative to the "soldier's council" that theoretically took over his unit during Bavaria's brief, brutal experiment with a Soviet republic. In June 1919, Hitler's idle days took a decisive turn, once again driven by outside fortune rather than inner conviction. The underutilized private was recruited by Captain Karl Mayr, the commander of a newly created intelligence and propaganda unit, to become a political education operative and an internal army spy (*Vertrauensmann,* or *V-mann*). Mayr's unit had been formed because army leadership was concerned about the growing "virus" of Marxism among the rank-and-file in the unstable postwar political environment. The army—now called the Reichswehr—wanted to "immunize soldiers against revolutionary ideas."[41]

To prepare his new operatives for the task of attacking Marxism and promoting German nationalism in the army, Captain Mayr sent Hitler and several other soldiers to a one-week course in history and politics[42] at the University of Munich. One of the university speakers was Gottfried Feder, a self-styled economics expert who already spoke the language that appealed to Hitler, blaming Germany's woes on "rapacious capital," a code for "Jewish finance capital." Feder denounced "capital slavery," claiming that Germany was enslaved to international (Jewish) "stock market capitalism." This notion appealed to both the populist and the anti-Semite in Hitler. Another speaker was conservative historian Professor Karl Alexander von Müller, who, after class, noticed Hitler lecturing other students in his animated, sharp-voiced manner. Müller told Mayr he thought Hitler had a talent for speaking.[43]

And indeed, Hitler's singular gift for oratory soon showed itself in a dramatic way, leading to the epiphany that Hitler claimed altered his life. If true—and most historians believe it is—this is the moment that turned the aimless war veteran from a soldier into a budding public speaker. This is the moment that gave Hitler a vision of his future vocation. This is the moment that created Adolf Hitler, the politician.

The life-changing experience occurred in August 1919, two months after Hitler's political lectures at the university. Hitler and several other graduates of the course were sent to inject nationalistic and anti-Bolshevist thinking into a Reichswehr barracks called Camp Lechfeld, located forty miles from Munich. There they gave five days of talks styled as "citizenship training" to the troops. Hitler threw himself into the task and, along with the course leader, carried a large share of the lecturing burden. His subjects ranged from Germany's alleged war guilt to "Social, Economic and Political Catchphrases." His lectures were rife with anti-Semitism. "I 'nationalized' the troops," he later wrote.[44] Hitler's passion, joined with his sweeping—if dilettantish and self-taught—grasp of history, made him a hit. "Herr Hitler is, if I may say so, a born popular speaker," wrote one participant in his after-course evaluation. "His fanaticism and popular style...commands the attention and cooperation of the audience." Another soldier noted that Hitler was "an excellent and spirited speaker....Once, when a long lecture wasn't finished on time, he asked [us] if he should stop or if [we] would agree to hear the rest of his talk after hours. Everyone immediately agreed."[45] At Lechfeld, Hitler was the star.

Hitler's skill and success were apparently a surprise even to him. He had always been prone to bossiness, insisting that he run all the childhood games with his playmates while growing up in Austria. "I was a little ringleader and did well in school at first, but I was a bit hard to handle," he recalled.[46] Hitler was a nonstop chatterbox and domineering conversation partner, said August Kubizek, his teenaged boyhood friend. Hitler "liked to talk, and talked without pause," but conversations with him, especially after their visits to Hitler's beloved Richard Wagner operas, were always one-way affairs, Kubizek recalled.[47] That these personality traits could be translated into a professional asset had not yet occurred to the ex–dispatch runner. Now, at Camp Lechfeld, Hitler became aware of his power over people. He uncovered what would become the defining force of his political life, his voice. "I could speak!" he wrote, as though describing a Damascus Road experience. Though he claimed to have intuited this skill earlier without having recognized it for what it was, he now saw his ability to influence others. He had been a nobody on the roiling Munich political scene. He was about to become a somebody.[48]

A month later, another serendipitous experience brought Hitler a step closer to finding his calling. Captain Mayr sent Hitler, in his job as *V-mann,* or army spy, to report on a fledgling political group called the German Workers' Party (*Deutsche Arbeiterpartei*). Founded with encouragement from the well-heeled, right-wing, cultish Thule Society, the little "party" was really more of a discussion group with a handful of members. Its first leaders were a disgruntled, anti-Marxist, anti-Semitic railroad machinist[49] named Anton Drexler and a politically active sports journalist named Karl Harrer.

Meeting on a September night in an unimposing pub called the Sterneckerbräu in the old part of Munich, the German Workers' Party drew only four dozen attendees.[50] Hitler's initial impression, in his secret role as petty intelligence agent (wearing civilian clothes, not his Reichswehr uniform), was "neither good nor bad—it was just another newly founded group in a time when everyone felt called upon to start a party," he wrote.[51] Near the meeting's end, however, when one participant stood to argue in favor of Bavarian secession from the German federation, Hitler's ire was aroused; his impetuous instincts took over, as they would so often in the future, and he left the role of incognito observer to become an impassioned debater. Rolling out his acerbic style and now-practiced arguments, Hitler launched into a fiery attack on separatism and a defense of the concept of Greater Germany, a union of Germany and Austria. In short order, he destroyed the other man's position and — according to his own telling — drove the poor fellow from the meeting "like a wet poodle."[52]

Hitler not only had proved that he could speak, but also had revealed that he could be a fast-on-his-feet demagogue.[53] His plain looks and modest stature, along with his exceptionally pale skin and what many remember as "luminous," piercing blue eyes, may have lent special intensity to Hitler's impassioned arguments.[54] In any case, the German Workers' Party cofounder, Drexler, was so impressed that he grabbed Hitler afterward and pressed upon him a copy of his own forty-page manifesto, "My Political Awakening." Drexler invited Hitler to return. To another attendee, Drexler said: "That guy has a mouth on him! We could really use him!"

After Hitler's confrontational evening at the Sterneckerbräu, events moved quickly. Unable to sleep early the next morning in his army barracks because of some noisy mice, Hitler had nothing better to do than to read Drexler's little pamphlet. With its anti-Semitic denunciation of "destructive Jewish influence" on German life, its attacks on "Big Capital," and its belief in closing the class divide between workers and the middle class, the short screed immediately resonated with Hitler. "I saw my own development come to life again before my eyes" while reading the pamphlet, he recalled.[55] But before he could decide whether or not to accept Drexler's invitation to return, Hitler received a postcard informing him that he was now a member of the German Workers' Party.[56] Hitler spent two "tortured" days thinking about the "ridiculous" little club, as he called it, before deciding to accept. "It was the most momentous decision of my life," he wrote. "Now there was no turning back." Hitler now had a party affiliation, a speaking platform, and a political base that he would turn, for a few years, into the most powerful political force in twentieth-century Europe.

For sending Hitler to his first party meeting, Captain Mayr later liked to claim that he was Hitler's spiritual godfather, the man who made it all possible. But the true role of intellectual inspiration fell to someone else, a hard-living, highly acclaimed intellectual named Dietrich Eckart. Hitler met Eckart through the German Workers' Party, and Eckart's influence on him would be profound. Considered the party's one-man brain trust, Eckart was a bohemian, poet, and sometime journalist whose translation and production of Henrik Ibsen's *Peer Gynt* in Germany had made him famous and prosperous. A raving anti-Semite, Eckart published an anti-Jewish weekly called *Auf Gut Deutsch* (*In Plain German*). With his bright blue eyes, high forehead, and totally bald head, Eckart cut a striking figure in the café culture of Munich's artistic and literary quarter, Schwabing. Despite an alcohol and morphine addiction that would lead to his death at age fifty-five, Eckart was regarded as an oracle of the anti-Semitic *völkisch* movement. He had once said of the new political party, "We need a leader who isn't bothered by the clatter of a machine gun....The best would be a worker who can also speak...and who does not run from somebody swinging a chair at him. He has to be a bachelor—then we'll get the women!"[57] It seemed an almost perfect description of the fearless former message runner who was becoming interested in politics. In Hitler, Eckart began to think he had found his man.

As Hitler would later remark, Eckhart quickly became the "polar star" of his intellectual development, refining his anti-Semitic beliefs and introducing him to both the bohemian and high-society worlds of Munich. Eckart dragged Hitler along on the budding politician's very first airplane ride—to Berlin—and he took the future dictator to meet, among others, the renowned and rich piano manufacturer Edwin Bechstein and, more important, his wife, Helene. Frau Bechstein became an enthusiastic financial backer and, later, when Hitler was in Landsberg Prison, a frequent visitor ("I wish he were my son," she once said).[58] She also presented him with a leather dog whip, one of three that he would eventually receive from various female admirers and carry with him as he moved around Munich.

While Hitler was making his first moves into party politics, he had another chance to flex his newfound rhetorical muscles on paper. In September 1919, Captain Mayr received a letter from Adolf Gemlich, a former student in the University of Munich course. Gemlich asked Mayr for more guidance on "the Jewish question." Mayr gave the letter to Hitler (still serving as an army private) to answer.

Hitler packed a lot into his nearly one-thousand-word response. He expressed, for the first time in writing, his deep-seated anti-Semitism, and laid out some of the key elements that would become the basis of his anti-Jewish policies all the way through his political ascension, the Third Reich, the Holocaust, and right into Hitler's final "political testament," written in 1945 just days before his suicide in his Berlin bunker.

Channeling stereotypes and clichés of the anti-Semitism that was widespread in Europe—and especially in *völkisch* thinking in Bavaria—Hitler gave his arguments an analytical gloss and extremism that set his letter to Gemlich apart. Hitler rejected an "emotional anti-Semitism" that, he said, was purely personal, led only to pogroms, and was therefore not politically useful, and chose instead an "anti-Semitism of reason" that was "fact-based" and intended to shape policy. Judaism was not a religion, he claimed, but a race. And the Jewish race functioned as a "leech" on the majority cultures in which it lived, since its entire raison d'être was the "dance around the golden calf" for the purpose of amassing fortunes. The Weimar Republic leadership, he claimed, was in thrall to Jewish money, which financed the unjust fight against "the anti-Semitic movement," meaning nationalist and *völkisch* (racist) parties. "[The Jew's] power is the power of money that in his hands constantly grows in the form of interest, forcing other peoples under the most dangerous yoke." In the earliest written record of his tendency to equate Jews with disease and parasites, Hitler described Judaism as "a racial tuberculosis." A reason-based response to this threat must inevitably lead to "a systematic and legal struggle and cancellation of the Jews' privileges," he wrote.

Germany, Hitler continued in his long letter, needed a "rebirth," but it could not move forward with an "irresponsible press," meaning Jewish-owned newspapers. Only through the ruthless efforts of "a leadership personality" would Germany reawaken, Hitler claimed, providing a glimpse of his emerging Messiah complex. He offered a simple solution to "the Jewish question" that chillingly foreshadowed events to come more than two decades later: "The final goal [of anti-Semitism] must be the irrevocable and complete removal of all Jews."

In its viciousness and candid brutality, the letter to Gemlich shows how fully Hitler's anti-Semitism was already developed by late 1919. Even before he had an official political platform, the letter pointed to the radical measures Hitler contemplated if he ever reached power. Now already thirty, Hitler was ready to embark on that quest.

CHAPTER TWO

The Charmed Circle

"From now on I will go my way alone."
—ADOLF HITLER, 1922[1]

"I must have a crowd when I speak," Hitler once told a friend, "in a small, intimate circle I never know what to say." In October 1919 on the night he made his debut as a speaker in the German Workers' Party, the turnout was only one hundred people, but they were sufficient to trigger Hitler's oratorical juices. Though Hitler was not the main attraction, his fiery words that autumn night dramatically boosted fund-raising, cementing his emerging role as a propagandist. From now on, he would speak; he would propagandize; he would be a "drummer," as he liked to put it, for "the movement," as he preferred to call it. At this point, Hitler did not yet see himself as the leader of a political force, but rather as its noisemaker and tent barker, building support for someone else who would emerge as the chosen strongman, a dictator for Germany. "Our task is to give to the dictator, when he comes, a people that is ready for him," he said.[2]

In February 1920, Hitler had his coming-out as a serious mass rabble-rouser. Later glorified in his overwritten manifesto, *Mein Kampf,* as a heroic Siegfriedian moment, the event in Munich's celebrated Hofbräuhaus beer hall was a bit more prosaic than that. Again the meeting was centered around another speaker; Hitler's name was not even mentioned on the party's flyers. But as an unannounced backup speaker, Hitler stirred the crowd of about two thousand listeners to a high pitch of enthusiasm. Even while presenting the party's banal if quirky twenty-five-point program, Hitler evoked cheers from supporters and jeers from a couple hundred Socialist opponents who had turned out for the speeches, transforming the gathering into a heated political rally; people climbed onto chairs and tables to harangue one another.[3] After some near-clashes between Nazis and Socialists, listeners left the beer hall arguing loudly in the streets, talking about Hitler, the speech, the issues. A defiant group of Communists and Socialists sang the "Internationale," the anthem of the Left. Hitler had accomplished exactly what he wanted—he had put the party on the map. "It makes no difference whatever whether they laugh at us or revile us," he wrote later. "The main thing is that they mention us."

The bigger the crowd, it seemed, the better Hitler performed. He had now discovered his knack for connecting with the masses, sensing their moods, speaking their language. "A great speaker... lets himself be carried by the masses in such a way that he develops a feel for the words that reach their hearts," Hitler wrote. "He can read on their faces...whether they are convinced."[4] The masses stimulated him with their attention and adulation. It was a reciprocal relationship—*the* relationship—that would define Hitler's political life. Sometimes "I spoke before two thousand people and eighteen hundred of them were looking at me through enemy eyes," he recalled. "Three hours later I beheld a surging mass filled with indignation and wrath" over the political outrage that Hitler had described.[5] Although he was a spin artist of the highest order, reports of his big-speech successes make this claim at least plausible.

Before the pivotal Hofbräuhaus gathering, there had been bitter debate in the German Workers' Party about the advisability of booking such a large hall. Party cofounder Harrer feared half the seats would be empty; the event would look like a failure. Hitler had argued the opposite, and now he had been proven right. After his success, the party would no longer shy away from mass meetings in huge halls, and Hitler would be the featured speaker wherever he appeared. His very name on the posters suggested excitement, political entertainment, and possible conflict. Returning to the Hofbräuhaus time after time, Hitler regularly attracted large crowds. In autumn 1920, he delivered to a packed house a frenzied speech called "Why Are We Anti-Semites?" The two thousand listeners interrupted him more than fifty times with applause.[6]

In his role as "drummer," Hitler stood outside the regular leadership structure of the German Workers' Party. But it was fast becoming obvious that propaganda was the heart of the party's activity. The party contested no elections, offered no candidates, sat on no commissions or official bodies. It simply made noise. Propaganda was its reason for being. And Hitler had become its chief propagandist.

As Hitler's star rose, Karl Harrer's dimmed. Stung by the newcomer's success in a venue where he had expected failure, Harrer resigned from party leadership. At Hitler's instigation the party's name was expanded: the German Workers' Party became the National Socialist German Workers' Party—NSDAP was the German acronym. By adding "National Socialist" (*Nationalsozialistisch*) to the party's name, Hitler aimed to give it resonance beyond its initial identification with workers. He sought a nationalist redefinition of socialism in contrast to the internationalist concept of Marxist socialism. He rejected the Communist concept of class struggle—he wanted to foster a national sense of community without class divides—and defended private property while thundering at the ravages of "Big Capital," a favorite whipping boy. In Hitler's mind, "national" and "social" were "two identical communitarian concepts." Hitler explained, "To be 'national' means above all to act with a boundless and all-embracing love for the [German] people.... To be 'social' means... that every individual acts in the interests of the community [and] is ready to die for it."[7] (Though "Nazi" is a natural abbreviation in German for _Nationalsozialistisch_—like "Sozi" for the Socialists—the Nazi nickname was not used until several years later and mainly by people abroad or enemies of the NSDAP. "Nazi" is employed throughout this book for its convenience and familiarity to readers.)

With Harrer gone, only Anton Drexler, the other party cofounder, stood between Hitler and the top leadership job in the NSDAP, and within a little more than a year after Harrer's departure, that was Hitler's, too, though not without drama and histrionics. In a bitter disagreement over a possible merger with another party, Hitler stormed out of a leadership meeting in July 1921 and, three days letter, sent a letter of resignation. Stunned, Drexler and other leaders realized they were losing not only their biggest draw but also their cash cow. The star of the Nazi mass meetings and magnet for mass donations was bolting. As if to make his point even louder, Hitler—acting on his own name alone—had within days filled the Circus Krone, Munich's largest indoor venue, with six thousand eager listeners.

Hitler's showdown worked. A week later, Drexler and other party leaders begged him to return to the Nazi fold, caving to his all-or-nothing demands for sole party leadership "with dictatorial powers." He had staged an internal putsch and won. A complete personal victory for Hitler, the decision also represented a strategic shift toward the *Führerprinzip*, the undiluted leadership principle that would dominate the Nazi Party and all of Nazi Germany throughout the Third Reich. This principle made the leader's word first, final, and infallible, eliminating any democratic internal processes or collegial controls. Ideas and initiatives were not always discussed or argued through: often they were put to Hitler and came back as fixed decisions. This power shift in summer 1921 marked the beginning of Hitler's reshaping of the Nazi movement into a *Führerpartei*—a leader-dominated party. It was also the first step toward the Hitlerian cult of personality. Unmarried and single-minded, obsessive, consumed with his own sense of mission, Hitler had no other life than politics.

Hitler's leadership made itself felt mainly on the propaganda front, where his decisions were painstaking and brilliant. As a manager, he was a disaster, moving around the city as whim dictated, forgetting appointments, showing up at odd hours at his favorite cafés or at the *Völkischer Beobachter* (The Nationalist-Racist Observer), his newly acquired newspaper. Hitler had such a "volcanic store of nervous energy" that "you could never keep him off the streets," remembered a close friend.[8] Rising late in his modest apartment, Hitler would sometimes hold a first conference while shaving or buttering a slice of bread for breakfast at 11 a.m. "Discussions always took place standing up," recalled Hermann Esser, an early party member who became editor of the *Völkischer Beobachter*. "He never offered coffee or tea. He shaved with a knife until later he had enough money to afford a single-edge shaving apparatus. He always cut himself [and] somtimes he would bleed all the way into the evening. That was well-known."[9]

Hitler was expanding his base. His message appealed not just to disenfranchised working-class people, but especially to the petite bourgeoisie who were one notch above blue-collar workers yet fearful of slipping down the ladder. He also had appeal to wealthy conservatives, especially anti-Semites — the fanatical "street public of the higher classes," as one observer put it.[10]

Adding to his speaking platform and his party newspaper, Hitler began developing other physical trappings of a real political group. With a fine feel for mass psychology and stirring symbols, he created a party identity based on the swastika, oceans of flags, and party uniforms. Drawn originally from auspicious Hindu symbolism, and used by many religions and cults over the centuries, the swastika motif had been adopted by race-minded groups like the ultra-Germanic Thule Society as an emblem of Nordic supremacy. After painstaking examination of numerous sketches and drafts, Hitler personally selected the party flag's primary colors: a red field, a white circle, and a starkly simple, tilted black swastika in the center. Given the complex and ornate swastikas then in circulation, Hitler's choice of the boldest, plainest look was a stroke of advertising genius. The Nazi flag made a strong statement, was easy to recognize, even at a distance, and, when necessary, inspired fear. Hitler explained his choices: "The red expressed the social-justice idea underlying the movement; white, the nationalistic belief. And the swastika signified the mission assigned to us — the struggle for the victory of Aryan mankind."[11] In addition, the red field was a sly provocation of the Communists and Social Democrats, who thought they owned that color. By misleading some leftists into gatherings advertised in bright red, thought Hitler, the Nazis could "demolish their positions and thus get into a dialogue with these people."[12]

Like most of the activist groups in Munich — including the Communists and the Socialists — the Nazis also had created their own version of a "hall protection unit." These were armed roughnecks who could start and stop beer hall brawls with competitors or any other disruptive elements. Originally tagged the "Sport and Gymnastics

Section" of the party, the unit's name, after a few mutations, became the *Sturmabteilung*—the Storm Section, or Storm Troopers, shortened to SA in German. Carrying brass knuckles and rubber truncheons, the Storm Troopers, with Hitler participating, displayed their chops in no uncertain terms in September 1921 when they attacked the meeting of a separatist group called the Bavaria League and beat its leader, Otto Ballerstedt, to a bloody mess. He later brought charges against Hitler, who was found guilty of breach of the peace and served one month of a three-month sentence (then was paroled) in summer 1922.

In forming the Storm Troopers, "I specially looked for people of disheveled appearance," said Hitler, describing a rough bunch that could take on dirty work. Such recruits were not hard to find in the postwar subculture of "militant ultra-masculinity" that sprang from the German army's rapid demobilization and the parallel growth of free-booting militias, wrote one historian.[13] These "jolly rogues," as Hitler called them, would play a critical role in the putsch that still lay more than a year in the future.[14] By then, they were operating under the command of a new member of the Nazi Party, Captain Hermann Göring.

The years that led to Hitler's 1923 putsch saw an accumulation of fol-lowers, hangers-on, and beer hall bruisers who would become his inner circle, his personal entourage and his fellow-putschists. Hermann Göring was one of its key members. A famous World War I flying ace with twenty-two kills and the *Pour le Mérite,* Germany's highest medal, Göring had returned to Germany after a few postwar years as a private pilot and barnstormer in Denmark and Sweden.* He was looking for a new adventure. Though enrolled as a student at the University of Munich, the flashy, large-living Göring was drawn to politics, a world

---

* *Pour le Mérite* was created in 1740 by Frederick the Great. He named it in French, the preferred language at his court.

in which he thought he might make a splash. Shopping around the Munich political scene, he finally chose the Nazis, not so much for their program and politics but because he thought he could be a bigger player in a smaller party—and history proved him right.

Hitler, for his part, was delighted the day the swashbuckling Göring walked into the run-down Nazi Party headquarters and offered his services. Within a short time, Hitler had put Göring in charge of the growing but disorganized Storm Troopers, which the former flier quickly shaped into a formidable force.

Another University of Munich student named Rudolf Hess, also a World War I airman, had already glommed on to Hitler. Born in Alexandria, Egypt, to a prosperous German businessman and his wife, Hess was under the influence of Professor Karl Haushofer, renowned for his theories of geopolitics. Through Hess, Hitler later incorporated Haushofer's views into his *Lebensraum* ("living space") policies, the justification for his World War II invasion of Russia.[15] Good-looking but moody ("I am an odd mixture," Hess wrote to his fiancée), Hess was involved with the Thule Society, which another attendee described as a wealthy "club of 'intellectualities' dealing with Germanic history."[16] Among the Nazis, Hess found his role as Hitler's personal assistant and amanuensis—a calling which would soon make him Hitler's closest comrade in prison and, later, deputy Führer of the Nazi Party. In Munich, neglecting his studies, Hess hung around Nazi headquarters and tried to keep the erratic and peripatetic party leader on schedule.

Hitler's brain trust also included Max Amann, the former soldier who had been Private Hitler's commanding sergeant on the western front in World War I. Amann, a "rough fellow" who relished a beer hall brawl, became Hitler's all-purpose publishing guru. Hitler made him business manager of *Völkischer Beobachter* and, later, his book publisher; *Mein Kampf* made millions for both of them. Amann was head of the iron-fisted Reich Press Association, which controlled the press during the Third Reich.

Besides Dietrich Eckart, the *Peer Gynt* translator and all-around roué who mentored Hitler, several other men of intellect were drawn to the fiery young orator and his dynamic movement. Alfred Rosenberg, an Estonian-German with a Russian education and pretensions to literary greatness, became a devotee and editor of the *Völkischer Beobachter*. Hitler read and was influenced by Rosenberg's anti-Semitic tract, *Die Spur des Juden im Wandel der Zeiten* (The Track of the Jew Through the Ages). The bald and severe Max Erwin von Scheubner-Richter, another well-educated German of Baltic origin, also added a touch of urbanity to Hitler's raw-edged crowd, providing both brainpower and connections to money through the wealthy Russian émigré network. Between them, Rosenberg and Scheubner-Richter strongly influenced Hitler's growing belief that "a gang of Jewish literary figures"—like Leon Trotsky and other Jewish Bolshevists—were behind the murders of "thirty million" victims of Communism in Russia. Increasingly, Hitler's anti-Semitism rested on invocations of the Russian horror and his reading of the scurrilous forgery *The Protocols of the Elders of Zion*, possibly given to him by Rosenberg. "The 'blood Jew' introduces a scaffold in the place of a parliament, [brings] the destruction of the intelligentsia and, finally, Bolshevism," he liked to say.[17] Rosenberg later played a key role in shaping the Third Reich's draconian race laws.

But Hitler's personal taste, like his political fascination with moving the masses rather than the elites, often trended socially downward. In his frequent after-hours gatherings in cafés around Munich, Hitler included his bodyguard, Ulrich Graf, a former butcher, and Christian Weber, an overweight former pub bouncer and horse dealer.[18] His sometime driver and frequent café companion was a darkly handsome watchmaker from northern Germany named Emil Maurice (who would later be discovered to be of Jewish origin and dropped from the inner circle). A photographer named Heinrich Hoffmann, who understood early that Hitler could be a gold mine for him, became part of Hitler's Munich rat pack. This merry band, in various mutations, could be seen afternoons or evenings in places like the elegant Café Heck adjoining the Royal Gardens on the Galerienstrasse; the old Café Neumaier in the central city (where Hitler had a regular Monday night table); and at the Osteria Bavaria, an Italian bistro that also served some Alpine dishes, just a couple blocks from the *Völkischer Beobachter* headquarters in the Schellingstrasse. One thing observers of the group always noted: Hitler did almost all the talking.

A late but important arrival to the charmed circle around Hitler was Ernst Hanfstaengl. A German-American art book publisher's son who had attended Harvard, Hanfstaengl stood out because of his height (six feet, four inches), his prognathous jaw, and his air of cultivation. Called Putzi ("little boy") as an ironic nickname, Hanfstaengl had been asked to attend a Hitler speech in November 1922 by his old Harvard friend Captain Truman Smith. Then deputy military attaché in the American embassy in Berlin, Smith had been in Munich and met personally with Hitler, and the young officer had been impressed with the Nazi leader's ability to deliver "a full-length speech" every time he was asked a simple question—"as if he had pressed a gramophone switch."[19] Smith wanted Hanfstaengl to find out how Hitler sounded when he gave a real speech. Hanfstaengl attended a Hitler appearance and was overwhelmed: he called it a "masterly performance" with "innuendo and irony I have never heard matched." Following the speech, Hanfstaengl introduced himself to Hitler, and the two found a quick affinity. "I agree with ninety-five percent of what you said and would very much like to talk to you about the rest sometime," said Hanfstaengl.

"I'm sure we shall not have to quarrel about the odd five percent," replied Hitler. At first, that would be true.[20]

Hanfstaengl soon joined Hitler's inner clique. Since he had leisure and means, he became Hitler's main walk-around guy in Munich. Because he spent so much time with Hitler, Hanfstaengl had more insights into the leader's ascetic lifestyle than most. Hitler "lived like a down-at-the-heels clerk" in his tiny rented room in the Thierschstrasse near the meandering Isar River, noted Hanfstaengl. The linoleum-covered floor had a few "threadbare rugs," but the large anteroom that Hitler shared with his landlady had only one redeeming feature, an upright piano. There, Hanfstaengl, an accomplished pianist, sometimes banged out tunes and learned Hitler's tastes. "I played a Bach fugue," wrote Hanfstaengl, with Hitler "nodding his head in vague disinterest." But when Hanfstaengl switched to Wagner, Hitler's favorite musical maestro and one of his political heroes, things changed. "I started the prelude to the *Meistersinger*. This was it. This was Hitler's meat. He knew the thing absolutely by heart and could whistle every note of it in a curious penetrating vibrato, but completely in tune." Not surprisingly, Hitler also thrilled to Hanfstaengl's old Harvard fight songs, ending in "Rah! Rah! Rah!"[21]

Hanfstaengl's relationship with Hitler became so close that the well-connected publishing scion found a way to lend the Nazi Party one thousand U.S. dollars. This was a whopping sum in inflation-racked Germany, and it enabled the *Völkischer Beobachter* to purchase two broadsheet rotary presses so that it could appear in a broader, more impressive format.[22] Hanfstaengl also introduced

Hitler to high society, inviting him to dinner and making connections to potential supporters and donors like the family of Fritz-August von Kaulbach, a renowned artistic clan.[23] Hitler's native Austrian charm emerged, and though he was sometimes mildly maladroit (Hanfstaengl caught him putting sugar in his wine), he was generally a hit, especially with the ladies.

Besides Helene Bechstein, the wife of the piano manufacturer, the women besotted with Hitler included another wealthy spouse introduced to Hitler by Dietrich Eckart. She was Else Bruckmann, the wife of Hugo Bruckmann, a conservative publisher who had a large mansion in Munich's monument district. Else Bruckmann, by birth a Romanian princess, was a noted salon hostess; an invitation to her soirées was a badge of arrival in Munich society—and Hitler received many, becoming a kind of prize curiosity at her gatherings. Both women, Bechstein and Bruckmann, managed to direct frequent infusions of their husbands' cash to Hitler. They sometimes found roundabout ways to move assets in his direction. One night at the luxurious Bechstein dwelling in Berlin, Edwin Bechstein rebuffed Hitler's entreaties over dinner for a new donation; funds were short, he said. Yet as Hitler was leaving, Mrs. Bechstein managed to press upon him some of her glittering jewelry for easy conversion to cash. Later she added pricey paintings from her private collection to her largesse. Though never openly involved with a woman, and unmarried until the last two days of his life, Hitler had a near-mystical appeal to many women.

By fall 1922, rumors of a Hitler putsch were already bubbling up in Munich, a full year before Hitler actually made his move. The talk of a coup d'état was fanned not so much by anything Hitler had said or done, but by a dramatic event outside Germany. In October 1922, Benito Mussolini and his Fascisti Party had managed to take over the Italian government with a sudden coup that began, people said, with a "march on Rome." As historians have since pointed out, the march was more symbolic than real and ended with a negotiated takeover. But the myth and vivid imagery of a popular march stuck, especially in Germany, and especially with a would-be revolutionary like Hitler. Viewing Mussolini's bold stroke as "one of the turning points in history," Hitler instantly translated the notion of a march on Rome into its German analog: a march on Berlin.[24] With dreams of gathering all the military forces in Bavaria behind him—the powerful right-wing paramilitaries plus the Reichswehr's Bavaria Division and the military-style Bavarian State Police—Hitler would stage a grand march from Munich to Berlin to spark a "national uprising" and take power. He would lead both a military force and a great moral cause—the German "rebirth" he longed for—to the gates of Berlin, toppling all before it. Hitler was a ruthless, brilliant propagandist and a hopeless romantic: The cinematic quality of a march on Berlin appealed to both those instincts. He did not just want to bring down the Weimar Republic, he wanted to replace it in grand style—as Mussolini had done.

Hitler was also inspired by the example of Kemal Pasha, later called Atatürk, who had mounted a successful coup against the Constantinople government from a provincial base in Ankara. In his own putsch attempt, Hitler would combine Mussolini's and Pasha's approaches, starting in the provincial base of Munich but with his sights set on the main prize in Berlin.

Hitler thought he had reason to feel good about his chances. Only a week before Mussolini's bold stroke, Hitler had mounted a brazen flanking move of his own. Invited to participate peacefully with a small delegation in a nationalistic celebration in the north Bavarian town of Coburg, Hitler had arrived on a special train with six hundred fifty Storm Troopers and, essentially, taken over the town. His forces violently attacked leftist groups that had also come for the parades, earning Hitler the reputation, for the first time, as "liberator" of a city from "red terror."[25] The heady experience raised Hitler's confidence to a new high. "From now on I will go my way alone,"[26] he declared.

Though he had made no preparations or given anyone a concrete reason to believe he was ready to strike (*losschlagen*), Hitler had clearly begun to contemplate the idea of a putsch that included a march on Berlin. "Mussolini showed what a minority can do if it is gripped by a righteous nationalistic drive," argued Hitler to his followers at a "discussion evening" in November 1922.[27] That was enough to get the rumor mill running and discombobulate the Bavarian authorities as 1923 began. Once implanted, the idea of an audacious move took root in Hitler's mind and became, said one adversary, an "idée fixe." Hitler's obsessions almost always were acted upon, sooner or later.

CHAPTER THREE

The Mounting Pressure

*"If [Hitler] lets his Messiah complex run away with him,
he will ruin us all."*

— DIETRICH ECKART, 1923

The year that would end with Hitler behind bars—1923—opened
with two dramatic events. The first was the January 11 French invasion of the Ruhr region, triggering the Berlin government's disastrous passive resistance campaign, bloody reprisals by French troops
against local saboteurs, and Germany's catastrophic spiral into
hyperinflation. The second, in the same month, was a pivotal confrontation between Hitler and Bavarian authorities over plans for
the Nazi Party's first "national" party convention, scheduled for
January 27 to 29 in Munich. Hitler announced a dozen marches
and rallies on a single day, with speeches by him at every one; the
Nazis would effectively take over Munich for a day, disrupting a city
of six hundred fifty thousand. The possibility of major clashes
between the Nazis and their archenemies, the Communists and the

Socialists, alarmed the commanders of the military and the state police, the ultimate keepers of internal order. General Otto von Lossow, a severe-looking man who commanded the Reichswehr's Seventh Division—known as the Bavaria Division—was a Prussian-trained Bavarian whose loyalty was more to Munich than to Berlin. Colonel Hans von Seisser, also a product of the Prussian officer class, headed the Bavarian State Police, a division-sized force that included infantry and mobile units. Apart from possible street battles between political adversaries, Lossow and Seisser were most concerned that Hitler might follow Mussolini's recent example and launch a putsch. They banned Hitler's twelve rallies.

All Hitler's bile, violent instincts, and do-or-die megalomania were aroused by the prohibition. In a stormy confrontation with authorities, Hitler threatened that if the ban were not lifted, he would "march in the first row and take the first bullets" should the army or police try to stop the marches by force. If that happened, he added haughtily, "the Bavarian government would be gone within two hours."[1] Storming out of a meeting with Munich police chief Eduard Nortz, Hitler let fly one of his typically grandiose historical metaphors, shouting: "We'll meet on the fields of Philippi!"[2] (Philippi was the Macedonian battlefield where, in 42 BC, amid unspeakable gore, Mark Antony defeated the forces of Marcus Brutus; Brutus, Caesar's assassin, then committed suicide. The event was dramatized in Shakespeare's *The Life and Death of Julius Caesar,* which Hitler had probably read.)

In a separate meeting with General Lossow, Hitler argued for lifting the ban and promised, on his "word of honor," that he had no plans for a putsch.[3] In 1920s Germany, a word of honor— *Ehrenwort*—was taken seriously as a binding promise. On the basis of Hitler's *Ehrenwort,* Lossow, Seisser, and Police Chief Nortz backed down, but they tried to preserve a shred of their authority by telling Hitler he could hold six, not twelve, rallies, and that his spectacular planned outdoor ceremony to consecrate the colors of the Storm Troopers must be moved indoors, to the Circus Krone. Hitler accepted this half-loaf, then blithely proceeded with his original plan; he held twelve meetings and an outdoor review of six thousand uniformed Nazis on the Marsfeld parade ground near the Circus Krone. Stunned by Hitler's audacity, the authorities did not interfere. Faced with the armed power of the state, Hitler had stood his ground and won, and everyone knew it. The stand-down by Lossow and Seisser was a major propaganda victory for Hitler, and an embarrassment for the men in uniform.

Hitler's aggressive posture caught the attention of no less a figure than General Hans von Seeckt, commander in chief of the Reichswehr, the German army. Based in Berlin, the country's top military man wielded huge political influence despite the truncation of the military class by the Treaty of Versailles, which limited Germany to one hundred thousand troops with only four thousand officers—a force thought to be large enough to suppress internal unrest, but not to wage war on Germany's neighbors. Despite its relatively small size, the Reichswehr under Seeckt gained the reputation of being a "state within a state."[4] In a moment of political turmoil, with the government under threat from restive paramilitaries and rebellious army units, the worried German president, Friedrich Ebert, asked Seeckt whom the Reichswehr stood behind; the unsmiling, monocled general in the stiff gray uniform replied: "The Reichswehr stands behind me." Seeckt was, in short, the man with the guns.[5]

In March 1923, Seeckt was persuaded to meet with the upstart former private who was causing Lossow and Seisser so much heartburn. For four hours, during a visit to Munich, the Prussian officer listened patiently, or stonily, to Hitler's familiar ravings about the "November criminals," the perfidious Jews, the need for a great man to take over. According to the accounts of Colonel Hans-Harald von Selchow, Seeckt's adjutant who was present, the Austrian high school dropout lectured Germany's top military officer on history and comparisons of Germany's fate with that of other nations that had saved themselves by drastic action. Swinging into his radical rhetoric, Hitler told Seeckt: "We National Socialists will see to it that the members of the present Marxist regime in Berlin will hang from the lampposts. We will send the Reichstag up in flames, and when all is in flux we will turn to you, Herr General, to assume leadership of all German workers."[6]

To many, this might have been a tempting offer. But even though the old-fashioned Prussian general favored a right-wing government, he wanted no part of lamppost hangings and extreme rhetoric from a fire-breathing beer hall politician. According to Selchow, Seeckt simply replied: "From today forward, Herr Hitler, we have nothing more to say to one another!" Seeckt left for Berlin.[7]

By now Hitler had built a reputation as an iron man who stood up to bourgeois politicians. Nazi Party membership, by local standards, was soaring—from twenty thousand to fifty-five thousand in 1923 alone.* A Hitler speech in Munich was now always promoted on wall posters as a *Riesenversammlung*—a "gigantic gathering"—and indeed it was. With his apocalyptic predictions, pat solutions, and unvarnished appeal to mass emotions, Hitler was able to fill the Circus Krone with up to six thousand listeners.

These listeners were eager to hear facile explanations for their mounting misery, and Hitler knew just where to place the blame. Pointing the finger at the stab-in-the-back civilians, especially Jews,

---

* By national standards, the party was weak, with only a small membership outside Bavaria. The Communists, by contrast, were a national party with more than three hundred thousand members and more than one million votes in federal elections.

who "betrayed" the "frontline fighters" in 1918 and thereby caused Germany to lose the war, Hitler vilified the current German government and the Weimar constitution as illegitimate. His was becoming the loudest voice among the numerous Weimar Republic rejectionists on both extremes of German politics—Communists on the left, ultranationalists and unreconstructed monarchists on the right. Hitler made proximate bugaboos of "Big Capital" and "internationalists," meaning all leftists who promoted the socialist international brotherhood. He denounced France and Britain and poured scorn on the "swindle" of Woodrow Wilson's unrealized Fourteen Points. He painted a rosy picture of prewar Germany in contrast to its current "disgrace and defeat."[8] He made complicated things simple. "Political agitation must be primitive," he said.[9]

Hitler's skill at galvanizing his audiences and striking deeper emotional chords than other politicians lay not merely in his demagoguery, but also in his ability to see beyond the political issues of the day to underlying themes and yearnings of his listeners. While he could rail with the best of them about the French occupation, inflation, unemployment, and the feckless government in Berlin, he also reached for something larger and broader—"a sense of greatness"—that resonated on a personal level among people feeling confused and buffeted by events beyond their control. "The question of the recovery of the German people is not a question of economic recovery," he wrote in an internal party memorandum. "Rather it is a matter of regaining an inner feeling among the people, the only thing that can lead again to national greatness and, through that, to economic welfare."[10] Hitler was selling the goodness and the potential of the German people, not just a stronger mark and fair wages. When he denounced the "outrages" of the Treaty of Versailles, ranted about "usury against the people," and rhapsodized about the "culture-creating" qualities of Germanic peoples, listeners felt he was talking about *them,* not about abstractions. Whatever the wrongs of World War I and whatever the merits of assigning "sole war guilt" to Germany as a collective, Germans as individuals did not feel that they were any worse than the French, the Belgians, or anyone else. Their self-esteem was shattered and offended, but Hitler's speeches offered them a different picture of themselves as strong and honorable people. He cleverly branded the Nazi undertaking a "freedom movement." This ingenious emotional strategy transformed his events into mass entertainments with an overlay of religious fervor, like revivalist tent meetings. Posters advertising the gatherings even had a negative religious tilt: "Jews not admitted," they read.

Hitler did more than appeal to emotions, though; he made arguments that had people nodding their heads. His heady brew of nationalism, social Darwinism, and biological anti-Semitism was served up with a stiletto intellect and a prodigious historical memory. "In a very short time I learned how to knock the enemy's weapons out of his own hands," wrote Hitler. Hitler's particular joy was preaching to his opponents and tormentors. Other politicians, he noticed, "made speeches to people who were already in agreement with them. But that missed the point: all that counted was using propaganda and enlightenment to convince people who…came from a different point of view." Hitler already understood the importance of wooing the independents.

The beer hall preacher was adding to his propagandistic bag of tricks, too: He used rousing music to warm up the crowds and rolling waves of flags and uniforms to induce a sense of shared community and militant purpose. He consciously staged prima donna–style late arrivals and approached the stage directly through the audience, not from the behind the podium. He began to fetishize the newly adopted raised-arm Nazi salute copied from Mussolini, who got it from the Romans. In a pre-radio, pre-television era, with no intermediating machine between speaker and audience, such crowd-pleasing devices were effective techniques for building a bond, even if momentary. Hitler's talents were ideally suited for a visceral connection with mobs of people, who went home with an afterglow of political enthusiasm undiluted by a television or radio report, or even by pictures in the next day's newspaper since almost none were printed at the time. And Hitler made sure his picture did not appear in those that were printed; he understood the value of maintaining an aura of mystery and initially forbade anyone to photograph him. When Heinrich Hoffmann, his future friend and court photographer, in 1922 attempted an unauthorized picture of Hitler on the street, the Nazi leader's bodyguards attacked Hoffmann and exposed his photo plate. It would be another year, in September 1923, before the world got its first look at Hitler from an Associated Press photograph taken at a rally in Nuremberg.[11]

Hitler had honed his speaking style as well: a slow start, wandering through history, followed by Wagnerian crescendos and bombastic finales. Practicing before mirrors (and later in front of Hoffmann's camera), he had developed a repertoire of theatrical gestures to dramatize his points—the extended fist, the pleading hands, a toss of his forelock as sweat poured from his brow. "His technique resembled the thrusts and parries of a fencer," noted Hanfstaengl.[12] Then, just as dramatically as he had entered, Hitler would depart through the crowd as a final anthem was played by a band. Lingering for argument and discussion could, he believed, "completely undo hours of oratorical labor."[13] People came to be carried away by the man who could speak from sketchy notes for up to three hours, and they were.

Wrote one woman in 1923: "You cannot imagine how quiet it becomes when this man speaks. It's as though thousands of listeners can no longer breathe. A cheer goes up that lasts for minutes when, full of rage, he skewers the acts of those who govern us and who now prevent him and his followers from dealing with the November Bigs. Until he waves his hand for quiet, so that he can continue speaking, there is no peace.... Adolf Hitler has such a firm belief in the honesty of his national socialist standpoint that he spontaneously transfers it to his listeners."[14]

Karl Alexander von Müller, the history professor who had noticed Hitler's oratorical bent during his "political citizenship" courses at the University of Munich, remembered his first experience, belatedly, of Hitler as a public speaker. It was at a 1923 rally in the large Löwenbräukeller beer hall.

"For hours, booming military music; for hours, short speeches by subordinate speakers. When was *he* coming—had something unexpected happened?" Müller wrote. "Nobody can describe the fever that spread in this atmosphere. Suddenly there was movement at the back entrance. Words of command. The speaker on the platform stopped in mid-sentence. Everybody jumped up, saluting. And right through the shouting crowds and the streaming flags *the one* they were waiting for came with his followers, walking quickly to the platform, his right arm raised stiffly. He passed by me quite close and I saw a different person from the one I had met now and then in private homes; his gaunt, pale features contorted as if by inward rage, cold flames darting from his protruding eyes, which seemed to be searching out foes to be conquered.... 'Fanatical, hysterical romanticism with a brutal core of willpower?' I noted down."[15]

Hitler was maintaining a frantic schedule in 1923. He spoke all over Munich—in the Hofbräuhaus, the Bürgerbräukeller, the Löwenbräukeller, the Circus Krone, even at out-of-town Nazi gatherings in Nuremberg, Bayreuth, Augsburg, and Regensburg, all in Bavaria. Once he spoke in Salzburg, just across the border in

Austria. Hitler, the indefatigable mouth, was already on his way to becoming perhaps the most prolific political speaker of all time, with a lifetime production of words to rival that of the most inexhaustible writer.[16] And he was increasingly hammering his central theme—the Jews.

From Dietrich Eckart, Hitler had learned early in his speaking career that he could always stir up a crowd by plucking at the widespread anti-Semitic sentiments then rampant in Europe, especially in Germany. His nasty swipes at "Jewish domination" and "Jewish usurers" unleashed the greatest applause.[17] Speeches with titles like "The World Jew and the World Stock Exchange" and "Germany at the Crossroads: The Jews' Paradise or German People's State?" drew large crowds eager to hear about the Jewish bugaboo, the root of all misery. One long-winded speech, titled "The 'Inciters' of Truth," laid blame for Germany's postwar downfall on Jews; a special reprint of the speech by the *Völkischer Beobachter* sold out, so it was reprinted again.[18] Among Hitler's favorite resources for his anti-Semitism were the works of American automobile magnate Henry Ford (*The International Jew*) and the notorious *Protocols of the Elders of Zion*. Even though Hitler soon knew that the *Protocols* were a forgery, he continued to invoke them in his speeches because they contained "the inner truth" about Jewry, he claimed.[19]

Gradually, Hitler had begun spinning his increasingly radical anti-Jewish views into an all-encompassing theory of the world. "Hitler and his associates...believed that anti-Semitism offered *the* explanatory framework for world history," wrote historian Jeffrey Herf.[20] By 1923, Hitler had developed a convenient, highly simplified, stereotype-based narrative of Jewish perfidy (*Werdegang des Judentums,* or "the path of the Jews"). Borrowing heavily from anti-Semitic writer Theodor Fritsch, Hitler outlined a tale of the cunning Jew. The story was, in Hitler's telling, a quick leap through the centuries that led inexorably to the Jews' full conquest of Germany, Europe, and the world. The path began with "court Jews" (*Hofjuden*) achieving positions of influence in Europe as personal bankers to nobility. Then came the "popular Jew" (*Volksjude*) who promoted democracy "and became everybody's friend" while espousing a "false humanitarianism."[21] But this good democratic Jew then mutated into the "blood Jew" (*Blutjude*), the merciless member of the Bolshevik leadership that took over Russia and unleashed a sanguinary reign of terror, Hitler claimed. "The Jew governs. He creates a dictatorship of the proletariat.... Instead of parliament, the gallows."[22]

Never mind historical details. Hitler's little story line was devoured by a crowd hungry for scapegoats. (It was also perfect preparation for what would become the most famous chapter of *Mein Kampf*, "Nation and Race.") Undergirding his paranoiac anti-Semitic construct of history was the message that Germans were the victims. He was not only painting the treacherous Jew as a target of hate and, eventually, extermination; he was first portraying Jews as the aggressor, an active enemy who was a mortal threat to Germans. As he told this story, over and over again, to rapt audiences, Hitler was laying the groundwork for a later message—convincing the German people that Jews had forced him to go to war. (In a 1939 speech before the Reichstag, he blamed Jews *in advance* for the outbreak of World War II and for their own coming mass extinction. If the "international Jewish capitalists" succeeded "in plunging mankind into yet another world war," railed Hitler, the result would be the "annihilation of the Jewish race in Europe.")

Even in the early 1920s, as he and Hanfstaengl were strolling home from a hugely popular movie, *Fridericus Rex,* which glorified Frederick the Great, Hitler made a comment that stunned his companion and foreshadowed his murderous future. Hitler said he especially liked the moment when the aging king threatened to have the crown prince beheaded. No sentimentality, indicated Hitler, should stand between a leader and his goals, a position often restated in later years. "Great deeds require harsh measures," Hitler told his walking companion. "What does it matter if a couple dozen of our Rhineland cities go up in flames? A hundred thousand dead would mean nothing if it assures Germany's future."

"I was thunderstruck," wrote Hanfstaengl.[23]

Hitler's expansionist bent was also beginning to show. He announced the Nazi belief in a Greater Germany encompassing all of German-speaking Austria and the Bohemian parts of Czechoslo-vakia, especially Sudetenland. He called for more "land and soil" for the German people, a harbinger of what would become his *Lebensraum* policy and, ultimately, his invasion of Russia.

While keeping his mad schedule, Hitler took time for a quick fund-raising trip to Berlin by car with Hanfstaengl, a trip that nearly brought the whole juggernaut down. Hanfstaengl's car, a not-so-shiny old Selve, was stopped in "red Saxony" near Leipzig by a Communist roadblock. Hitler was already known as the Communists' archenemy; had the armed men realized who the small mustachioed man was, the scene could have ended with Hitler's arrest, or worse. But the quick-thinking, theatrical Hanfstaengl—a dual American and German citizen—whipped out his U.S. passport and "affected an atrocious accent" in German, he wrote. Declaring himself an important international businessman, he described the fellow sitting silently in the backseat as "my man" (valet). The Communists waved them on.[24]

Hitler was by now, in mid-1923, unafraid to flaunt his extreme and anti-democratic views to the outside world. In an interview with an American newspaper, *The World,* he stated plainly: "Democracy is a joke.... History has always been made by an organized minority which seized power for the benefit of the majority." Elsewhere, he wrote: "The National Socialist movement is...the mortal enemy of today's parliamentary system. We oppose the concept of democratic majority rule and promote a Germanic democracy based on the authority of the leader."[25] Hitler told the *American Monthly* that "Marxism is not socialism, but a Jewish invention [and] no healthy man is a Marxist."[26]

The next showdown between Hitler and the ruling powers came on May 1, 1923, the traditional International Workers' Day. Informed that Communists and Socialists planned big rallies for May Day, Hitler and the Nazis decided to thwart and attack them. Drawing their weapons out of the Reichswehr arsenal—where they had been stored under special arrangement with the army—Hitler's men assembled on Theresa's Meadow, the massive field where the Octoberfest is held every year. But the Nazis were kept a great distance from their leftist adversaries and were eventually surrounded by police and the Reichswehr. Along with their right-wing allies, Hitler's men were forced to stand down and return their weapons to the Reichswehr armory. This was a victory for Lossow and Seisser and a nasty propaganda defeat for Hitler—the only one he would suffer in the months leading up to his putsch. Nursing his wounds, Hitler withdrew for several weeks to his preferred Alpine retreat, Berchtesgaden, near the Austrian border.

Staying at a bed-and-breakfast called Pension Moritz under his preferred and oft-used pseudonym Herr Wolf, he was joined on "his magic mountain," as one observer called it, by various members of his retinue.[27] Rudolf Hess, in a letter to his parents, said the leader's time in the mountains was doing him good. "What an unusual sight to see him ambling around in old lederhosen with bare knees and a short-sleeved shirt. He looks a lot better than before."[28]

Not all of his followers agreed. There were no rooms left at the

Pension Moritz when Hanfstaengl arrived in Berchtesgaden, so he had to bunk in with Eckart, the Munich muse, who seemed to be cooling to some of Hitler's extremist positions and antics. Eckart was put out with Hitler for marching around the courtyard of the little inn, cracking his leather whip and showing off to the proprietor's comely wife while spouting revolutionary predictions and declamations. "I must enter Berlin like Christ in the Temple of Jerusalem and wipe out the moneylenders!" shouted Hitler.

Eckart confided to Hanfstaengl: "Something has gone completely wrong with Adolf. The man is developing an incurable case of *folie de grandeur*. If he lets his Messiah complex run away with him, he will ruin us all."[29]

CHAPTER FOUR

A Hot Autumn

"Tonight the balloon goes up!"
—STORM TROOPER, 1923

Hitler's days in the mountains, it turned out, were balmy times before the coming storm. By autumn 1923, Germany was an explosion waiting to happen. The sitting national government under Chancellor Wilhelm Cuno had just collapsed, its policy of passive resistance a massive failure. Its replacement would be another center-left government under Gustav Stresemann. Inflation continued to gallop out of control, moving into the trillions of marks per U.S. dollar. Talk of civil war was in the air, and even of foreign invasion from the east (Polish and Czech forces) and from the west (French and Belgian forces). Besides assorted hints of aggression by the French military if Germany began falling apart, the French ambassador Pierre de Margerie had explicitly told Chancellor Stresemann that France would intervene if a right-wing dictatorship took over Germany—a major braking factor on potential putschists in Berlin.[1]

Just to Bavaria's north, the states of Thuringia (a land of rolling forests and cultural centers like Weimar and Eisenach) and Saxony (with major cities like Leipzig and Dresden) were in upheaval; they had just admitted Communists into their coalition governments who wanted to stage uprisings to grab the whole cake and stage a Communist revolution in Germany. Their plan was directly supported by the Communist International in Moscow, modeled after Russia's 1917 October Revolution. The plan was prospectively and aspirationally called the "German October." In response to these rumblings, General Seeckt and the Reichswehr were preparing to invade Thuringia and Saxony to oust the Communists. There was even talk of using Bavaria's Reichswehr forces to suppress the neighboring Communists. Germany was, in short, an unstable place with centrifugal forces in play.

In Bavaria, the desperate state government had appointed a *Kommissar*—a commissioner general—with near-dictatorial powers to lead the way out of the misery. Gustav Ritter von Kahr, a stolid, square-faced man with an upturned mustache, was supported by the two pillars of armed forces in Bavaria, General Lossow of the Reichswehr and Colonel Seisser of the Bavarian State Police. In fall 1923, the three leading men—Kahr, Lossow, and Seisser—were effectively a triumvirate ruling Bavaria, politically the most important state outside Prussia (the Weimar Republic had eighteen states and city-states). The military leaders—Lossow and Seisser—saw themselves in an isolated but strong position: They aimed to bolster Bavaria's border defenses to the north, keeping the Thuringian and Saxon reds out, and to strengthen their position on the ground by integrating the extra-legal paramilitaries directly into the Reichswehr Bavaria Seventh Division, nearly doubling its strength. They were even prepared for conflict with Reichswehr troops sent from Berlin.

Germany's turmoil was Hitler's gain. The more dazed and disillusioned people were, the more they responded to his extremist message. For the Nazi leader, the fall 1923 political season had gotten off to a good start. On September 1, returned and refreshed from his mountain retreat, Hitler found himself standing shoulder to shoulder with the vaunted General Ludendorff at a bombastic "German Day" rally in Nuremberg, Bavaria's second city. The odd couple—the stolid general and the unpredictable beer hall politician—shared the reviewing stand with seventeen-year-old Prince Ludwig Ferdinand of Prussia,[2] representing Germany's deposed but, in some quarters, still-loved royal dynasty. As the trio reviewed the marching by of an astonishing one hundred thousand people[3] expressing their nationalist sentiments and distaste for the Weimar Republic, Hitler's standing as the leading political celebrity in the right-wing movement was confirmed. With Ludendorff's blessing implied, Hitler gave a fiery speech that pulled no punches. "We need another revolution in Germany, not that Socialist, bourgeois, and Jewish revolution of 1918 but a nationalist revolution today to restore Germany's might and greatness.... We need a revolution, bloodshed, and a dictatorship.... We need no parliament, no government like the present," he said, pouring out his disdain for the creaky parliamentary process and its "weak majorities," as he liked to put it.[4] Majority rule, he believed, was equivalent to mediocre rule; it weakened strong leadership. Hitler's contempt for parliamentary democracy was so complete that he refused to let the Nazi Party participate in elections. His was a purely revolutionary party whose only imaginable path to power was the overthrow of the existing order.

On the following day, September 2, while still in Nuremberg, Hitler's Storm Troopers joined forces with two hard-line nationalistic paramilitaries—the Bund Oberland, led by a veterinary professor named Dr. Friedrich Weber, and the Reichskriegsflagge, led by Captain Ernst Röhm, a scar-faced World War I officer who was still an active member of the Reichswehr. Together, they formed the Kampfbund, or Fighting League. Its military chief was retired Lieutenenat Colonel Hermann Kriebel, a tall, bullet-headed, hardened veteran of World War I. Mincing no words, the Kampfbund immediately called for the abrogation of the "disgraceful" Treaty of Versailles and the overthrow of the Berlin government.[5] Hitler would soon be named the Kampfbund's political leader, dramatically expanding the forces at his disposal just at the moment when he was contemplating a grand strike.

These developments were only the beginning of a hot political autumn of moves and countermoves that would culminate, within two months, in Hitler's play for power. The chessboard jousting was among three forces: Hitler's team, including the paramilitaries; the Bavarian triumvirate of Kahr, Lossow, and Seisser, with their control over the Reichswehr's Bavaria Division and the Bavarian State Police; and the national government in Berlin, including the German army, though its loyalties were often uncertain.

The explosions began on September 26 when the new national government under Gustav Stresemann announced the end of the failed passive resistance to the French occupation of the Ruhr region. This unleashed peals of protest from *völkisch* nationalists. It also triggered the creation of the dictatorial commissioner general's job for Kahr, the former governor who had earlier proclaimed Bavaria a "bastion of order." Known as a cautious bureaucrat—"a man of eternal preparations," complained Göring—Kahr's new powers rested entirely on the support of the Bavarian State Police and the Reichswehr. That meant Lossow and Seisser. Thus, they found each other in a common embrace that made them an unofficial but iron triumvirate.

Declaring the appointment of the indecisive Kahr "a heavy blow" to the *völkisch* movement, Hitler also attacked the Stresemann government for lifting the passive resistance policy. To protest the changes, he announced fourteen rallies and fourteen speeches for the following day, September 27. Commissioner Kahr's first official act using his new dictatorial powers was to declare a state of emergency in Bavaria, automatically banning Hitler's rallies. This drastic step was soon followed by another move that, by contrast, played favorably with the Nazis—the forced expulsion from Bavaria of more than one hundred families of oft-vilified "Eastern Jews." In Berlin, Chancellor Stresemann denounced the Bavarian action as "medieval."[6]

Now it was Berlin's move. By early morning on September 27, the Stresemann government had announced a *national* state of emergency, placing full executive powers in the hands of the defense minister—which effectively meant in the hands of General Seeckt, the Reichswehr chief of staff. Figuratively, Berlin and Bavaria were looking down their gun barrels at each other.

But by late morning, the order of battle had shifted again. Into the war of words and indirect armed standoff came the element of public insult. In its edition of September 27, Hitler's *Völkischer Beobachter* published a front-page article headlined "The Stresemann-Seeckt Dictators." Credited to the newspaper's Berlin bureau, the story denounced the national government's state of emergency as a bald-faced attempt to wipe out the *völkisch* movement. But the offending lines were personal. Driving General Seeckt's decisions, the *Völkischer Beobachter* declared, was the political influence of his Jewish wife, "née Jakobsohn, born in 1872 in Frankfurt and registered on her birth certificate as *mosaisch* [Jewish]." Chancellor Stresemann's wife, the article mentioned, was also Jewish.[7]

In fact, Seeckt's wife was half Jewish, but the very mention of her name, much less her religious preference, infuriated the aristocratic general. He struck back. Using his executive powers, he ordered the *Völkischer Beobachter* shut down. As Reichswehr chief of staff, he told his commanding general in Bavaria, Lossow, to execute the ban on Hitler's mouthpiece. Lossow, a good German officer but an even better Bavarian, refused to carry out the order. His fig leaf was a refusal by Commissioner Kahr to recognize General Seeckt's right to intervene in Bavarian affairs. General Seeckt, in turn, fired General Lossow, effective immediately. But Lossow would not go. Citing overriding authority from Kahr, the Bavarian-born general defied his own commanding officer. Kahr announced that Lossow and the Reichswehr Seventh Division now worked for *him* and that Bavaria "must in this hour serve as the besieged bastion of true Germanness."[8] Lossow swore an oath to the Bavarian government, implicitly breaking his oath to the Weimar constitution. On October 22, at 11 a.m., the entire Bavarian Division was marched onto its drill grounds, where every soldier—almost all of them Bavarians to begin with—happily swore an oath to Bavaria.[9] Lossow and the Seventh Division were now in full mutiny against General Seeckt, shaking Reichswehr morale throughout Germany.[10] Seeckt wrote a letter to President Ebert warning of "civil war."[11] The only remaining question in some parts of Germany, wrote a spy working for Lossow in Saxony, was: "When will Bavaria march? Any delay is considered dangerous."[12]

But just because the Bavarian triumvirate had broken with Berlin did not mean it had joined with Hitler and his newfound ally, Ludendorff. On the contrary, the Hitler-Ludendorff camp continued to joust with Kahr, Lossow, and Seisser over how to deal with Berlin. Hitler wanted to proclaim a national putsch and march on Berlin. But he first needed the Bavarian Reichswehr and triumvirate on his side, and that seemed to be a question of timing. Hitler's intellectual sidekick, Scheubner-Richter, wrote in a September memo to Hitler: "The popular mood is such that *any* political change would be welcome. It's just a matter of finding the right psychological moment to take advantage of this mood."[13]

To Hitler, the psychological moment was now. He was ready to *losschlagen*. Inspired by the Mussolini model of a march on the capital, Hitler would mount a putsch in Munich, proclaim a new national government, then stage a 379-mile march on Berlin to topple the old one. The plan, informed and guided by Scheubner-Richter, seemed infallible.

But it was not the triumvirate's plan. Though they shared Hitler's desire for an authoritarian right-wing government in Germany, they were deeply ambivalent about an armed march on Berlin. Among the three, Lossow was the most conflicted, declaring at one point, with a bang of his fist on a tabletop, "God knows, I want to march—I really want to march!" But, he added, he would do so only with "a fifty-one percent" chance of success—just the kind of equivocation that drove the all-or-nothing Hitler to outrage. One thing the three triumvirs agreed on: They did not want hotheaded Hitler at the fore of any march or takeover in Berlin, not even with Ludendorff by his side. And rather than a dictatorship led by a strongman—especially a strong-headed one like Hitler—the triumvirate wanted a group leadership in Berlin, what they called a *Direktorium,* or directorate (utterly overlooking its negative associations with the brutal excesses of the French Revolution).

Hitler's quixotic and bristling team—with its battle-hardened Kriebel, bespectacled veterinarian Weber, disfigured Röhm, dour Rosenberg, conspiratorial Scheubner-Richter, and even debonair Hanfstaengl—were by now spoiling for action. Hermann Göring, the high-spirited leader of the Storm Troopers, had blood in his eyes. In a Munich meeting with his commanders from around

Bavaria, he laid out a murderous scenario: even before the coup began, he said, he wanted all unit leaders to prepare lists of people in their towns and districts "to be eliminated" as soon as the putsch was sprung. "At least one of them will have to be shot immediately after the proclamation [of the putsch] to set an example," he said.[14]

Göring was not the only conspirator who envisioned a quick reign of terror if and when the Nazis succeeded in their takeover. Theodor von der Pfordten, a Bavarian state Supreme Court judge and a crypto-Nazi, drafted for Hitler a draconian provisional constitution to replace the Weimar constitution the minute the putsch succeeded. The new constitution would have abruptly ended democracy and substituted a radical dictatorship, starting with dissolving the parliament. The constitution draft banned strikes and union activity, removed all Jews from public jobs, confiscated Jewish money and holdings, and forced "unproductive consumers" or people regarded as "security risks" into labor or "collection camps," a euphemism for concentration camps. Freedom of the press, assembly, and speech were suspended. Worse, the draft constitution was rife with threats of the death penalty. It would be applied for such crimes as refusing to work, participating in illegal meetings, or not turning over funds "earned from the suffering of the German people during the war"—another swing aimed at alleged Jewish profiteers. All violations and sentences were to be dealt with in fewer than three days by summary courts-martial, with no appeal. "The death penalty shall be executed by hanging or shooting," von der Pfordten's draft constitution read.[15]

Throughout October, the jousting between Hitler's team and the triumvirate continued. One of its greatest ironies was the high level of cooperation between the Kampfbund paramilitaries and the established forces of the Reichswehr and the Bavarian State Police—even as their political leaders squabbled. In order to take any serious action, such as ousting the French invaders from the Ruhr region (which they considered), holding back the reds now agitating in Thuringia and Saxony, or marching on Berlin, they knew they needed one another. Weber, leader of the Bund Oberland, the best-armed of the Kampfbund militias, was approached about moving his heavy artillery into Reichswehr and Bavarian State Police units on Bavaria's northern border—"apparently because they didn't have any of their own," he noted, a plausible scenario given the postwar restrictions on the Reichswehr's size and budget.[16]

In addition to such prospective force-sharing, Hitler's men were regularly trained in Reichswehr barracks, sometimes even wearing Reichswehr uniforms. Kampfbund weapons were stored in official arsenals; paramilitary troops spent their off hours drilling with the regulars. Lossow sent orders to all his commanders around Bavaria to prepare for integrating paramilitaries from the so-called Patriotic Leagues into their units. Since the whole business was a glaring violation of the Treaty of Versailles, in October Lossow called for an "Autumn Exercise" to disguise the melding process from Allied observers assigned to enforce the treaty.

While the triumvirate prevaricated about marching on Berlin and joining political forces with Hitler, the would-be rebels were gearing up for action. In a November 1 meeting arranged by Weber in his own apartment, Hitler confronted the state police commander, Seisser: "The time has come. Economic misery is causing such despair among our people that we must act or they will swing over to the Communists."[17] Seisser replied that he was traveling to Berlin the next day to find out if General Seeckt would support a march on the capital or some other takeover by force. He pleaded with Hitler to refrain from any solo acts of revolution, at least until he returned from Berlin. Hitler responded: "Colonel Seisser, I will wait until you return, but then you must take action and get the

Commissioner General [Kahr] to take action. If you return and nothing happens, I will be forced to act on my own."[18] According to some reports, Hitler also retracted his earlier pledges not to stage a putsch.[19]

Four days later, Seisser was back in Munich. General Seeckt, he reported, had dismissed the idea of a march on Berlin out of hand. While the old general favored takeover by a right-wing directorate, he would support it only if it followed "the legal path"—a declaration by President Ebert under Article 48 of the Weimar constitution. This was, to the triumvirate, confirmation of the slippery ways of the Berlin leadership. Lossow had earlier expressed his frustrations in dealing with the men in the capital: "If there are only eunuchs and castrati in Berlin who are too cowardly to make a firm decision, then Germany cannot possibly be saved by Bavaria alone!"[20] Strong words, but still no action.

By now, the external pressures on Hitler to act had become nearly irresistible. For months, the men in the paramilitaries and the Storm Troopers had been primed for action—trained, indoctrinated, and given hope of a historic role in "chasing out that gang in Berlin" and restoring German national pride. But pressure was also building from within, and Hitler was highly responsive to his own inner needs.

After four years of ranting against the "November criminals" in Berlin, after continuously forecasting the imminent doom of the nation, Hitler had essentially nothing to show for his bombast. By strictly forbidding Nazi Party participation in elections—since he opposed parliamentary rule—he had made even small victories impossible, apart from beer hall altercations. Though it had a growing membership, the party could not point to growing *voter* support or elected representatives. This political stagnation, combined with his restless personality, kindled in Hitler a burning compulsion to act.

When faced with high-risk situations, Hitler's instinct was almost always to take the leap. Action was his aphrodisiac, his catnip, his default. His impetuosity often overwhelmed all other considerations, as the world would later learn, to its horror and sorrow. Hitler had whipped his audiences, as well as himself, into a frenzy of expectation. His increasingly grandiose self-image demanded that he go for the bold stroke. He had recently compared himself to Martin Luther, Frederick the Great, and Richard Wagner, his heroes and role models: "I will fight on and never lose sight of the goal I've set myself to be the pioneer of the great German liberation movement," he said.[21] In another conversation, Hitler had even styled himself as a latter-day Napoleon. "He identified himself with Napoleon's march on Paris from the Isle of Elba, which also began with a small following but won all of France," said Colonel Otto Freiherr (Baron) von Berchem, General Lossow's chief of staff. "He wanted Bavaria's military might brought against Berlin, which we all considered hopeless. We rejected it out of hand."[22]

Finally, there was the pressure from above. Hitler began to sense that the triumvirate might, somehow, get its act together and make a move—but without him. Whether by putsch or by negotiation, the Bavarian threesome might maneuver itself into a position to grab the reins of power in Germany. Hitler's fears were confirmed by a meeting Commissioner Kahr called in his office on Tuesday, November 6, to which he invited all the paramilitary chiefs with one big exception: the Nazis. Neither Hitler nor Göring was present. But the Kampfbund leaders—Colonel Kriebel, Dr. Weber, and others—were there; Kahr knew they would make a beeline for Hitler as soon as his meeting ended. The ostensible purpose of the meeting, Kahr said, was to put full brakes on the rumored plans of the paramilitaries, including Hitler's Storm Troopers, to make a premature move against the Communists in Thuringia.[23] Yet in the meeting—which included all three members of the triumvirate—Kahr was more focused on Berlin: he declared that any move to create a dictatorial directorship had to be carefully prepared and had to include some strong figures from North Germany who had not yet been found. "The key point was that we would have a nationalistic government in Berlin, free of parliamentary interference," reported Max Kühner, a factory owner who was present. "Dictatorship was the most important thing. Stresemann's administration had to be fought. Liberation from the [1918] revolution and all its effects. Liberation from the unions and the trusts."[24]

To accomplish regime change in Berlin, Kahr told the group assembled in his office, there were two choices: the "normal path" and the "abnormal path." The normal path ran through Article 48 of the Weimar constitution, allowing President Ebert to declare an emergency and create a directorate. This seemed unlikely, especially in view of Seisser's unsuccessful overtures to General von Seeckt. "Therefore, the abnormal path is prepared," continued Kahr, meaning an armed takeover: "the preliminaries are done." Then, sounding like the man of eternal preparations that Göring called him, Kahr added: "But action can be taken only according to a unified and meticulously worked-out plan." And such a plan had to be led by Kahr himself. "Only I will give the order to begin," he said. The commissioner hinted that it might happen within two weeks.[25]

Lossow added, "The Bavaria Division is ready."[26]

All these details reached Hitler's ears within hours. Finally, he realized, Kahr seemed serious about acting—but not yet quite ready to *losschlagen*. Still, Hitler was beginning to feel outflanked. Kahr seemed to be trying to neutralize him into inaction by waiting. Meeting that evening with Scheubner-Richter and The-odor von der Pfordten, Hitler told the men their moment had come. He had made his decision: after four years of dreaming about revolution, they were finally going to get one, and it would carry them to the pinnacle of power.

First, they would seize power in Munich. By usurping the Bavarian instruments of control—the government, the military, and the Bavarian State Police—Hitler could establish an unassailable power base in Bavaria. He would then proclaim a new national government and march to the German capital. Modeled on Napoleon's 1815 trek from the Isle of Elba to Paris, Hitler's march would trigger a "national uprising," he believed. But the undertaking could succeed militarily, Hitler knew, only if he forced Kahr, Lossow, and Seisser into his corner. Hitler intended to capture the Bavarian triumvirate at gunpoint and make them his co-conspirators, pushing them to finally do what they had been saying they would do: march on Berlin. He wanted to "help them make the leap," as he put it. Colonel Kriebel described it as "giving them a little push into the water." The plan was bold, complicated, oddly inspired—and highly risky. The penalty for failure could be death.

Following his meeting with Scheubner-Richter and von der Pfordten, Hitler planned his storming of the barricades for the coming weekend, November 10 and 11. "All the people in the administration are then away from their offices and the police are only at half strength. That is the time to strike," Hitler told Hanfstaengl.[27] Colonel Kriebel suggested announcing night exercises by Kampf-bund forces on Saturday, with troops then marching into the city on Sunday morning, their bands playing—all common enough occurrences in Munich. Those smartly marching troops would then turn into coup makers, seizing key government buildings, police stations, and communication centers. But as Hitler and other Kampfbunders discussed this plan on Wednesday morning, November 7, news arrived that dramatically altered the timetable, shifted the order of battle, and may have determined the outcome of events. Hitler learned that Commissioner Kahr would be making a speech on the following night, Thursday, in the Bürgerbräukeller, a large beer hall where Hitler had often spoken. Kahr was hardly a rabble-rouser, but beer halls were the venues of choice in 1920s Munich, as much public meeting places as drinking and eating establishments. Though "few other places are so democratic" as a Munich beer hall, wrote one American visitor in 1909,[28] the capacious watering holes could of course become scenes of nasty brawls among political factions. Many a skull had been cracked with a flung beer stein. Drinking, like 1920s politics in Bavaria, was a contact sport. For the last few years, Hitler had been cutting his teeth on just such confrontations. But no fireworks were to be expected on this Thursday night.

Organized by a nationalistic Munich businessman to shore up support for Kahr, the meeting was meant to give the new commissioner a chance to rail against the Bolshevist threat while explaining his economic program, which had so far failed to bring relief to Bavaria.[29] Even the prices of beer and bread — the two economic issues that the government could directly influence and that were uppermost in Bavarians' minds — were out of control.[30] Last-minute invitations to Kahr's speech were delivered by hand to all the Munich elite: the business community, leading politicians, city officials and parliamentarians, academics, the top newspaper editors. Bavarian governor Eugen von Knilling, who supported giving his executive powers to Kahr, was coming. So were Justice Minister Franz Gürtner, Baron von Berchem, and Count Soden, a representative of the deposed, but still widely respected, Wittelsbach royal house of Bavaria. Among the business elite, of course, were Jews like

Ludwig Wasserman, a factory owner. The Bavarian Industrialists Association sent notices to its members with a comment: "This gathering is intended to be a historically significant moment."[31] The meeting would feature the establishment talking to the establishment.

Best of all, Hitler was told, both General Lossow and Colonel Seisser would be present. Under one roof, in one hall, at one time — the triumvirate would be there for the grabbing. He could finally act on a line he'd often said to Hanfstaengl: "We have to compromise people into joining our cause."[32] The Bürgerbräukeller was like a theater waiting for a play, and Hitler was going to be its star. On Wednesday morning, he moved the putsch up from the weekend to the very next day, Thursday, November 8. He had to move fast.

For two days, November 7 and 8, Hitler and his closest confederates were in a whirl of secret preparations. They held war councils and dashed around Munich. The Kampfbund's assorted armed units, including many outside Munich, needed to be put on alert without knowing what for. Hitler insisted, for good reason, on tight secrecy; any leak of his putsch plans could foil the plot. Only a handful of fellow schemers were drawn into the circle of secrecy. One of those was Röhm, the former World War I army captain (and future head of the Storm Troopers), who headed the Reichskriegsflagge paramilitary. Röhm was told to invite his three hundred men to a "comradely evening" of drinking and singing at the cavernous Löwenbräukeller on the Stiglmaierplatz and await a signal from Hitler's men in the Bürgerbräukeller. If the initial putsch succeeded, the code words for the night would be: *"Glücklich entbunden"* (a charming but ambiguous phrase meaning "happily relieved" or "baby successfully delivered"). Röhm's beery social evening would then turn into an attack on key buildings in Munich.

Even as he was giving these orders, Hitler did not know that General Lossow was making his own preparations for the possibility of an uprising in the coming days. On November 7, Lossow ordered all the Reichswehr unit commanders in Bavaria to Munich, informing them that "a Hitler-Ludendorff Reich dictatorship" was brewing and that their troops should be put on highest alert. Lossow told the commanders he had let Hitler know that if he prematurely staged a putsch, "he would have the Bavarian Reichswehr against him." He added: "We're not going to be part of this craziness."[33]

While Lossow was girding his forces for trouble, however, others were paving the way for Hitler's success. One of the key military institutions in Munich was the Reichswehr's Infantry School — the training academy for future infantry officers. A hulking, four-story edifice with its own drilling grounds in the Blutenburgstrasse, not far from the Löwenbräukeller, the Infantry School had about five hundred cadets. The place was a hotbed of youthful enthusiasm, nationalist sentiment, and Nazi leanings. Speakers like Ludendorff and Captain Hermann Ehrhardt, the former Kapp putschist and Organisation Consul leader, had lured the cadets toward the *völkisch* movement. In one speech, Ludendorff had called Hitler a "fabulous person."[34] One Infantry School officer, Lieutenant Gerhard Rossbach, was secretly a member of the Nazi Party and did not hesitate to spread his beliefs through the school's humming grapevine.[35] Rossbach's spadework would pay off on the night of the putsch.

On November 8, the day of the planned putsch, Hitler moved through Munich trying to make preparations without making noise. Von der Pfordten had worked out a detailed plan for takeover of Munich's main telephone exchange — "six men enter the Residenzstrasse door, take the stairs to the right, arrest Director Wild on the second floor."[36] At midday, Hitler showed up at the cramped offices of the *Völkischer Beobachter* and told its editor, Rosenberg, the disorganized Baltic German, what was up. "Tonight we strike," he said. Hanfstaengl was there, too. Hitler told both men to meet him at eight o'clock in the evening at the Bürgerbräukeller — "and don't forget to bring your pistols."

Hitler made a quick visit to Hermann Esser, the slightly unsavory member of Hitler's inner clique whose bullying style alienated many, though Hitler found it useful. Esser lay sick with jaundice, but Hitler persuaded him to rise from his bed. "I need you tonight," he insisted. Esser, the good soldier, pulled himself up and hurried to join Röhm at the Löwenbräukeller.

As evening fell, some of Munich's blue-uniformed city policemen — not to be confused with the green-uniformed military-style Bavarian State Police — noticed armed men, some in steel helmets, assembling in company-sized units on small squares near the Isar Gate, not far from the Bürgerbräukeller. Some were Nazi Storm Troopers. One Twelfth District officer, Georg Albang, overheard a passing bicyclist say: "You guys know something? Tonight it's happening!" By six o'clock, with the evening chill setting in, Officer Anton Zauner had seen seventy men in mixed uniforms, many carrying bayonets or short daggers, marching across the Maximilian Bridge in the general direction of the Bürgerbräukeller. Officer Joseph Bömerl, dressed in street clothes, noticed gatherings of paramilitaries on the Gärtnerplatz and at the Nazi offices in the Corneliusstrasse. Twice he heard someone say, "Tonight the balloon goes up!"[37] Clearly Hitler's obsessive secrecy had sprung leaks; the paramilitaries knew why they were assembling.

With its formidable intelligence operation, the Munich City Police always maintained a tight watch on just such activities; they received detailed overnight reports on every significant political meeting in town, sometimes several per night. Even the street cops were trained to report suspicious activity. But on this of all nights their system failed: when Officer Bömerl phoned the political division at police headquarters at 6:45 p.m., he was told: "Don't worry. The Nazis are invited to that big meeting [at the Bürgerbräukeller]. There's probably nothing to these rumors that something is going to happen tonight."[38] Forewarned, the police—who had fended off unfounded putsch rumors for years—took no action.[39] This time, however, the sky really was about to fall.

CHAPTER FIVE

The Putsch

"I will never let those swine take me. I will shoot myself first."
—ADOLF HITLER, NOVEMBER 11, 1923

With his stumpy build and bureaucratic style, Gustav Ritter von Kahr was anything but charismatic; certainly, he was no crowd-pleaser. The last thing Kahr was expected to do was draw a large turnout to a beer hall.

But in the crisis-ridden atmosphere of 1923, people in Munich, like everywhere in Germany, were desperate for a ray of hope. So many people showed up for Kahr's appearance on this cold and soon-to-be-snowy November night that they could not all fit into the Bürgerbräukeller. The plainspoken Kahr had drawn three thousand people to hear a hastily organized speech in defense of his new regime. Even Hitler was surprised.

When the Nazi leader arrived in a red Mercedes at the beer hall's gates at 8:30 p.m., he could barely get inside. A contingent of police had closed the doors, explaining to a clamoring crowd in the street

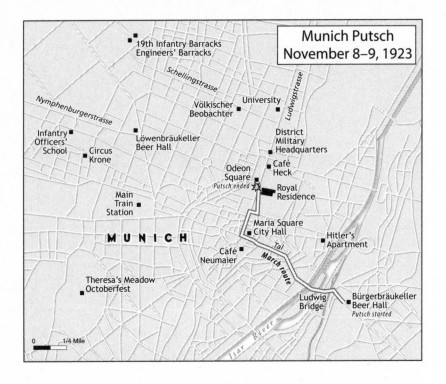

Munich Putsch
November 8–9, 1923

that the hall was filled to bursting. "It was so tight that you couldn't have fallen over," remarked one man standing near the podium.[1]

At the dais, Commissioner Kahr was droning away about "state authority" and the "nationalist spirit" and "the will to act."[2] The distinguished audience, their beer steins filled, listened in polite silence.

Suddenly, the doors to the capacious hall flew open. A platoon of uniformed men pushed their way inside, their military gear clanking. At their head was Hitler, his eyes flashing and his face "wildly distorted" with excitement. Wearing a frock coat pinned with his two World War I Iron Cross medals, he looked like, depending on whom you asked, an operatic hero or a "forlorn little waiter," as one observer put it. Turning to his bodyguard, Ulrich Graf, Hitler said, "Make sure I don't get shot in the back."[3]

The crowd was so thick, Hitler recalled, that he had to "use my fists and elbows to clear my path" to the podium. Commissioner Kahr, interrupted in mid-sentence, stood stock-still, his face a mask of indignation. The room erupted in confusion and outrage.

"Quiet!" shouted Hitler. "Silence!" The room roared.

Jumping onto a chair, Hitler raised his Browning pistol and fired a single shot into the twenty-five-foot-high coffered ceiling. "Silence!" he shouted again. "The national revolution has begun."

Now "dead silence reigned," said one man present. Hitler had the meeting's attention. His pistol still held aloft, he warned: "The building is surrounded by six hundred heavily armed men! No one is allowed to leave. If you don't stay calm, I will have a machine gun placed in the balcony!" Many in the audience thought they had a madman in their midst.

As Hitler spoke, a platoon-strength unit led by Hermann Göring had occupied the main entrance with a heavy machine gun. They blocked all the side doors. Through the windows to the beer garden, people could see steel-helmeted men carrying carbines. Hitler had gotten the drop on three thousand of Munich's finest, turning a dignified if boring event into a massive hostage-taking. Kahr was now "trembling and pale."[4]

From atop his chair, Hitler continued to shout: "The Bavarian government is deposed. The national government is deposed. A provisional government is being formed. The Reichswehr and Bavarian State Police barracks are occupied. Reichswehr and police units are marching here under the swastika flag."[5]

Much of what Hitler said was exaggerated (he did not have six hundred men, but perhaps half that many), untrue (the Reichswehr and Bavarian State Police barracks were not occupied), or only aspirational (Hitler *hoped* to create a new government in the next hour).

But, like so much Hitler would do in his political career, he painted the dream first, then tried to fill in the facts.

Besides Kahr, the two most important men in the room were those in uniform, General Lossow and Colonel Seisser. Seated near the podium, they looked on in disbelief and fury, unable to defend themselves or anyone else. Lossow's first thought when he heard commotion at the door was that a leftist coup must be in the making. "It never occurred to me that men of nationalist politics would attack a gathering of nationalists," said Lossow. "I hadn't even brought a sidearm."

As Hitler approached the podium, a police officer, Major Hunglinger, moved into his path, his hand in his pocket. But the fiery-eyed Hitler was quicker; he lifted his pistol to the major's head and growled: "Take your hand out of your pocket." The major's hand came out empty.[6]

Commissioner Kahr stood like a statue at the podium, his interrupted speech still in his hand, his face betraying nothing. Hitler gruffly addressed the triumvirate: "Gentlemen, I must ask you to come with me to the side room. I guarantee your safety. It will take only ten minutes." At close range, Lossow noticed that Hitler seemed carried away, in "a state of ecstasy." As Hitler marched the three men through a gauntlet of Storm Troopers toward the Bürgerbräukeller's side room, Lossow whispered to Kahr and Seisser: "Play along!" The words in German are *Komödie spielen*—"playact," "make theater," or "create comedy." What was about to happen was part comedy, part tragedy.

As Hitler herded the three men into the side room, Göring, the Storm Trooper commander, took over the main room. Shouts of disgust and derision rose again from the restless crowd: "Theater!" "Mexico!" "South America!" Hitler was being ridiculed as a tinpot insurrectionist. Göring stopped the shouting with another pistol shot into the high ceiling. Assuring the assembled dignitaries that the Nazis' actions were not an attack on Kahr but the beginning of a "national uprising," Göring asked the audience to be patient for a while.[7]

"And, besides, what are you worried about? You've got your beer," he said.

In the Bürgerbräukeller's side room, Hitler faced the thorniest part of his improbable undertaking: converting his three chief hostages into his three closest collaborators. Hitler seemed still in a kind of rapture, according to those present. "He was covered with sweat," said the general. It was true: when Hitler made speeches, holding forth for two or three hours at a time, he always ended up soaked in sweat.[8] Tonight, in the midst of the greatest gamble of his political life, the putsch leader was drenched in a matter of minutes.

Despite Göring's anodyne assurance that Kahr was not under attack, Hitler was threatening his three hostages. "Nobody leaves the room alive without my permission," he said. Calling Bavaria "the springboard for the Reich government," Hitler told the men their new roles: General Lossow would become Germany's new defense minister, Colonel Seisser the head of the new "national police," and Commissioner Kahr the chief regent of Bavaria. Hitler would assume "political leadership," he added, without specifying a job. To lead a new "national army" with the Storm Troopers and other paramilitaries at its core, Hitler had chosen General Ludendorff. As the former hero of World War I—he won the great battles of Liège in Belgium and Tannenberg in East Prussia that knocked Russia out of the war— Ludendorff was still a demigod to many Germans. He was also the chief promoter of the infamous stab-in-the-back legend, disingenuously claiming that Germany's army had been near victory in 1918 when it was betrayed from behind by craven civilians, especially Socialists and Jews. Ludendorff's name and military heroism were the perfect cover for Hitler's chief biographical weaknesses: he was uneducated and he had never achieved noncommissioned officer's rank, despite two medals for bravery. But, as the putsch unfolded, Ludendorff was not yet at the Bürgerbräukeller.

In the tense standoff in the beer hall's side room, Hitler now became more menacing. "Each of us must accept his assigned role," he growled, waving his pistol. "Otherwise he has no right to live. You must fight with me, win with me or die with me. If things go wrong, I have four bullets in my pistol: three for my collaborators, if you desert me, and the last one for myself." Hitler suddenly lifted the Browning to his own head.

Kahr, who had been silent since the putsch began, seething with "disgust and hatred," finally spoke up: "You can arrest me, you can have me shot, you can shoot me yourself. Dying or not dying is unimportant."

Hitler was stuck. Ten minutes had passed, and the triumvirate was not playing the game he had planned. Ludendorff, his trump card, had not yet arrived (Hitler had sent Scheubner-Richter to pick him up). Hitler's threats of violence, even suicide, as well as his appeals to patriotism—none of these had moved the triumvirate to join Hitler's adventure. The impetuous putschist was left with only one weapon, but it was his strongest: his voice.

Leaving the triumvirate under guard—the three men were not allowed to converse with one another—Hitler returned to the raucous main hall, where the Bürgerbräukeller beer maids were still busily delivering one-liter mugs to the tables. More shouts of "Cowboy tactics!" "Mexico!" and "South America!" Again, Hitler silenced the crowd with a pistol shot.

Now Hitler was on his home turf. At a beer hall podium, with an audience spread before him like a carpet, Hitler shifted into gear. In his usual evangelical style, he told the crowd of his plans for the new government led by the men from Bavaria. The time had come, he said, "to march on that godless Babel called Berlin. We must use all of Bavaria's power...to save the German people." Exactly five years earlier, Hitler noted, Germany had suffered the "greatest disgrace" when the 1918 revolution was proclaimed. "Today that disgrace comes to an end!"[9] Already, the assemblage that had been jeering was beginning to cheer—loudly (the *Münchener Zeitung* called it *stürmischer Beifall,* "stormy applause"). "In the other room, Kahr, Lossow, and Seisser are wrestling hard with their decision," said Hitler. "I ask you now: Are you in agreement with my proposed solution to the German question? You can see that we are not driven by selfish motives or personal gain, but only by the battle for the fatherland in the eleventh hour." More *stürmischer Beifall.*

Finally, Hitler added an appeal to local sensibilities: "In a free Germany, there is also room for an autonomous Bavaria. One thing I can say to you: either the German revolution begins tonight or we will all be dead by dawn!"[10]

The crowd went wild. In the space of a few minutes, Hitler's rhetoric had won the approval of much of the Munich establishment, including those who only moments before had dismissed him as a half-baked caudillo. "It was an oratorical masterpiece," wrote historian Karl Alexander von Müller, who was present. "He swung the temper of the crowd with just a few sentences. It was like turning a glove inside out. Hitler left the hall with the total endorsement of the gathering to tell Kahr that if he joined Hitler's coup, he would have everyone behind him."[11]

As if on cue—he had arrived late on purpose—Ludendorff, the Lion of Tannenberg and Liège, entered the hall. Shouts of *Achtung!*

("Attention!") and *Heil!* ("Hail!") rose from the crowd. Though dressed in civilian clothes, the upright general was unmistakable and, through his appearance alone, commanded men to their feet. As Ludendorff passed to the side room, it was as though the imprimatur of a righteous Germany with an honorable past had been stamped on the proceedings.

Hitler followed the general into the side room. Kahr, Lossow, and Seisser heard the cheering; they knew the temper of the crowd. Still, they hesitated. Ludendorff addressed the three men: "Gentlemen, I am just as surprised as you are by what has happened."[12] That was probably not true, but Ludendorff obviously felt confronted with new facts on the ground. "What's done is done," he said. "The issue is the fatherland and the great *völkisch* cause. I can only advise you to join with us in this undertaking."

Looking directly at his fellow German general, Ludendorff said: "Okay, Lossow, let's do it." Lossow apparently felt bound to take orders from Germany's greatest living soldier. With tears in his eyes, Lossow clicked his heels and said: "Your Excellency's wish is my command."[13] The men shook hands. Seisser, a mere colonel, had no choice left. He, too, shook Ludendorff's hand, a classic silent agreement.

Only Kahr held out. Hitler pressed: "The deed is done. There is no going back. This is an historic moment." The crowd outside would "carry you on their shoulders,"[14] Hitler told Kahr. Finally, the equivocating commissioner general found a way to take Hitler's assignment of Bavarian regent: "Gentlemen, in the end we are all monarchists. I'll accept the job [of leading Bavaria] as a placeholder for the [deposed but possibly returning] king."

Hitler, whose mood and appearance had gone from agitated revolutionary to delighted schoolboy, insisted that the men carry their newfound unity onto the public stage. As he returned to the main hall, his face "was beaming," said one observer. Hitler had clearly won the first round.

But victory wasn't enough. Hitler needed to set his actions in a historical context to limn their appeal and justify their meaning in a larger time frame. Speaking to the crowd, Hitler said: "Tonight I want to fulfill the promise I made to myself five years ago today as I lay, blinded and crippled, in a military hospital—never to rest, never to give up until the criminals of November [1918] were toppled and the German people had risen again on the ruins of today's troubled Germany, with power, greatness, freedom, and joy. Amen!"

Hitler's words were greeted again by stormy applause, even though they were a perfect example of Hitler's rewriting of history. He was never crippled by the gas attack that temporarily blinded him, and he never again made such a claim. And most historians doubt his melodramatic story about having sworn to reverse the revolution right after it happened. More likely he was presenting a myth he'd created about himself. But no one in the Bürgerbräukeller knew that.

Ludendorff added his share of sentimentality, claiming to be "deeply touched by this momentous event" and ready to serve again. "Today it's about the highest possible stakes (*Es geht heute um das Ganze*).... This hour is a turning point in German history."[15] Ludendorff later said that he was in the grip of "barely contained inner excitement."

The other men spoke briefly but with seeming sincerity, pledging themselves to the new cause. Gazing deeply into one another's eyes, they all exchanged what appeared to be heartfelt handshakes. Obviously moved, Hitler placed his left hand on their joined right hands; some observers compared it to the historic hands-atop-hands

"Rütli oath" that formed the Swiss confederation in the sixteenth century. Tears were shed on the stage and in the crowd. Finally, the entire assemblage burst into a robust rendition of the "Song of Germany"—*"Deutschland, Deutschland über alles."* According to historian Müller, many people were "so choked up that they couldn't sing at all."

But the final uplifting scene of nationalist fervor and comradely unity masked brutal aspects of Hitler's putsch that were unfolding in the Bürgerbräukeller and elsewhere. Göring's prediction of widespread arrests, with the underlying threat of targeted assassinations, was becoming reality. Now that the performance was over, Kahr, Lossow, and Seisser were escorted back to the side room under guard. The crowd was free to leave—except for certain people. Storm Troopers and other Kampfbunders began pulling people out of the Bürgerbräukeller crowd as Rudolf Hess read out their names from a list he and Hitler had drawn up. The surprised captives were hustled off under guard to an upstairs holding room, where they became hostages with no inkling of their fates. These included members of the Bavarian government and legislature, even Governor Eugen von Knilling—all of them invited guests to Kahr's speech. They were now theoretically out of their jobs; their administration had been deposed. In some cases, as with the representative of the Bavarian royal house, a sly game of courtliness was played until it became obvious that the aristocrat had become a hostage. The hostages were transported to the suburban villa of conservative publisher Julius Lehmann, a gilded cage.

In other cases, especially involving Jews, courtliness was replaced by nastiness and rough treatment. Ludwig Wasserman, the factory owner, was pulled out of the crowd and placed in isolation in a small room—with the warning that if he tried to flee, "he would be shot." Two Nazis told him he would be hanged the next morning in front of city hall on Marienplatz, Munich's central square.[16] Other Jews were dragged from their homes in Bogenhausen, a prosperous neighborhood thought to be home to many Jews. The Nazis and Kampfbunders picked out Jewish-sounding names from a telephone book, or off the nameplates on house doors, breaking in, firing shots into ceilings, and terrorizing the inhabitants. More than twenty Jews were eventually held hostage at the Bürgerbräukeller, including one seventy-four-year-old gentleman who was brought in with his daughters. One Nazi suggested executing them all immediately, but Göring told him: "We don't have the right to shoot them yet."

Across the Isar River, in the heart of old Munich, another scene of pillage and destruction was unfolding at the offices of the *Münchener Post,* the Social Democratic newspaper that vocally and often criticized Hitler and his Nazis. With Social Democratic politician Erhard Auer as a key editor, the *Münchener Post* was one of the few publications that had, early on, spotted Hitler's views and extremism for the danger they represented. The *Post* consistently denounced the message, the messenger, and his methods. To Hitler, the *Münchener Post* was a "poison kitchen" that had to be eliminated at the first opportunity—and tonight the opportunity had come. Sent by Göring and led by Storm Trooper Josef Berchtold, the Hitler Shock Troops smashed every window, trashed every desk, destroyed or stole every typewriter, and wrecked the presses and typesetting equipment of the *Post* in an orgy of anger and destruction. They smashed a revered symbol of the newspaper's philosophical origins, a bust of August Bebel, one of the 1869 founders of the Social Democratic Party. Scheubner-Richter sent law student Hermann Fobke to Auer's office on the third floor. "There's an entire file cabinet full of papers here!" Fobke gleefully reported. Gathering up stacks of personal and political documents, Fobke proudly delivered them to Hitler in the Bürgerbräukeller.[17]

Destroying the newspaper was not enough. The Nazi wrecking crew also forced its way into Auer's apartment in Munich; but the editor had heard of an impending putsch and fled. Deprived of their target, the housebreakers (with Hitler's driver, Emil Maurice, in the lead) manhandled Auer's wife, frightened his two daughters, and led away his son-in-law.[18]

From his new command post in the Bürgerbräukeller, Hitler was trying to oversee his putsch's planned operations around town. News had arrived of at least one successful operation. After receiving the code phrase, "baby safely delivered," Röhm had departed the Löwenbräukeller and marched his three hundred men to the Reichswehr district headquarters. Located on the grand boulevard of the Ludwigstrasse, right next to the Bavarian State Library, this was General Lossow's command post. At the head of the march, carrying the banner of the Reichskriegsflagge, strode a new member of Röhm's detachment, a bespectacled and expressionless young man named Heinrich Himmler. A trained agronomist, Himmler was fanatically attached to Röhm and, in time, would feel the same way about Hitler (Himmler would become chief of the SS during the Third Reich and a chief perpetrator of the Holocaust). At the Reichswehr district headquarters, Röhm's men quickly convinced General Lossow's thin guard that they had valid orders to take over the building. Stringing barbed wire around the edifice, they soon had full control of a strategic installation at a key location.

Things were not going so well elsewhere. Neutralizing Lossow's Reichswehr command post was not the same as capturing and converting the actual arms and troops of the Reichswehr in Munich.

These were chiefly located in the barracks of the First Battalion, Nineteenth Infantry, and the Engineers' Barracks on the northwest edge of the city. But when Kampfbunders arrived and tried, like Röhm's men, to talk their way into control of the barracks, they were rebuffed by sentries who said they had their own orders to obey. Their steadfastness proved crucial to reversing the tide of the putsch. When word of this unexpected opposition arrived at the Bürgerbräukeller, Hitler impulsively decided to solve the problem himself. Just as he had earlier turned the resistance of the crowd at the Bürgerbräukeller "inside out like a glove," he believed he could, with his always persuasive rhetoric, talk the skeptical Reichswehr troops into his arms. He left his command post for the trip across town to the barracks. Fatefully, he left Ludendorff in charge of his still-captive "co-conspirators," Kahr, Lossow, and Seisser.

It was the wrong move. Ludendorff respected Hitler's new pawns as fellow officers and gentlemen (even Kahr had been commissioned during World War I). A lifelong military man (he began cadet academy as a teenager), Ludendorff was schooled in the Prussian rules of duty and honor, not the sordid wiles of hardball politics. Even in the *völkisch* movement, where he had been agitating for several years, Ludendorff served more as a father figure than as an on-the-ground tactician. That the political game was played with ever-shifting rules and alliances of convenience was foreign to him. When Kahr, Lossow, and Seisser asked for their freedom—giving their *words of honor* that they needed to carry out their duties as members of the new government—the old general smelled nary a rat. He set the hostages loose.

Meanwhile, other Storm Troopers and Kampfbund units were carrying out orders from above. One company marched, puzzled, to a church attached to a monastery on St. Anna Square. Then the troops understood: man after man was coming out of the monastery's cellar door carrying a carbine. After a while, they formed a relay line, handing the weapons up to men on trucks. In all, more than three thousand rifles were retrieved from the underground vaults of the monastery, all illegally stashed there by Bavarian militias. Another weapons cache was opened near the university. In the basement of a fraternity house called Palatia, more than one hundred rifles were retrieved by Storm Troopers; they had been hidden there a week earlier by Röhm, nicknamed the "machine-gun king" for his skill at procuring and caching weapons.[19]

Yet for all their preparations, the ill-coordinated putschist units were unable to capture any more ground. Although they outnumbered the government forces — the putschists had roughly four thousand armed men while the Reichswehr and state police combat units numbered only twenty-six hundred — Hitler's troops did not successfully mount another attack.[20] Even Röhm's attempt to seize Kahr's administrative headquarters a few blocks from the military command post had met with stiff resistance; he withdrew without firing a shot. Only the police headquarters was successfully commandeered for a while by the former police chief and his deputy, now part of the putsch. But in less than two hours, the police building flipped back into the hands of the constituted authorities, who arrested the putschists.

Hitler had arrived at the infantry and engineers' barracks. But his vaunted persuasive powers had finally met their limit. Barracks guards refused him admission. Hitler admitted defeat and left. When he returned to the Bürgerbräukeller, he was appalled to learn that Ludendorff had let his hostages go *on their words of honor.* Hitler exploded. He began a stream of abuse that was abruptly cut short by the general. "I forbid anyone to challenge in my presence the word of honor of a German officer."

The worm had turned, and Hitler knew it. The freed hostages soon renounced their very public and—to everyone who was there—apparently very sincere statements of collaboration with Hitler's putsch. It took the slow-footed Kahr longer than the other two to recant, and he made a few odd moves that left his staff wondering which side he was on. Lossow's turning of his coat back to its original side was hastened by the confrontational question of one of his top officers as he walked into the Infantry Barracks: "Well, General, that scene in the Bürgerbräukeller, that was all just a bluff—right?" Lossow knew his answer: of course, it was all *Komödie spielen*—just playing along. Lossow began sending orders for Reichswehr units around Bavaria to march on Munich. The battle against Hitler's putsch had begun.

Near midnight, the upheaval in Munich was reverberating in the outside world, starting in Berlin. General Seeckt had been immediately notified of the coup and reacted swiftly, mobilizing troops around Berlin. He was prepared to attack Bavaria if necessary, finally inaugurating the civil war many had feared. Other countries took note as well. Already, the *New York Times* was preparing a banner headline across its entire front page: "Bavaria in Revolt, Proclaims Ludendorff Dictator; Its Monarchist Forces Reported Marching on Berlin; Capital Cries Treason and Masses Troops for Defense." The headline was full of errors, and notably left out Hitler, but captured the gravity of the situation. Benito Mussolini's envoy to Munich even paid a call on Kahr before he switched his allegiance for the second time, congratulating him on the coup and the anticipated march on Berlin.

There was also the battle of the wall posters. In the lively print age, before the arrival of radio for the general public, every European city had a slew of newspapers—Munich had more than ten—and a daily stream of posters on public walls and special street columns where news and events were announced. Fast-printed wall placards were a key means of communication, especially between government and citizenry. For this part of the battle, the Hitler putsch had been prepared. The Nazis and Kampfbunders let loose with a quick broadside designed to convince Munichers that a new era had dawned. "Proclamation!" read the headline in huge black letters. "The government of the November criminals in Berlin is deposed. A provisional government has been formed." This straightforward statement of regime change was anemic, however, compared to other bloodcurdling announcements plastered around town by the putschists. One proclaimed a new "National Tribunal" as the highest court in the land. The court would pass sentence on unspecified "crimes against the nation or the state." Only two verdicts were possible: guilty or innocent. "Innocence means freedom, guilt means death," read the statement. "Sentences are to be carried out within three hours. There is no appeal."[21] But even three hours was too long to wait for Hitler and his henchmen to apply their form of justice to the "villains of November 1918." A decree was prepared that named top government officials, including President Ebert and former chancellor Scheidemann, declaring them "outlaws" (*vogelfrei*) who could be shot on sight. "Every German...has the duty to deliver them dead or alive to the national government," stated the decree.[22]

Incredibly, Hitler and his eager putsch-planners had overlooked one of the first rules of any modern revolution: capture the communications system. Despite von der Pfordten's detailed plan for seizing the Munich telephone and telegraph exchange, no one was deputized to do the job; Kahr, Lossow, and Seisser were able to communicate freely with their allies outside Munich and in Berlin. Even at the lowest level—at the switchboard inside the district military headquarters that Röhm had seized—the putschists left the military in charge of the telephones for several hours, a move they would come to regret.

His political coat now turned twice in a single night, Kahr was at pains to erase from history the Bürgerbräukeller drama of the previous evening, especially the emotion-laden scene at the end, with its sincere handshakes and emotional rendition of *"Deutschland, Deutschland über alles."* He ordered all Munich newspapers to refrain from reporting the event. Some, like the nationalistic *Münchner Neueste Nachrichten,* Munich's biggest paper with a circulation of one hundred thirty thousand, would have been happy to comply—but it was too late. More than twenty thousand copies of the next day's edition had already gone out, its front page filled with detailed stories from the Bürgerbräukeller. Another newspaper, the *Münchener Zeitung,* was only able to insert a short version of the triumvirate's latest statement atop its long story on the putsch and its political implications. Kahr's remarks on the previous evening were quoted in boldface type: "With a heavy heart...and for the good of our beloved homeland, Bavaria, and the German fatherland, I accept the position of regent for the monarchy." There was no erasing history, and Kahr's ambivalent role on this night would haunt him in the months and years to come.

Back at the Bürgerbräukeller beer hall, dawn was breaking on a morning-after scene of despair and petty destruction—smashed beer mugs, broken furniture, and garbage. "Cigarette smoke, nighttime dust, and fatigue hung in the air as men sat around tables or lay on pushed-together chairs," recalled a young putschist named Hans Frank.[23] Hitler was eating two eggs and a slice of meat loaf with tea.[24] Ludendorff sat silently, "like a raging war god on his throne," sipping red wine for breakfast.[25] Curiously, the podium was stacked with 14,605 *trillion*[26] German marks—money that Hitler had had "appropriated" from two printing houses that printed money for the government. The Nazi thieves duly signed a receipt for the funds stolen from Parcus Brothers, a Jewish-owned printer, though none of it was ever repaid. Hitler claimed the money was taken "as a reminder of the [1918] revolution that confiscated hundreds of billions in gold from the German people."[27] Hitler used the cash to pay some of the Kampfbund troops—about two dollars per man. Each also received two liters of beer (more than half a gallon), no unusual amount in Bavaria. On the bandstand, a paramilitary band, working unhappily under direct orders, squeaked out half-hearted marches in a vain effort to raise spirits.

The hopelessness of the situation was sinking in on Hitler. Earlier in the evening, with typical melodramatic overreach, he had said to Ludendorff and other co-conspirators: "If this works out, fine. If not, we'll all hang ourselves." Politics, and life, was an all-or-nothing game for Hitler. He thought only in terms of monumental success or dismal failure. With this Manichean worldview, Hitler frequently spoke in either-or terms, always outlining "only two possibilities." Thus the exalted grandeur of his initial goal—an audacious march on Berlin supported by a heroic "national uprising"—and the abjectness of the alternative: total failure and suicide. Hitler could now glimpse the abyss. Besides Röhm's now-useless takeover of Lossow's headquarters building, Hitler could chalk up only one other accomplishment: the mutiny of the Infantry School. Led by Lieutenant Rossbach, almost all the officer cadets enthusiastically joined what they had been told was the liberation of the fatherland. After putting the school's commander under house arrest, they formed up into a large company and were rechristened the Ludendorff Regiment. Their military band playing, they marched across town in a light snowfall to the Bürgerbräukeller. The smart young cadets in their neat uniforms cut a sharp contrast to the disarray at the beer hall. Arriving at first light, they were ceremoniously reviewed and saluted by Ludendorff. Hitler, as always, knew a captive crowd when he saw one; he gave a short but impassioned speech, ending with a quick ceremony in which the young officers took an oath to Ludendorff. Then they marched off again, this time to attempt a takeover of Kahr's still unoccupied headquarters in the Maximilianstrasse.

The glow of this momentary success didn't last. Hitler, Ludendorff, and the other putsch leaders sat around like beaten dogs in an upstairs room at the Bürgerbräukeller, contemplating their options. Reports poured in of Reichswehr and Bavarian State Police units taking up strategic positions all around Munich, including on the Ludwig Bridge over the Isar River just a few hundred feet west of the beer hall. The bridge was the only thing that stood between the Bürgerbräukeller and the rest of Munich. Someone suggested retreating in the opposite direction, toward Rosenheim, a small Nazi-leaning town about forty miles away. Ludendorff angrily rejected the notion: "The movement must not end as street filth in a ditch," he barked. Hitler had something else in mind. Ever the propagandist, he reached for his very last card: public support. If the coup-makers could somehow rally the public to their cause, they could perhaps face down the coup-stoppers by sheer force of numbers and popular enthusiasm. It was a variation on Hitler's march-on-Berlin fantasy. The best way forward, it seemed, was to carry the cause to the people, straight into the heart of Munich. Yet resistance from the Bavarian State Police was almost certain. Though Ludendorff's safety was a concern, when Hitler warned the general that he should perhaps stay out of harm's way, Ludendorff replied with finality: "We'll march!"[28]

By late morning all the Kampfbund units called from the countryside had made their way to the Bürgerbräukeller. A long parade column began forming up outside the beer hall. Twelve or sixteen abreast, they shaped into three companies according to their paramilitary affiliation—the Bund Oberland on the right, Storm Troopers in the center, and the Hitler Shock Troops on the left.[29] Most men were armed, though some were not. Hitler claimed to have ordered that all weapons be unloaded—though that is disputed by other evidence. One firearm was surely loaded and later used—a machine gun mounted atop a truck in the middle of the march. Festooned with flags from all participating Kampfbunders, the truck bristled with armed men positioned on its roof.

In addition to fighters, the march initially included many of the hostages taken during the night. The hapless prisoners were placed in the march line by Göring, who viewed them as both shields and targets. Besides the government officials and random Jews hauled in overnight, Göring's Shock Troops had staged a morning raid on city hall, taking hostage the Social Democratic mayor and seven Socialist and Communist city council members for refusing to fly the swastika on the city hall tower. They were thrown into the parade, too. "The first time a shot comes from the other side," blustered Göring, "we will execute the hostages." This order was quickly changed; the city councilmen should "have their heads smashed in with rifle butts" instead. Hitler initially supported Göring's move, but Ludendorff did not like it at all. He ordered the hostages removed from the march.[30] Some were later taken by Shock Troopers Berchtold and Maurice to a forest outside Munich, where they expected to be shot. Instead, several were forced to disrobe and give their clothes to their captors, who wanted to return in disguise to Munich. The hostages were eventually set free.[31]

At noon the march began. Stepping off slowly from the Bürgerbräukeller, the long parade resembled a ragtag mix of out-of-step militiamen, some in uniform, some not. "It looked more like a funeral procession than a military march," remarked one observer. But somehow the parade smartened up as old soldiers and new recruits found their military cadence. The column was led by a line of flag bearers carrying the swastika and other banners, accompanied by armed skirmishers. Then came the show row: Hitler, Ludendorff, Scheubner-Richter, Göring, Kriebel, Dr. Weber, and von der Pfordten.[32] Hitler later claimed the leadership intentionally led the marchers so they would be among the first ones hit if shooting broke out.[33] This row, if any, was the one that would sell. As they lined up, and Scheubner-Richter linked his arm in Hitler's, he remarked: "This will be our last walk together."

But sell it did. After a rough scuffle on the Ludwig Bridge against a police line that yielded, the long march wound its way into the inner city. Up the Tal, a tight street aimed straight at the city hall, the march entered the famed Maria Square (*Marienplatz*), with its St. Mary statue and the giant glockenspiel in the city hall tower high above. To the delight of the marchers, the Nazi flag was now flying atop city hall, raised by Shock Troops who had taken over the building. A noisy Nazi rabble-rouser from Nuremberg, Julius Streicher, was speaking to a large crowd. The marchers were now singing patriotic songs.[34] Hitler's ploy seemed to be working: the crowds on the sidewalks were cheering. Feeling confident, Hitler thought: "The people are behind us.... The people are ready to settle accounts with the November criminals."[35] The public was throwing support behind the putsch, or at least behind the two thousand men marching through their streets. "It was clear that the feeling of the crowd was all for Hitler," reported the English consul general to London.[36]

Turning right at city hall, Ludendorff impulsively decided to march toward the Reichswehr district headquarters, still held by Röhm. After a zigzag turn, Ludendorff led the procession into the

Residenzstrasse, the street beside the sprawling royal palace. Behind him, marchers were belting out *"O Deutschland hoch in Ehren"* ("O Great and Honorable Germany"[37]). But as the narrowing Residence Street debouched into the Odeon Square, beside the famous Italianate Field Marshals' Memorial (*Feldherrnhalle*), the march suddenly confronted a new line of Bavarian State Police; they formed a blocking cordon. Unlike the weak detachment on the Ludwig Bridge, these policemen did not seem inclined to yield. But the putschists, emboldened by their earlier success at breaking through a police line, did not slow down. "After the encounter at the Ludwig Bridge, we did not even consider the possibility of being stopped by the state police," said Dr. Weber.[38]

"Halt!" yelled a police commander as a line of his men knelt into firing position. The marchers continued, their rifles held at port arms. "Don't shoot!" shouted someone in the march. Ulrich Graf, Hitler's bodyguard, who had been marching directly behind Hitler and Ludendorff, stepped forward and, pointing with his right hand at Ludendorff, yelled directly at the police troops: "Ludendorff! Do you want to shoot your own general?"[39] In the background, said Graf, he could hear marchers singing, *"Deutschland, Deutschland über alles."* Then fighting and chaos broke loose.

As marchers and policemen closed in on one another, hand-to-hand combat began—the marchers using rifles with fixed bayonets, the police using rifle butts and nightsticks. According to Lieutenant Michael Freiherr von Godin, who commanded the police line, a shot was fired. "A Hitler man who stood one half step left of me fired a pistol at my head," he reported. "The shot went by my head and killed Sergeant Hollweg behind me. For a fraction of a second my company stood frozen. Then, before I could give an order, my people opened fire, with the effect of a salvo. At the same time, the

Hitler people commenced firing, and for twenty or thirty seconds a regular firefight developed."

The half-minute of violence left four policemen dead. The damage was worse in Hitler's ranks. Next to him, Max Erwin von Scheubner-Richter, Hitler's bright, intellectual star, had taken a fatal shot in the chest; two feet to one side and the bullet would have struck Hitler instead. As Scheubner-Richter fell, his arm tightly linked with Hitler's, Scheubner-Richter had jerked the Nazi leader to the hard pavement; Hitler's shoulder was severely dislocated. In the same row, Theodor von der Pfordten, the Bavarian Supreme Court judge who carried a copy of Hitler's new constitution in his coat pocket, was also killed. Göring took a severe wound to the thigh. Hitler's bodyguard, Ulrich Graf, covered Hitler's prone body and was struck multiple times by bullets that would otherwise have found Hitler. Graf survived. Besides the four policemen, thirteen of Hitler's men and one bystander were shot to death. The putsch was over. Hitler had stormed the gates and failed.

Ludendorff, despite the hail of fire, was unscathed. When the shooting ended, he was walking directly into the arms of the police, who arrested him on the spot. Pompously outraged, the giant of the German officer corps sputtered: "I'll never respect a German officer's uniform again."

With help from some of his followers and "looking deathly pale," said Hermann Esser,[40] the injured Hitler made it toward the back of the march, which had scattered in all directions. He was taken into a yellow car driven by Dr. Walter Schultze, a Nazi sympathizer and physician who had joined the parade for just such an eventuality.[41] Even as Schultze drove away with his newest patient — Hitler was moaning in pain — Göring was, ironically, being treated in a house near the Odeon Square by a Jewish physician who may have saved his life. Göring was later spirited out of Munich and, after briefly being arrested and hospitalized in the Bavarian Alps, made his escape into Austria, where many of the putschists had taken refuge.

Did Hitler consider fleeing to Austria? It was the easy and obvious way to go, though slipping through some unguarded border crossing in the woods or mountains could have been difficult with his injured shoulder. But if the idea of fleeing to Austria crossed Hitler's mind, it may just as quickly have left it. Austria was, after all, not exile for him, but his country of origin. Once back in his homeland, he might not so easily get out again. Worse, exile to the little rump republic of the former Austro-Hungarian empire could spell political oblivion to the man who thought of himself as a modern Napoleon.

It seems more likely that Hitler was considering the ultimate exile, suicide, rather than cross-border exile; suicide was always Hitler's plan B. As his rescuer drove south toward the Alps, Hitler asked him to turn off toward the tiny town of Uffing on Lake Staffel. There, he knew, Hanfstaengl had recently bought a villa. When Dr. Schultze knocked on the door, Hanfstaengl didn't open it—he, too, had fled to Austria—but his wife did.

Helene Hanfstaengl was one of the joys, and frustrations, of Hitler's life. A striking beauty of German-American extraction, Helene had met Putzi Hanfstaengl while he was running the family art book business on Fifth Avenue in New York (and taking his meals at the Harvard Club, where Franklin Roosevelt also dined); Hanfstaengl had brought her back to the land of her forefathers.[42] During the period that Hanfstaengl was showing Hitler around Munich's high-society scene, he often invited him to his Munich home for meals, and Hitler developed a special affection for Helene. Hanfstaengl once walked into the living room to find Hitler laying his head in Helene's lap and saying, "If only I had someone like you to take care of me." Helene gently rebuked Hitler and removed his head. She swore to her husband later that Hitler was no man for any woman: "Believe me, he is an absolute neuter."[43]

Now, Helene had another chance to take care of Hitler, at least briefly. She could hardly turn away a friend in severe pain. Only dimly aware of events in Munich, she installed Hitler in an attic bedroom, where he spent the next two days and nights under two "English travelling rugs" — thick blankets — that Hanfstaengl had bought as a student. Helene warned Hitler that the police would surely come looking for him there, and he was trying to arrange for pickup by his other wealthy friends, the Bechsteins. But on Sunday evening, the police arrived. Already deeply depressed, Hitler now went into a frenzy, according to Helene. Hitler "pulled out his revolver with his good hand and shouted, 'This is the end. I will never let those swine take me. I will shoot myself first.'" But Helene was quicker, wresting the pistol from Hitler and throwing it into a nearby flour bin. Unable to do much because of his dislocated shoulder, Hitler gave up. Accepting the fact that he was about to go away, perhaps for a long time, he began writing instructions for Helene to pass on to his confederates.[44] One of the most surprising and, for the Nazi Party, most portentous was to Alfred Rosenberg, the unruly intellectual who was editor of the *Völkischer Beobachter:* "Dear Rosenberg, From now on you will lead the movement."[45]

Still in his white pajamas, his painful left arm in a sling, his Iron Cross First Class medal pinned to his coat, he descended the stairs and greeted Lieutenant Rudolf Belleville of the Bavarian State Police Weilheim station. Belleville apologized to Hitler but said he had to do his duty. Hitler responded, according to some sources, with a handshake, according to another with a tongue-lashing.[46] Either way, Belleville had to look around for a driver for his police van to ferry Hitler forty miles away to Landsberg Prison. He finally found a local beer-truck driver willing to do Sunday afternoon service; the man was, the police report noted, "a Social Democrat." Belleville loaded his prisoner into the van and trundled him off to the year that would change his life, his strategy, and his sense of self.

CHAPTER SIX

Hitting Bottom

"It's over! Let them see how well they do without me.
I'm giving up."

—ADOLF HITLER, 1923[1]

"There was something in the air," wrote prison guard Otto Lurker about the cold autumn night on which Adolf Hitler arrived in Landsberg Prison. "A storm ripped over the rooftops and watchtowers of the prison, shaking the gates and bars as though it were angrily trying to force its way in. Down in the cell blocks, all was dead silent except the occasional pacing of the night watchman."

If ever a chapter in history called for a dark-and-stormy-night opener, the night of Hitler's arrest and delivery into prison, November 11, 1923, would seem to be it. Another prison guard, Franz Hemmrich, wrote in his memoir: "It was a starless night, and a feeling of tense uncertainty had come over the wardens and guards." Into this fraught atmosphere, around 11 p.m., walked a pale, distraught, and silent figure with his left arm in a sling and a shopworn gray trench coat over his shoulders.[2] "A strand of dark hair fell across his washed-out visage, weakened by overstimulation and sleepless nights," wrote Hemmrich. This down-and-out character was incongruously dressed in a formal frock coat—with an Iron Cross still pinned on its front[3]—the same outfit he'd worn for the putsch, for his failed march to Odeon Square, and during his escape to Ernst Hanfstaengl's villa. Beside him, "their shadows flickering and dancing in the darkness before them," walked Landsberg Prison warden Otto Leybold and two police officers, one of them leading a "strong dog" on a chain. The prison was still, except for the slamming of iron doors behind the men. In the dead of night, Adolf Hitler had arrived at what would be his home for most of the next thirteen months.

Located thirty-eight miles west of Munich, Landsberg Prison was a modern penal institution in a charming, small municipality on a meandering Alpine river called the Lech. The medieval town had the requisite cobblestoned streets and bubbling fountain, once the source of village drinking water, along with several bakeries and pubs on the main square; it could have been any of the rustic Bavarian market towns that dotted the region. What made Landsberg-on-Lech special was that it had a state prison on the edge of town and, nearby, a Reichswehr garrison. In years to come, Landsberg would become a hotbed of Nazism, a place of pilgrimage and—to its shame—the center of a collection of World War II slave labor camps.

But on this wind-lashed night, Landsberg was just a sleepy burg of no special renown. Its prison, a state-of-the-art penitentiary that housed five hundred convicts, had been opened in 1909. Though it had a brownish, faux-fortress main gate—two fat onion-domed towers with an arched entryway—the prison's interior was thoroughly modern, consciously modeled on the latest American "panopticon" design: four large wings, four stories high, joined in the middle by a central watch station with easy access to all cells in all four directions.

Yet there was one difference: Landsberg Prison had a special wing for special prisoners. It was called *die Festung*—the fortress. The so-called fortress was, however, nothing of the sort; it was simply a contemporary (in 1909) two-story, rectangular, whitewashed building with an orange tile roof connected by a corridor to the main prison.* The building originally had been designed for small prison industries,[4] then became a prison wing for political inmates. The name, *Festung* (fortress), derived from Germany's nineteenth-century tradition of putting political offenders, prisoners of conscience, and members of nobility, such as duelists, into a local fortress tower for an "honorable" imprisonment under relaxed conditions (dueling was a semi-tolerated crime of honor). In modern times, the name had remained, codified in law, but the fortress towers had not. Adolf Hitler, like many other political prisoners during the 1920s, would serve his time under "fortress arrest"—better translated as "honorable imprisonment" in a minimum-security facility (also called *custodia honesta* in some countries).[5] Hitler's "fortress" looked more like a dormitory than a castle, though the dorm had two-foot-thick walls and bars on the windows. "Anyone who expected to find a romantic whiff of mossy castles with damp vaults...was bitterly disappointed," wrote one prisoner.[6]

A striking political irony awaited Hitler in Landsberg. The only prisoner in the fortress[†] at this time was Count Anton Graf von Arco auf Valley. The nationalist nobleman, in a fit of what he considered

---

* Numerous books have mistakenly referred to an old fortress at Landsberg, but there was none there.

[†] "Fortress" will be used from now on without quotation marks to denote the modern square building described above.

patriotism, had shot dead Bavaria's governor, Kurt Eisner, on a Munich street in 1919. By killing the Socialist governor, Arco-Valley (as he was generally called) helped unleash the political tumult that led to a three-week Communist takeover of Bavaria in April 1919 by a council republic. That short-lived republic ended in an appalling bloodbath, stirring up a far-right backlash that nurtured, among other groups, the Nazis. For murdering Eisner, the nationalistic Arco-Valley had been sentenced to death, only to have his term commuted to life under fortress (honorable) arrest. He occupied the only cell in Landsberg's fortress building that was considered suitable for incarceration of a "notable figure"—"with space for a guard in the anteroom," wrote Hemmrich, the prison guard.

On the notability scale, Hitler now outranked the near-forgotten count. With his name splashed across Munich's and Germany's front pages, the pale man with the stubby mustache was clearly more prominent than the nobleman lying in fortress cell number five.[7] Like a garden-variety rich person being evicted from a hotel's best suite to admit a suddenly arrived movie star, Arco-Valley was "unceremoniously dragged out of his sleep and installed in a cell in the prison hospital," remembered Lurker. The awakened assassin "swore a blue streak" over his eviction and shouted that "if he had the chance he would kill this Hitler exactly as [he had Eisner] because this 'painter's apprentice' was Germany's greatest disaster!" wrote Hemmrich.[8] Still, Adolf Hitler got the best room.[9]

But the best room was still spartan. Only about nine feet wide and twelve feet deep, cell number five contained a simple white metal bunk with mattress and blankets, a nightstand with a lamp, a small wooden writing table, two wooden chairs, and a wardrobe. Although he was locked in at night, Hitler's cell had a real door that afforded more privacy than simple cell bars.[10] The room's best features were two five-foot-high windows that opened inward and admitted a great deal of light. From these windows, Hitler could see the twenty-foot-high stone wall surrounding the prison, standing about seventy-five feet away. Over the wall, from his second-floor vantage point, Hitler saw farm fields and the gently rolling countryside beyond; he liked to watch cars on a distant highway and dreamed of once again owning a luxury automobile like those he saw passing.[11] No doubt the bars on the windows often served to bring him out of such reveries. One sunny-day photograph showed the barred double-casement windows casting a gridlike shadow on the wall above Hitler's bed and reflecting off a large picture frame on the opposite wall, giving his cell the hemmed-in appearance of having barred windows on three sides.[12] It may have been better than a standard-issue cell, but it was no hotel room.

Hitler's reputation had preceded him on this blustery night, sending the prison into an uproar of preparations. Word of the putsch had filtered into the provincial newspapers; everyone knew who Hitler was, and that he and his Nazis were capable of serious mischief. "We have to be prepared for anything," Warden Leybold had told Lurker and Hemmrich. "His followers may attempt a rescue." Given the brazenness of the putsch attempt, the fears were not unfounded. "We had only sixty prison guards, some quite old, and a twenty-man security detail outfitted with World War I weapons," noted Hemmrich. "If we'd been assaulted by a massive force led by former officers, our little troop would have been too weak to defend the big prison complex."[13]

As they were fretting over security, Leybold got a reprieve: a phone call from Munich informed him that the Reichswehr would take over guard duty for Adolf Hitler and the fortress. The Nazi Party leader was too important to leave to the inadequate resources of the prison. Within half an hour, the prison corridors echoed with the tramp of boots and clang of military equipment. Rifles, machine guns, steel helmets, even hand grenades were laid in by the thirty-two-man Reichswehr detachment from the Landsberg garrison. The guard unit's commander, Lieutenant Imhoff, set up his post in the cell next to Hitler's. A direct telephone line to the Reichswehr garrison was run out of Imhoff's headquarters, yet it was repeatedly cut during the night, according to Lurker.

For all the excitement, the prison guards' chief job on this historic night was helping Hitler out of his clothes. His dislocated shoulder was still causing him great pain. "He was just about all in," reported Hemmrich. "He refused a bite or even a sip of soup, but lay down on the cot. His sole request was for a glass of water. I put a full pitcher on his table. I went away after securely locking him in."

Hitler's lack of appetite turned out to be more than a function of exhaustion. It was also political, and a function of depression and desperation. Hitler fully expected, he said later, to be shot for his misdeeds, just as so many revolutionaries before him had been—and just as he would have done to anyone who attempted a coup against him when he was in power.[14] Given the waves of political violence since World War I, it was no idle fear. Nor was it a surprise that Hitler, buffeted by his sense of failure and physical collapse, was still contemplating suicide. His chief reason for living—the Nazi movement—seemed to be at an end.

Hitler was a man of dramatic mood swings. He had already spoken of death or suicide four times in the past three days. Now his volatile psychological state triggered turbulence and drama in the prison. Besieged by court officials trying to get testimony from him, Hitler's temper vacillated wildly. The temperamental prisoner had at first clamored for a chance to make an official statement to investigators; he wanted to put his version of events on the record. Hitler's goal was to exact revenge from those he believed had betrayed him: Kahr, Lossow, and Seisser. But when investigators arrived at Landsberg, Hitler repeatedly clammed up, "acted fresh, or broke out into crying fits," reported an official.[15] During attempted interrogations, Hitler's shouts and screams "could be heard all over the building."[16] Guards standing outside the second-floor interrogation room feared that fisticuffs would break out. Both defiant and dejected, Hitler was a problem prisoner from the start. Then came the hunger strike.

At first, Hitler ate the food Hemmrich brought him—"but didn't touch the meat." Hitler had become a vegetarian. As part of his "honorable" incarceration, a fortress prisoner received the same food that the prison staff ate, not the plainer fare served to the five hundred inmates in the main prison. But one morning, when Hemmrich arrived with Hitler's breakfast, the inmate's dinner from the night before still stood untouched on his table. "Herr Hitler, what's the matter?" asked the guard. "Why aren't you eating? Are you sick?"

"Just leave me alone!" cried Hitler. "I'm not eating anymore."

Prison Warden Leybold told Hemmrich to leave each meal in Hitler's cell nonetheless, and pick it up only after bringing the next meal. But when Hemmrich delivered breakfast the following morning, Hitler flew into a rage. His dinner from the night before again stood untouched on the table. Hitler "howled like a madman at me," said Hemmrich.

"Take it away!" shouted Hitler. "Otherwise I'm going to throw it against the wall!"

Hitler then broke into his classic political rant, yelling at Hemmrich about "liars and traitors." A shouting match erupted; Hemmrich issued disciplinary threats. But he removed Hitler's spurned meals.

Not eating day after day, Hitler became weak. He looked "like a heap of misery, crestfallen, poorly shaved, and listening to my simple words with a tired little smile and no interest," wrote Hemmrich.[17]

It was bad enough that his party was banned, his newspaper shuttered, and his comrades arrested, hunted, or in exile. But Hitler, who had always put great store in his personal dignity, now faced ignominy. He heard that people were calling him crazy, or drunk, or megalomaniacal on the night of the putsch.[18] He was roundly denounced and derided by all but his own fanatical followers, and even by some of them. Hermann Esser later claimed that many Nazi adherents were deeply angered that their leader had not stayed with his people at the Odeon Square.[19] The *New York Times* captured the consensus: "The Munich putsch definitely eliminates Hitler and his National Socialist followers."[20] U.S. diplomat Robert Murphy, based in Munich, soon wrote, "It is to be expected that Hitler, who is not a German citizen, will be deported from the country after serving his prison term."[21] As historian Othmar Plöckinger put it, "Hitler's fall was steep; in the first days and weeks it was uncertain whether he would ever be able to return to the political stage."[22] And the stage itself was suddenly cleared of all the smoke and clamor that Hitler and his Nazis had been generating. "The swastikas and Storm Troopers disappeared, and the name of Adolf Hitler fell almost into oblivion," noted Austrian writer Stefan Zweig, who traveled often to Germany.[23]

With his world shrinking and his future closing down, Hitler again sought the melodramatic way out. With no gun, no defiant marches, and no rope for making a noose, Hitler chose the only weapon left to him: death by starvation. He would punish himself and die like a martyr, succumbing for his cause (*die Sache*).

Several days after he began his hunger strike, alarmed prison officials moved Hitler to the hospital wing, where he was continuously watched and strictly isolated from other prisoners. Drinking only water, Hitler spent most of his time reading beside his barred window. He asked Hemmrich to bring him materials from the little prison library;[24] he said he found peace in rereading philosopher Arthur Schopenhauer. But he was increasingly pale and frail, his voice growing hoarse. Hemmrich began to notice an odd odor, a "cloyingly sweet smell that surely came from his stomach."[25] The malodor became so "penetrating" that Hemmrich had to hold his breath to avoid nausea while delivering packages to Hitler. After a week, Warden Leybold was concerned that he "might not be able to keep his most precious prisoner alive for trial." The warden ordered hospital staff to prepare to begin force-feeding of Hitler by "synthetic nutrition." The future ruler of Germany was about to have a tube forced down his throat.

But on that same day, November 19, the prison's teacher and "practical psychologist," Alois Maria Ott, decided to pay Hitler a visit.[26] "It was a gray Monday morning, and I went to the hospital around 10 a.m.," Ott later wrote. "I unlocked the door and found before me a short, darkly staring man whose appearance was, at first, rather disappointing. He looked like an ordinary person with a very mannered way of combing his dark hair over his forehead.... Most noticeable were the prominent cheekbones and strong chin with a stubbornly closed wide mouth and a broad, slightly indented nose.... His eyes betrayed his hostility, shooting daggers at me."

Ott, a devout Catholic and firm believer in the power of good-will,[27] had made up his mind to break through Hitler's wall of resistance. He had a plan: Ott brought the angry inmate a Munich newspaper featuring a story by one of Hitler's former friends; it accused the Nazi leader of "falling victim to the devil of his own vanity and a prima donna complex." Handing Hitler the newspaper—the conservative *Bayerischer Kurier* (Bavarian Courier)—Ott said, "Herr Hitler, I give you my word that I've told nobody in the prison that I was coming to see you, and nobody will learn anything of this conversation. You and I are about the same age and have both lived through war and misery. I'm coming to you man to man, to be of assistance, the same way I do with every inmate. But, here, read what your old friend has written about you!"[28]

Hitler read while the prison psychologist paced up and down the narrow hospital room—"ten paces long by three paces wide," he recalled. It was silent in the room.

Suddenly Hitler jumped up and smashed the crumpled-up newspaper onto the table. In a shrill voice, "with his unique guttural rolling 'R,'" Hitler began shouting: "This [German] people are a bunch of bums! What a poor excuse of a nation! What a bunch of know-it-alls! You put your life on the line for the greatest cause and then they betray you!... It's not worth the sacrifice. I'm tired of going on. It's over! Let them see how well they do without me. I'm giving up. If I had a revolver, I would take it."

Ott was stunned: "[Hitler's] mouth was flecked with white foam, his eyes were rolling, the whites of his eyes were moist. The man was hysterical."

Nonetheless, Ott lectured Hitler on the need for patience if he really meant to help people find jobs and security instead of just offering vague promises. Ott's little sermon didn't work: "He exploded again and shouted at me: 'Germany cannot wait! I tried to help the country with an appeal to its dignity and its honor. But these cowardly fools won't listen! They betray anyone who tries to lift them out of the slime of subservience. History has shown again and again: those who want the best [for their people] are always crucified and burned at the stake.'"

Ott let Hitler rage on. Asking him if he didn't perhaps follow the wrong role models — given Austria's recent history with the fallen house of Hohenzollern — Ott touched another nerve. Hitler hated the Austro-Hungarian monarchy, so now he gave Ott "a long private lecture" on history, revolution, and role models "from Sparta to Frederick the Great to Nelson and Garibaldi."

Hitler's silence was now broken. And he was on familiar ground. He could not resist a chance to pontificate on history and politics. The prisoner and the prison teacher fell into a classic colloquy, debating issues of the day and of the past. Hitler claimed the only two institutions he ever respected were the Prussian army general staff and the College of Cardinals at the Vatican. "Then you must know," said Ott, "how long it took the Prussian general staff to prepare for the last war, and that revolutionaries like Garibaldi and Mussolini need the will of the people behind them. Slogans, especially ideological ones like anti-Semitism and anti-clericalism, won't bring starving people to the barricades.... Why do you and your followers spread hatred toward Jews and toward papal authority? We can be political opponents, but if you want to lead a whole nation into a better future, we need one another."

Hitler interrupted and contradicted Ott, but stayed engaged. In the end, Ott concluded that Hitler's hatred for "those who think differently" could not be attenuated: "I could feel his demonic obsession with an ideology that unleashed the psychopath in him." Hitler was filled with "vanity and brutal dogmatism," wrote Ott. The next day, however, Ott "heard that Hitler had ended his hunger strike."

Whether he did so because of his encounter with Ott is uncertain. Anton Drexler, the Nazi Party cofounder whom Hitler had replaced, visited Hitler at around the same time and claimed that after a "one-and-three-quarter hour struggle with a man who had given up on life," he had talked Hitler out of dying for the sake of the movement. According to Putzi Hanfstaengl, his wife, Helene— the woman who took the pistol out of Hitler's hand just before he was arrested—played a decisive role, too: "She sent a message through to say that she had not prevented him from committing suicide in order to let him starve himself to death."[29] One other woman may have made a difference: Frau von Scheubner-Richter, the young widow of the man shot dead beside Hitler as the putsch- ists marched into Odeon Square. She arrived heavily veiled and dressed in mourning to visit Hitler; her presence meant forgiveness and may have convinced Hitler that his followers still supported him. Hitler's attorney, Lorenz Roder, also visited him on November 24 and afterward told Hemmrich that Hitler had just agreed to end the strike.[30]

Hitler's first meal, recalled the guard, was a bowl of rice. The pris- oner had regained "his will to live," thought Hemmrich, despite the report of one visitor just a day before that Hitler's left arm "was still unusable."[31] But Hitler was again interested in sharing his thoughts, or at least writing them down; Attorney Roder wrote within a week to the state's attorney, requesting permission to take to Hitler "the dictionary of the German language by Weber, five volumes of Scho- penhauer, along with paper, pen, pen holder and a pencil."[32]

Hitler soon received yet another confidence boost from yet an- other female admirer. Winifred Wagner, the English-born daughter- in-law of composer Richard Wagner (deceased 1883), had taken a shine to Hitler a few months earlier when he paid a reverential visit to the Wagner home and gravesite in Bayreuth. Along with her brother-in-law, the English-born racist writer Houston Stewart Chamberlain,[33] Wagner went out of her way to signal support for Hitler and his cause. After the putsch failed and Hitler landed in prison, Wagner organized a gushing letter that attracted one thousand signatures. "We cherish more keenly than ever our love for you," it began. Wagner appended a personal note, delivered on December 1, to "Honorable Dear Herr Hitler," a more endearing form of address than usual. She enclosed as a gift an opera libretto written by her husband, Siegfried Wagner, who, like his father, had become a composer. It was called *The Smith of Marienburg.* "If this little book can help you through some long hours, then it will have done its duty," wrote Winifred.[34]

Hitler's hunger strike was over, but his resistance to questioning was not. Among the officials rudely rebuffed by Hitler was Ludwig Stenglein, the state's attorney responsible for prosecuting Hitler and the other putschists on charges of high treason for their attempt "to overthrow the government by force." As a last-ditch effort, Stenglein decided to send his much younger deputy, Hans Ehard, to try to interview the mulish Nazi. Only thirty-six, two years older than Hitler, Ehard reckoned he might be able to break Hitler's wall of silence. But when the deputy prosecutor arrived on December 13 with his stenographer and a typewriter, Hitler was just as willful as before. "I'm not a criminal, and I won't let myself be questioned like a criminal," he snorted.

Warming to his own indignation, Hitler challenged the very legitimacy of the official's presence and rejected the jurisdiction of the court, reported Ehard. He had no need to tell Ehard any details about the putsch, he said, because he intended to "play his trump cards...only in the courtroom." But the sensitive Ehard wisely played his own little trump card: he sent the stenographer and typewriter out of the interview room on the second floor of the fortress. Having shed the aura of officialdom and criminal investigation, the young prosecutor settled down face-to-face with Hitler, two men in a small room, with no other listeners. Now they were brain-to-brain — the kind of setting in which Hitler could not resist running his mouth. And he did.[35]

For five hours, during the morning and part of the afternoon, Adolf Hitler and Hans Ehard had a rambling open discussion. In their long chat, Hitler spilled his guts, at least on the matter of the putsch, on the entanglements of the Bavarian triumvirate, on his role in history, and on his plans for his upcoming trial. "I never pulled out a pencil or a piece of paper," remembered Ehard. "Hitler gradually came out of himself. 'When I talk, I can find the right word, but not when I write,' he said. Dictation didn't work for him either, [Hitler] said. Yet I could never get him to give a simple, short, clear answer to a clear, unambiguous question. He held endless political lectures."

Hitler "talked a blue streak, and with so much spittle flying that I almost needed an umbrella," said Ehard. Out of all the verbiage, Ehard was able to distill the arguments Hitler would likely use in what was sure to be a sensational trial.[36] Hitler laid out his full defense for Ehard. First, he said, one could not commit high treason against a state such as the Weimar Republic that was itself, in Hitler's view, founded on high treason. Hitler considered the Socialist-led 1918 November revolution a betrayal of the German people. None of the subsequent elections, he argued, had legitimized the republic because they had not posed the question: was the revolution legal?

But the core of Hitler's argument wasn't about his own alleged treason; it was about the treason of his "mortal enemies," Kahr, Lossow, and Seisser. After all, they had been colluding for months with Hitler and his Kampfbund allies about a putsch and a march to Berlin; they were fully complicit. If they had been truly against his undertaking, asked Hitler, why hadn't they — as the governing authorities—arrested this "dangerous Hitler" before anything had happened? To the contrary, he continued, the triumvirate had been part of the putsch "in their hearts" (*innerlich bei der Sache*).[37] Hitler also threatened to reveal previously confidential details about secret Reichswehr plans to mobilize not only for a march on Berlin but also for a possible attack on French forces in the Ruhr region. The chatty Hitler was showing his hand: he would turn the trial on its head, putting his adversaries—Kahr, Lossow, and Seisser—into the dock. As it stood, they were scheduled to appear as prosecution witnesses.

As for the timing of the putsch, Hitler told Ehard, he had felt pressure from his men; he had known Kahr and Lossow could never make a firm decision to *losschlagen,* and he worried that one of the other nationalistic groups might upstage him with some spectacular action—"like grabbing a dozen Jews and hanging them."[38] This jaw-dropper put Hitler's casual cold-bloodedness on full display.

Hitler seemed ready to fight. Even though his left shoulder was still bothering him—it was too painful to hold down a sheet of paper with his left hand while writing with his right hand, he said—the injured leader claimed he was feeling vigorous and "tough as a wildcat" when it came to saving his own skin and making his enemies' lives "sour." His trial presentation—probably in the form of a memorandum, said Hitler, despite his aversion to writing—would "rip the masks off the faces of his mortal enemies...and force them to end up where he was, namely in prison." As soon as he could escape Hitler, Ehard reconstructed the entire conversation on paper. The result, a nine-page, six-section, single-spaced document when it was later printed in a book, became a seminal text on Hitler's trial, state of mind, and political framework.

By mid-December, five weeks after entering Landsberg, Hitler was coming out of his post-putsch depression and preparing for his trial, bolstered by the expressions of support that continued to flow into the prison from his admirers. Although the Nazi Party was now officially banned and operating underground behind thinly veiled cover, the committed Nazis were fanatical in their devotion. Hitler received piles of mail, packages, gifts, and flowers. A flood of Christmas "love gifts,"[39] mostly fine foods, came from people like Winifred Wagner. In early December, one visitor had noticed a package from Bayreuth that included a "wool jacket, woolen long underwear, socks, liqueur, zwieback, sausage, books...."[40]

Warden Leybold initially forbade Hitler from sharing his overflow of sweets and delicatessen foods with other prisoners, so Hitler donated his extras to a nearby Dominican cloister for distribution to the poor. It became a banner year for the nuns and their flock. "Never has the 'poor wayfarer' who knocked on our doors had it better than during the time Hitler was in Landsberg Prison," one nun told Hemmrich.[41]

Hitler also began receiving a stream of visitors. The demand to see the Nazi Party leader was so great that prison officials conferred with Hitler in advance of every visit to determine how long the caller would be allowed to stay. Sometimes, if the visitor was simply a passerby claiming to be an admirer of Hitler's, a three-to-five-minute visit was allowed. If the visitor was someone like General Ludendorff, Hitler's comrade in (failed) arms and co-defendant in the upcoming trial, a visit might last four or five hours. Unlike the poor devils in the main prison, who were given only fifteen minutes of visiting time every three months, fortress inmates were allowed six hours of visiting time every week—a limit that Hitler apparently often exceeded.

Hitler's most invigorating visit came not from a general or any other two-legged devotee, but from his German shepherd, Wolf. Attorney Roder had made special application to the state's attorney's office, asking if he might take Hitler's beloved pet on a visit to the prison. When they arrived, the dog leapt onto Hitler as only a large animal can, triggering the "first full laugh" that Hemmrich had heard since Hitler had arrived in prison.

Though Hitler maintained distance from his family, and rarely spoke of them even when talking of his youth, he was visited around Christmastime by his half-sister, Angela. She spent a half hour with him "that I will never forget," she wrote afterward. She described a man clearly on the mend. "He was intellectually and spiritually (*geistig und seelisch*) on top again. Physically, he's in good shape. His left arm caused him a lot of trouble, but should be healed by now. The support being shown him these days is touching."[42] (Hitler, on the other hand, showed "every sign of horror" when Rudolf Hess suggested that Hitler's younger sister, Paula, ought to move from Vienna to Munich to be nearer and safer. "He suddenly became nervous, squirmed in his chair, ran his hand through his hair," wrote Hess. "For God's sake, no! Even though he loved her, she could become a burden and cramp his style.")[43]

Things were busy in Landsberg Prison. Told to expect more arrestees from the putsch fiasco, Warden Leybold began renovations to create more cells in the fortress building. Meanwhile, he housed the new group of putschists in a special section of the main prison; it had a makeshift wall and a ceiling over the corridor in front of their cells to shield them from contact with the regular convict population. In splendid isolation, they could still enjoy their special privileges, such as having their cell doors open all day. The covered corridor became their dayroom and eating area, but since the ceiling blocked natural light from the skylights of the four-story cell wing, their space was always in semi-darkness.[44]

The new prison arrivals included Dietrich Eckart, Julius Streicher, Fürst Karl Philipp von Wrede,[45] former Bavarian justice minister

Dr. Roth, and even German Workers' Party cofounder Anton Drexler, the man who had first invited Hitler to join his movement.[46] Hitler continued to live in his hospital cell apart from the other putschists, who constantly pestered Hemmrich for information about their leader. Hemmrich was under strict orders from Leybold to share nothing about Hitler; the new arrivals felt stiffed and pelted the luckless guard with niggling insults.[47] Still, life behind bars was quite bearable for the inmates. Their daily privileges included several hours in the prison courtyard and garden, where they could walk up and down a five-hundred-foot-long gravel path. On December 22, Baron von Wrede wrote home to one of his children: "There are seven other gentlemen here with me. We can spend the whole day together if we want to. Our rooms are nice and clean. . . . They give onto a hall-like room where we can spend our days and take our meals. There's already a Christmas tree in the room. . . . The food is supposedly good and plentiful, say my mates, so that, as you can see, things are not bad here."[48]

Landsberg Prison became the last place where Hitler and Eckart were together, though they never met while there. Arguably Hitler's most important intellectual and political mentor, Eckart had, more than anyone, shown Hitler the power of anti-Semitism as a political tool. Often called the spiritual father of Nazism, the hard-drinking, morphine-addicted Eckart was still cranking out his political vitriol; when arrested, he was working on an anti-Semitic tract called "Bolshevism from Moses to Lenin: Dialogues Between Hitler and Me." Probably reconstructed from multiple discussions with Hitler, Eckart referred to the work as his "Hitler pamphlet."[49] Yet in the months before the putsch, the two men had drifted apart. The Nazi leader no longer treated the star of the Munich bohemian-*völkisch* scene as his better, or even as his equal; Eckart had been ejected from Hitler's brain trust. Eckart spent the night of the putsch in one of his watering holes, the Fledermausbar (Bat Bar), and slept late the next morning. Hearing of the march to the Odeon Square, Eckart joined in—but only by car.[50] It was enough to get him arrested and now imprisoned in Landsberg, but he did not stay for long. Within ten days of his incarceration Dietrich's already declining health led to his premature release. Several weeks later, on the day after Christmas, in the small alpine town of Berchtesgaden that he and Hitler loved so well, Eckart died at age fifty-five.[51] Hitler later dedicated the second volume of *Mein Kampf* to him.

Spending Christmas 1923 behind bars must have impressed upon Hitler the gravity of his situation. Yet given his unsentimental personality, it seems unlikely to have been an especially difficult season for him. Hitler had no close family that he would miss; he was an utterly political animal. To an old boyhood friend who wrote to him three weeks before the putsch, Hitler had replied: "As far as a family is concerned, mine consists so far only of my wonderful German shepherd dog. I haven't been able to carry it any farther than that. The old ringleader of yesterday is still the ringleader of today and not refined enough yet for the gentler bonds of life."[52]

The most exciting moment of the holidays came a week later on New Year's Eve. Just past the stroke of midnight, the loud pealing of the prison's church bell was overwhelmed by a "hellish crackling," Hemmrich recalled, the sound of explosions from outside the prison walls. The Bavarian State Police jumped into action and doubled the guard around the prison—but it was a false alarm. Exuberant soldiers at the Reichswehr barracks were just firing off their "excess ammunition," wrote Hemmrich.

The Reichswehr fireworks may have been a false alarm, but there was indeed reason to celebrate the coming of 1924 and, especially, the going of 1923. The fifth year in the life of the new German republic had been its most disturbing and unstable. The annus horribilis of 1923 had begun with the Franco-Belgian invasion of the Ruhr region and gone downhill from there, reaching its nadir in autumn with the spiking of the inflationary spiral and with an assault on the state and its constitution — Hitler's putsch. And there the descent had stopped. Hitler's botched coup d'état marked the finale of a turbulent political era in Germany — uncertainty, extreme violence, near civil war, revolutionary activities, and runaway inflation. Just as Hitler was entering prison, Germany began a period of both exhaustion and calm that eventually led to renewal and stability.

Germany's comeback had begun with the introduction, in mid-October 1923, of a new currency called the *Rentenmark,* based on a new institution called the Rentenbank. The new mark was exchanged for the devastated Reichsmark at the rate of one Rentenmark for one billion Reichsmarks. Soon after Hitler's putsch, the currency began to regain the buyers' and sellers' confidence, and brought inflation to a standstill. The new stability was soon supported by the Dawes Plan, an American-led restructuring of Germany's reparations debt signed later in 1924. With the currency stabilized, unemployment began to ease. The French even hinted that they might be prepared to evacuate the Ruhr region, and there was talk of Germany being admitted into the League of Nations. The quashing of the putsch had lanced the boil of revolution and insurrection in Bavaria, averting the Berlin-Munich collision that had seemed inevitable in fall 1923. Even Kahr, Lossow, and Seisser, the other players in the 1923 conflict, were soon on their way out. A corner had been turned; Germany seemed to be on the upswing.

The new year also brought changes inside Landsberg Prison. Warden Leybold had been given a new project; he was to renovate the fortress building into a cell block for an expectedly large number of putschist prisoners, far more than could be held in his small special facility in the main prison. More challenging was another order: he was to turn the fortress's second floor into a courtroom. The much-anticipated "Hitler-Ludendorff trial," as it was often called, would take place within the walls of Landsberg Prison. Along with Hitler and Ludendorff, eight other putsch leaders— including Colonel Kriebel, Captain Röhm, and Dr. Weber—would be tried together in February. Their trial would be followed in a few weeks' time by a second trial for the smaller fry, the forty foot soldiers from the Storm Troopers and Kampfbunders who were charged as accessories to high treason and for sundry offenses such as vandalizing the *Münchener Post* offices, taking hostages, and mishandling people like the wife of the *Münchener Post* editor. Because it was impossible to know who among Hitler's many marchers had fired the shots that killed four police troops, no one was charged in their deaths.

Having done the battle of the streets, and lost badly, Hitler was now preparing for the battle of the courtroom. A crisis junkie, Hitler responded best when cornered and confronted. His years of rampant reading, his reportedly excellent memory for broad concepts as well as for details, and his growing belief in his own infallibility began to flow into a thought process for legal (and political) combat that would turn his trial into something more than a judicial process. It would become a platform for his solidifying worldview as well as an ex post facto rationalization of his attempt to overthrow the German state.

To prepare the fortress for the trial, Warden Leybold quickly set carpenters and painters to work. Walls were ripped down, rooms were designed for the press and the police, and a broad wooden railing was installed as the court bar, dividing spectators from those involved in official proceedings. In the watchtower overlooking the fortress building and courtyard, new shooting slits and a machine gun emplacement were installed. Barbed wire was added atop the barrier separating the fortress building from the prison church. Drivers bringing construction materials began calling the road inside the prison "Hitler Street." Noted Hemmrich: "The 'fortress' was finally turned into a fortress in the military sense."[53]

These renovations included one unusual touch: Leybold knew he might need a special space for General Ludendorff. Arrested and released after the putsch on his word of honor, Ludendorff would have to serve time if convicted and sentenced at the trial. But even if found guilty of high treason, nobody—not the prosecutor, not the judge, not any prison official—could bring himself to treat Ludendorff as a normal mortal. He would have to have something better.

Surveying his options, Leybold saw the solution right in front of him: he would give Ludendorff his own rather spacious conference room in the administration building, far from the prison hoi polloi. Workers began converting and furnishing the space as a "two-room cell" for the general: a sitting room where he could work and receive visitors, and a "bedroom" behind a newly installed archway with a heavy curtain. Leybold even designated one prison guard to be Ludendorff's manservant, since no German general could be expected to do without one. The guard cleaned his best suit and patent-leather shoes and began preparing for the assignment of a lifetime.[54]

Behind the planning for Hitler's trial, a political backstory was unfolding. Hitler and his accomplices were charged with high treason for an attempt to "violently change the constitution" not only of Bavaria but of the German Reich as well.[55] At the national level, the offense fell under the 1922 Law for the Protection of the Republic— passed following the assassination of Foreign Minister Walther Rathenau. Strictly interpreted, the Hitler trials should therefore have been held at the newly created State Court in Leipzig, in Saxony. At first, even Hitler favored that venue, thinking he might receive a fairer trial and — best of all — get his bitter enemies, Kahr, Lossow, and Seisser, charged with treason alongside him. Moving the trial to Leipzig would deprive his tormentors of their special influence in Bavaria, he thought. But Bavaria looked out for its own: Justice Minister Franz Gürtner adamantly refused to remand the defendants to the State Court in Leipzig, claiming that the Bavarians — Kahr, Lossow, and Seisser — could not be safely transported through Saxony. In the end, the Bavarians won: they kept the putsch, the imprisonment, and the trial an all-Bavarian affair. They would try the accused traitors before their own People's Court, a special institution created to mete out swift justice during the bloody upheavals of 1918 and 1919. The People's Court was supposed to have been dissolved by now. It was kept alive for the express purpose of holding the Hitler trial.

At Landsberg Prison, builders were debating which shade of green to paint the new courtroom walls when their exertions were brought to a sudden halt. Word had come from on high that Landsberg was too small for a proceeding that would have multiple defendants, numerous lawyers, and a large press corps from all over Germany — maybe even from foreign countries. The decision had been made to hold Hitler's trial in Munich after all. Leybold went back to building an enlarged cell block.

As for Hitler's preparations, the autodidact did what he had done ever since his life's first big setback when, as an eighteen-year-old in October 1907 in Vienna, he was rejected by the arts academy: he read.

"For my friend, it was books, always books," wrote Hitler's boyhood friend Kubizek in his memoir. "Hitler arrived in Vienna with four cases full of books.... I could not imagine Adolf without books.

He stacked them in piles around him. . . . Whenever he went out there would usually be a book under his arm . . . he would rather abandon nature and the open sky than the book. . . . Books were his whole world."[56] Kubizek, who had for a time been Hitler's roommate in Vienna, claimed that his friend read the great classics of German literature and philosophy: Schopenhauer, Nietzsche, Goethe, Schiller, Wagner, Herder, Lessing—plus German heroic legends, as well as Dante's *Divine Comedy*.[57] Hitler claimed to have read "endless amounts," including all five hundred books in a Viennese bookshop, which gave him the "granite foundation" for his worldview.

Yet because he almost never attributed his ideas or statements— in speeches or in *Mein Kampf*—to any books or persons, Hitler has forced the world to rely on secondary sources for clues about what he actually read and who influenced him. Such clues include a list of more than one hundred books—including works by Rousseau, Montesquieu, and Kant—that Hitler borrowed from the private collection of a Nazi dentist who lived in a nearby town. Then there was the list of forty-two mostly anti-Semitic books "that every National Socialist must know" that was printed on Nazi Party membership cards starting in 1922; it included six works by Alfred Rosenberg and the just-published 495-page bible of pseudo-scientific racism, *Rassenkunde des deutschen Volkes* (Racial Typology of the German People), by Hans F. K. Günther, who had earned the nickname "Race-Günther."[58] In addition, Hans Frank, Hitler's future legal adviser and governor-general of occupied Poland, wrote that, while in Landsberg, Hitler had read everything he could get hold of: Nietzsche, Ranke, Treitschke, Marx, Bismarck, and Houston Stewart Chamberlain.[59] Further underlining the bookish legend is a rare photograph of Hitler in his Munich apartment standing before an overfilled bookshelf with numerous volumes stacked wildly on top.[60]

* * *

Yet, as with so many parts of the Hitler legend, there are holes, gaps, and inconsistencies in the received wisdom. Serious doubts have been cast on Hitler's reputation for deep reading. Historian Ian Kershaw has noted that though he was "capable of conversing on the comparative merits of Kant, Schopenhauer, and Nietzsche...this is no proof that he had read their works." And Vienna-based historian Brigitte Hamann considered it "utterly doubtful" that Hitler read the books Kubizek said he read; Kubizek's memoir was written many years after the fact, in part for Nazi consumption, and apparently with a ghostwriter. Hamann suggests Hitler picked up pithy quotes from the "famous 'German wise men'" who were often cited in pamphlets and free literature in the cheap cafés that Hitler frequented. "Hitler did not have to read a single book to make himself appear to be an expert in literature," she wrote.[61]

As for the weighty tomes that Hitler borrowed from the Nazi dentist, the dentist said, "I noticed that Hitler was rather hasty and undirected in his studies—he cannot possibly have digested all that." Likewise, historian Sven Felix Kellerhoff questioned how a young man "who left school after the eighth grade with very poor grades" could have "actually worked his way through such demanding books and understood them."[62]

Still, there appears to be no doubt that Hitler read, or at least skimmed, a great deal (especially if one also counts his pleasure-reading of the cowboys-and-Indians novels of storyteller Karl May). Hitler's style was to cherry-pick materials for the items that suited his developing worldview and his political purposes. In *Mein Kampf* he lectured the world on "the art of proper reading." Reading, he insisted, was "no end in itself, but only the means to an end." That end was, in his case, the confirmation of his own prejudices and previously held beliefs.[63] Hitler's recommended method was combing "every book, newspaper or pamphlet" for material to "increase the correctness or clarity" of one's own point of view. In a conversation with Hans Frank, Hitler asserted that, after all his reading in Landsberg, "I recognized the correctness of my views"[64]— yet another step in Hitler's growing conviction of his infallibility.

In Landsberg, Hitler certainly had books. Visiting his friend, Hanfstaengl said Hitler's cell, besides resembling a "delicatessen and flower shop," also looked like "a regular little library." Hemmrich described Hitler's room as "a scholar's study." Most of Hitler's books came as gifts from admirers. Rudolf Hess, who became Hitler's closest prison pal and amanuensis after the trial, mentioned three books in particular: Oswald Spengler's *Decline of the West*, Professor Karl Haushofer's book on the geopolitics of Japan, and a humorous put-down of the United States melting pot called *Amerikaner* (Americans) by Erwin Rosen, a pseudonym for writer Erwin Carlé.

Whatever his reading list may have included, Hitler was getting ready to fight. He had everything at stake. Despite his faith in himself, he knew that if he missed his mark, his career really could be over, and worse: he could be convicted and receive a sentence of up to life in prison. Or Hitler could be given a medium term of, say, ten to fifteen years and fall off the political map. Still another bad option was that he might be deported to the backwater of Austria, sent there to languish into a historical footnote. (Given his still-valid parole status in the 1921 beating of Otto Ballerstedt, plus the wording of the 1922 Law for the Protection of the Republic, he should have been deported in any case.)

In the coming months, Hitler became a dervish, more productive with words than ever before in his life, reading constantly and writing a memorandum on the putsch that ran to more than sixty pages.[65] "With the warden's permission, Hitler had a typewriter sent to him," wrote Hemmrich, who also purchased writing paper for

Hitler in the town. Hitler had clearly worked himself into a state of high dudgeon as he wrote. "I'm letting my resentments pour into my defense statement," he said in a letter.[66] Angry or not, Hitler was boosted by the adulation of his admirers. "The gushing hero-worship and even deification that has come his way has probably contributed to his getting good control of the situation," wrote his attorney Lorenz Roder. One Nazi visitor from the Sudetenland in Czechoslovakia wrote a report comparing Hitler with Jesus.

Hitler was beginning to see his trial appearance as another beer hall performance—but the beer hall performance of a lifetime. As he read and reflected and wrote, Hitler realized he had two tasks: One was to implicate Kahr, Lossow, and Seisser in the putsch conspiracy. The other was to sell his anti-Marxist, anti-Semitic politics and Nazi Party brand by laying out his grand design for solving the problems Germany faced. In this boldly aggressive fighting style, he would also be selling himself. For that he needed a courtroom version of his beer hall stump speech.

Hitler also began conceiving his defense in personal terms, framed by his own biography, conflating his own fate with Germany's. His life, with its odd twists, chance intellectual discoveries, and self-taught insights, he decided, was the perfect metaphor for his movement, his plans, his understanding of the great questions facing the nation. His personal awakening and leadership of the Nazi Party would become the story of the putsch—and the proof of his innocence. Or it would become his swan song.

Done right, the stump speech would redeem Hitler even if his attempt to implicate the triumvirate failed. He would establish himself, at least rhetorically, as a committed soldier in the cause of saving Germany from the Marxist scourge. If convicted of treason for the putsch, Hitler would go down in a blaze of his own glory in the eyes of Germany's nationalist-minded community; he would become a martyr. He would write his own epitaph and it would be a glorious one. For the courtroom stage, he had an almost fail-proof strategy.

On February 22, 1924, Hitler was piled into a police van and trundled, for the first time in nearly four months, back to the town he loved, the platform of all his greatest successes and his worst failure: Munich. There he was housed in the Infantry School, which had been converted into a court.

The trial was set to begin in four days.

CHAPTER SEVEN

A Trial for Treason

"Why isn't Hitler's trial listed among the most important trials in history?"
—OTTO GRITSCHNEDER, MUNICH, 2001[1]

Adolf Hitler's trial for high treason began in Munich on a snowy Tuesday, February 26, 1924.

Lawyers, journalists, and jurists arrived at the Reichswehr's former Infantry School to find a scene like a military siege. For fear of violence by nationalistic paramilitaries or demonstrations by Hitler's fanatical supporters, a detachment of steel-helmeted Reichswehr soldiers and Bavarian State Police had been deployed around the building. The hulking, dark-brick pile was temporarily serving as a Bavarian People's Court and as a provisional jailhouse for Hitler and several other defendants.[2] Stamping their feet and puffing into their gloves on a day described by one trial attendee as "ice cold," the soldiers patrolled behind a cordon of concertina wire and tank traps (*cheval-de-frise*). The militarized aspect of the block caused some

Munich wags to call the area "occupied territory"—a play on the French invasion of the Ruhr region.[3] Another observer compared the Infantry School to an armed "Roman *castello*."

In front of the old building—it had been Bavaria's nineteenth-century War School before becoming the Reichswehr's academy—checkpoints forced every attendee to show identification twice and to undergo a weapons check. A special room was set aside for frisking females. "Women who have been looking forward to daily thrills in connection with the trial got one wholly unexpected when they were compelled to undergo a personal search for arms before entering the court," reported the *New York Times*. "Their hair, hats, purses, muffs and even stockings were inspected for daggers, hand grenades and bombs [and] hatpins exceeding the limit allowed."[4]

The *New York Times* wasn't the only foreign newspaper covering the trial. Besides the London *Times* and Paris's *Le Temps,* nearly fifty foreign journalists were present, a Swiss newspaper reported. "The eyes of the world are on Munich during these days," noted the paper. For the Germans, this could only mean bad news. "Doubtless the foreigners who read about and study this trial will find plenty of material with which to attack the whole of Germany," lamented a Munich columnist.[5]

Of course, German reporters outnumbered all others. The journalists were crammed into sixty of the one hundred twenty spectator seats in the refurbished formal officers' mess, now a courtroom. But that wasn't enough; an overflow press room was created down the hall. The place was crawling with reporters "along with their relief colleagues, their secretaries and messengers." One German journalist complained that court officials had installed only five telephone lines, then claimed them all for themselves. "There is nothing for the newspapers and the public they serve," he groused. In the weeks to come, messengers would rush newspaper copy from courtroom to press room with alacrity and zeal; stories on events at the trial appeared *on the same day* they occurred in multiple editions of fast-moving newspapers in Munich, Berlin, and elsewhere.

Located on the Blutenburgstrasse, the military academy had been chosen for Munich's most sensational trial in many years partly because it was away from the crowded courthouse in downtown Munich, thus easier to surround and defend. But there was another reason: the school was empty. Because the school's five-hundred-man cadet corps had enthusiastically joined Hitler's insurrection, General von Seeckt, high commander of the Reichswehr,[6] had shut down the Munich school and moved the academy to a small town in Thuringia where the cadets could make less mischief.[7] Now the school that had been so gladly in Hitler's pocket during the abortive coup had him in its own pocket. He was imprisoned in a former cadet's room, awaiting the judgment that would shape the rest of his life.

He was being tried with nine fellow putschists, including the war hero, Ludendorff. Some, like Colonel Kriebel and Dr. Weber, were imprisoned with him on the second floor of the Infantry School. They lived well, each in a simple single room, their meals served "on white tablecloths" at a table in the hall. They even had two hours of outdoor time per day in the school's inner courtyard if they wanted it. Along with Hitler, Ludendorff, Kriebel, and Weber, the other defendants included Captain Röhm, Ernst Pöhner, Wilhelm Frick, Wilhelm Brückner, Robert Wagner, and Ludendorff's stepson, Heinz Pernet. One defendant, Pöhner, Munich's former police chief, suffered a recurring illness and had just barely made it to the trial. Hitler, as usual, was flooded with gifts. When his old walk-around buddy, Ernst Hanfstaengl, paid a visit, bringing along his four-year-old son, Egon, Hitler allowed the delighted boy to have his pick of the "sweets and cakes" that cluttered the room.[8]

It had been nearly four months since the spectacular failure of Hitler's putsch, and he faced, in theory, a simple trial for treason; he had already practically confessed to the deed. But the proceeding in the People's Court was to be about much more than the discovery of guilt or innocence. The chief defendant would do everything in his power to recast his trial as a morality play about Germany's future and "the salvation of the fatherland," with himself in the role of savior. He would use a courtroom packed with journalists to sell himself, still unknown in most parts of Germany, to the largest audience he had ever had.

Already that audience was eager to hear from him. "The [leftist] democratic press is bubbling with anticipation,"* wrote Stuttgart's nationalistic *Süddeutsche Zeitung*,† "hoping for a self-destruction drama among the nationalist forces to beef up the republicans' notoriously weak platform in the days before the next election." Word had been leaked that Hitler would make a multi-hour opening speech. "All the preparations to satisfy a hunger for sensation, like press, film and photography, have been made," wrote the newspaper. "Now it can begin."[9]

It began with a long march down the second-floor hall of the Infantry School. Housed in "cosy"[10] rooms on the western end of the building, Hitler and his fellow defendants, with Ludendorff in the lead, walked nearly three hundred feet "in a ceremonial procession" to the building's eastern end, where the converted officers' mess was located.[11] Ludendorff, journeying to the trial every day from his villa on the outskirts of Munich, had arrived by

---

* Democratic in this context is code for Socialist or left-leaning.

† Not to be confused with the highly respected postwar Munich newspaper by the same name. Today's *Süddeutsche Zeitung* is Germany's leading center-left daily.

chauffeured car and was cheered as his vehicle turned into the Infantry School courtyard. Journalists in the press overflow room were on lockdown as the procession passed.[12] Every door of the long hallway was closed and guarded by a soldier in a steel helmet or in the classic German spiked headgear commonly called a *Pickelhaube,* or "pick bonnet."[13] Hitler was again decked out—as on the day of the putsch, as on the moment of his arrival in Landsberg Prison— in what had become his revolutionary outfit, a frock coat with his World War I medals pinned on. Ridiculed on the night of the putsch for his formal attire that made him look like "a forlorn little waiter" in a beer hall, Hitler now appeared to be arriving as a star performer—which he was.

The converted courtroom looked the part of a judicial chamber. Fifty-two feet long and thirty-eight feet wide,[14] the refitted dining hall had simple chandeliers hanging from the heavy-beamed ceiling. A newly installed judicial bench skirted with dark baize stood at one end. Natural light from the high windows augmented the new electric fixtures. The courtroom "glowed red" from the weak February sun, noted one observer.[15] The only complaint was that the chairs were packed in too tightly and the room was sometimes overheated.

Hitler entered the courtroom like a hungry animal. His eyes darted "back and forth, looking all around,"[16] taking in the scene: lawyers, journalists, spectators. One journalist noted that "he is shorter than his photographs make him look."[17] Ludendorff, the picture of calm reserve, strode silently to his place at a defense table. For other defendants, it was like old home week; friends hailed, greetings exchanged, handshakes and smiles all around. The spectator seats seemed mostly filled with Hitler supporters.[18] The relaxed treatment of the Nazis and their allies was in stark contrast to the much rougher handling meted out to trial defendants from Communist or Socialist groups who were prosecuted in the People's

Courts around Bavaria. The Socialist *Münchener Post* bitterly noted that in Hitler's trial "the accused carried on animated conversations with one another until they were asked with great tact if they wouldn't mind taking their seats. No sign of guards." Only two months earlier, wrote the newspaper, sixteen Socialists had been brought into a People's Court where "they arrived manacled and departed manacled...each had a guard on either side...they were not allowed to speak with one another...even those whose sentences were already covered by time served were led away afterwards in chains...that's the kind of tact the court shows to Socialists."

The trial's opening day was the political event of the season for those in public life. The two dozen seats reserved for witnesses had been designated on this day for Munich's elite, including members of parliament, high government officials, and prominent members of the judiciary.[19] Clearly everyone wanted to be there for the showdown at the Infantry School and, most important, to hear Hitler's speech. Many expected the courtroom to be a perfect setting for one of his bravura performances.

The show started with the arrival of the judges. Three jurors, called "lay judges" (plus one alternate), and two professional judges (plus one alternate) were led into the courtroom by the chief judge, Georg Neithardt.[20] A bald man with a pointed gray goatee who arrived at the Infantry School in a high fedora and black overcoat, Neithardt was a decidedly nationalist member of the Bavarian judiciary. Later a beneficiary of Hitler's office-giving powers, the judge had a track record in the People's Court for coming down hard on leftists but going easy on rightists. It was Neithardt, for example, who had commuted Count Arco-Valley's sentence (for his back-of-the-head assassination of Kurt Eisner in 1919) from death to life in prison under the easy conditions of "fortress arrest." The commutation was justified, stated Neithardt, because of the murderer's "glowing love of his people and fatherland"[21] and, incredibly, because of "the widely felt antipathy for Eisner" in Bavaria. A political murder, Neithardt signaled, was not quite a real murder, especially if the victim was performing poorly at the polls (Eisner had received less than 3 percent in the most recent election). Providentially for Hitler, Neithardt was also the judge who in 1922 had given Hitler early parole after he served only one month of a three-month breach-of-the-peace term ("too hard,"[22] Neithardt called it) for the brutal bludgeoning of Bavaria League leader Otto Ballerstedt. In Neithardt, Hitler and his lawyer, Lorenz Roder, knew they had a friendly face on the bench. Despite the presence of the other judges, Neithardt — wearing the traditional chief judge's high beret and judicial robe — was the man in charge. (Before the trial ended, many would say that Hitler was in charge.)

The prosecution came prepared to wage heavy battle against Hitler and his nine co-conspirators. Hitler, like many others, may have been taken aback when Deputy State's Attorney Hans Ehard, the man who had chatted with him in prison for five hours without a stenographer, rose to present the government's case — with a thirty-nine-page document in his hands. Based on interviews and depositions from scores of participants and witnesses, Ehard had meticulously reconstructed the events of the attempted coup. For the next ninety minutes, Ehard led the courtroom back through the harrowing experiences of November 8 and November 9, 1923, carrying his listeners through the maze of meetings and confrontations leading up to the putsch and its botched execution, untangling a thicket of testimony and recollections that brought the misbegotten events vividly to life again: Hitler's gunshot into the Bürgerbräukeller ceiling; his proclamation of a new government; his seizure of hostages; his assaults on military installations; his theft of billions of marks from two print shops; and, finally, his last-ditch "propaganda march" through the center of Munich to the Odeon Square, where the procession ended bloodily. "In the end," intoned Ehard flatly, "the Bavarian State Police stood fast and had to make use of their firearms."*

Then came Ehard's central point, the comment that focused the trial on Hitler. For all its complications, convolutions, and numerous participants, said the prosecutor, the putsch was essentially the work of one man. "Hitler was the soul of the whole enterprise," said Ehard.

On the surface, Ehard's statement was damning, to be sure, but Hitler could not have asked for a better setup for the most important speech of his career. Not only was he supposedly guilty of treason, not only had he played diabolical political games, not only had he arrogated unto himself the right to take over Germany, but he had become the *soul*—the spirit, the heart, the very intellectual marrow—of the whole undertaking. Despite the great efforts of Kriebel, Weber, and all the others, Hitler, as far as the state was concerned, was *it*. Even the vaunted Ludendorff wasn't the soul of the enterprise—Hitler was. A politician who constantly sought to separate himself from mere *politicians,* who considered his mission more spiritual than materialistic, who felt a kinship to Napoleon and Frederick the Great and the sainted Richard Wagner, Hitler could have hoped for no higher compliment. As the man whose entire political striving until now—and again in the very near future, as we shall see—was to make himself the irreducible center of things, the beating heart of his own movement, the X factor in Germany's future, what could be better than being called in open court, before the world's press, the *soul* of the show? Hitler must have been ecstatic.

---

* Ehard did not mention the fifteen dead Nazis, the four dead policemen, and the one dead bystander. Everyone already knew. Besides, there had been no indictments for homicide; it was impossible to know who shot whom in the melee.

But before Hitler could speak, the prosecution moved that the entire trial be held in camera — behind closed doors. Secret sessions, maintained State's Attorney Ludwig Stenglein, were necessary to prevent sensitive details about the putsch preparations, especially the Reichswehr's complicity in preparing for a march on Berlin, from reaching the public and especially foreign ears — mainly French ears. After all, these measures were in violation of the Treaty of Versailles. The defense objected; it wanted Hitler's story and that of his co-defendants to reach the widest possible audience to generate the pressure of public support. Hitler knew that his upcoming speech was his chance to reestablish himself as a credible figure in German politics. In a secret session about the secret sessions, one defense attorney argued that the trial needed to serve as a kind of civics class for the nation. "This trial arises from the collision of two worldviews on November 8 and 9. . . . We will be committing a grave injustice if we don't let these two points of view have their say in public."[23] (Of course, he really meant letting Hitler's point of view have its say.) Judge Neithardt split the difference. After a long discussion, he ruled that some topics would be reserved for closed sessions, some would not. The witnesses and defendants themselves, he argued, would know when to save material for the closed-door sessions. This sounds like putting the fox in charge of the chicken coop, and it was: after all, everyone was in on the deal — the putschists and the triumvirate. For Hitler, this was a nearly ideal decision. He could lay out his politics and populist style before the world while revealing the most incriminating details of the triumvirate's involvement in coup planning behind closed doors.

Ironically, Neithardt had nearly scotched Hitler's hope for long public sessions even before the trial began. The judge had made it known that he saw no reason to hear witnesses at all; a judgment could be reached based on the defendants' confessions alone.[24]

Fortunately for Hitler, Neithardt had changed his mind. He decided to allow full and long testimony, he wrote later, because the defendants, unlike the prosecution, had not yet been allowed to have their say and "defend their honor."[25] After all, the Nazi newspaper, the *Völkischer Beobachter,* like the Nazi Party itself, as well as Dr. Weber's Bund Oberland, had been banned after the putsch. Because of the prohibition on the defendants' publications, argued Neithardt, "the accused have been unable to defend themselves in public against official and semi-official versions of events." Since those versions, "in the opinion of the accused...do not correspond to the facts and are likely to influence public opinion against them," Neithardt felt Hitler and his confederates deserved to have a go at swaying public opinion—as if a court of law is supposed to have anything to do with mass mood.

Stunningly, Neithardt went further, citing personal "bitterness" and political pressures as grounds for a long, open trial. "As a result [of their inability to influence public opinion], the hearts of the accused were filled with bitterness which threatened to explode," wrote the judge. "If one were going to have a trial at all, one had to allow the accused the opportunity to vent their resentments to the fullest and in broad public view."[26]

Grimly, Neithardt's legitimization of public opinion as a trial factor reflected reality; the judge knew the supreme importance of popular emotions in 1920s Germany. And so did Hitler.

On the trial's first day, at two thirty in the afternoon, Hitler rose from one of the ten small defense tables arrayed at the front of the crowded courtroom. After nearly four months off the speaking circuit, after many weeks without raising his voice to oratorical pitch, and no days and nights of declaiming and hectoring, Hitler had to plunge into his showcase moment from a cold start. In the press corps and the audience, as well as among the judges on the bench, expectations were high. The man who had held half the Bavarian government hostage, who had led fifteen of his men to their deaths, who made his living by speaking (and shouting) but who had not spoken publicly since November—that man was finally ready to talk. "Herr Hitler, I call upon you to give us a statement of your position and how you got involved in this matter," deadpanned Judge Neithardt.

In his black frock coat and war medals, Hitler drew himself up to his full five feet nine inches. "May it please the court!" he began in perfect lawyerly fashion, setting a pattern of pointed politeness toward Neithardt that he maintained throughout the trial. Hitler immediately fired his planned autobiographical opener, pointing out that he'd served "four-and-a-half years" in the German military and received a performance rating of "very good." Why, then, he rhetorically wondered, would a man trained in "blind obedience to his superiors" find himself in the "highest possible conflict in public life, that is, with the so-called constitution"? Why was he accused of high treason?

Already taking shots at the hated Weimar government, Hitler launched into an answer that would consume the afternoon. His rambling, melodramatic peroration recalled for many one of his political speeches, except that it was even longer. According to contemporaneous reports, Hitler's speech lasted nearly four hours, although the trial transcript suggests that it lasted about three hours.[27] At the beginning, even the seasoned rabble-rouser spoke "almost nervously," reported one observer. But soon he was on his game, pouring forth a deluge of words, gestures, anecdotes, historical allusions, and personal biography that overwhelmed the courtroom and seemed to carry his audience along on resurgent waves of outrage, passion, and self-righteousness—the familiar Hitlerian torrent. When Judge Neithardt was later criticized for not interrupting Hitler to keep him somewhere close to the topic at hand, he threw up his hands and answered lamely, "It was impossible to block his flood of words."[28]

Hitler's flood made the story of Nazism the story of himself. It even had a classic hard-luck beginning. "As a young person of sixteen-and-a-half years of age, I had to begin earning my daily bread," he said. The statement was a typical exaggeration (young Hitler lived on family money at that age; he was eighteen before he left home and almost twenty-one before he earned any money[29]) and it contained one of Hitler's favorite images—"daily bread." Yet the claim gave him an easy segue into politics. "At seventeen I went to Vienna and learned three important things." Those three things, he said, were social injustice; the "race problem" (by which he meant Jews, whom he always described as a race, not as a religion or an ethnic group); and the perfidy of Marxism. Within another sentence he had joined Judaism and Marxism into one evil force whose goal, he had concluded, was "the downfall of the entire modern state." Jews he called "the greatest enemy...of Aryan humanity." The result of this eye-opening youthful experience, said Hitler, was that "I had arrived in Vienna as a citizen of the world and left [after five years] as an absolute anti-Semite."[30]

Hitler's statement was blunt and bald-faced. In the first few minutes of his discourse, Hitler had laid down the key tenets of his political ideology. He planned to build a huge target on the political stage and then attack it. He had thrown down the gauntlet of race-based politics, labeling himself a card-carrying anti-Semite (as though he had earned a graduation certificate from an apprenticeship on the mean streets of Vienna). Yet calling himself an "absolute anti-Semite" conveyed little of the shock value those words would imply today. As reprehensible as the term may be, and as strongly as many educated Germans of the period rejected it, anti-Semitism was nonetheless a widespread and openly debated political issue of the era. As "a mortal enemy of the entire Marxist *Weltanschauung*," he had sketched his apocalyptic vision of Germany's future and offered a path to salvation: "Either this racial poison, this mass tuberculosis prospers in our nation and Germany dies of a sick lung, or we cut [the disease] out and Germany can thrive." The antidote to this "racial poison" (read: Judaism) is not "calm analysis," he said, but a politics of "hot, merciless, brutal fanaticism...to bring the [German] people back from slavery."

Those who came to see fireworks in the old Infantry School on this wintry day were not disappointed. The trial of former private first class Adolf Hitler for high treason was clearly not going to be boring. It would follow no formal or legalistic path to its uncertain outcome. The beer hall agitator would not sit back and let the biggest legal proceeding in Germany in years rest in the hands of lawyers and judges. This was a *political* event—he would see to that. Though Hitler had nine co-defendants, including General Ludendorff, this was *his* trial. "For Hitler, the trial was the continuation of political propaganda by juridical means," wrote historian Ernst Deuerlein, echoing Clausewitz's dictum that war was the continuation of politics by other means.[31]

Hitler was now playing to a different audience. In the courtroom and through the Munich newspapers, he would finally reach people who would never attend one of his rowdy mass meetings. Even better, through Germany's dense thicket of newspapers in the pre-radio age, he would reach many who might never hear his voice directly—the general German public outside Bavaria. It didn't hurt that Berlin's most prestigious newspaper, the *Berliner Tageblatt*—the voice of the establishment, the *New York Times* of its day in Germany—ran a banner headline across the top of page one on the first day: "The Beginning of the Munich High Treason Trial."[32]

Despite its discursive nature, Hitler's opening speech—and his speaking style—held his audience rapt. "He knows how to use all modulations of his sometimes raw voice," noted the respected *Frankfurter Zeitung.* While no friend of the Nazi leader—the sophisticated newspaper was committed to a liberal-democratic order in the new Germany and had endorsed the Treaty of Versailles—the Jewish-owned daily nonetheless let its reporter give Hitler his due as a performer, and explain to an unknowing audience some of the magic of Hitler's method. "He softens his voice, then gradually raises it to a dramatic shout, even a hoarse screech. His voice then cracks in sorrow over his fallen comrades. He scornfully mocks the trembling timidity of his enemies. Shaping his words with a lively play of his hands, Hitler rounds off his periods with both hands, emphasizes an ironic or offensive comment by shooting his left index finger towards the state's attorney, and uses his head and even his body to undergird his speech. The rhetorical impact is strong." It sounded as though a visitor from the world of high culture and lofty ideals had gone slumming and discovered that the sideshow was better than expected.

Hitler's goal, as he talked his way through the afternoon, was to establish himself and his movement as the last bulwark against Germany's descent into chaos —what he called, in a typically classical reference, a "Carthaginian end" (Carthage, on the North African coast, was brutally leveled by the Romans in 146 BC). "We are lost unless Germany awakens from its lethargy and recognizes that politics...is not done on this earth with a palm frond but rather with a sword." The Nazi Party, he pointed out, was founded "for the specific aim of saving Germany" in its "eleventh-hour struggle." The Nazi movement offered the two essential requirements for Germany's salvation: "the brain and the fist." The brain, in Hitler's dream palace, was propaganda—an all-purpose concept that, for him, included everything from speeches to posters on the wall to marches through cities to music, slogans, and the very uniforms he and his supporters wore (it also included Hitler's trick of entering a hall from behind the audience, not from behind the podium). Propaganda was, in effect, all the trappings of politics and was the proper job of all who wanted to work with their brains.

The fist was another thing—force, might, muscle, the work of the hands. Waving his arms before the attentive court, he described "our Storm Troopers" as "the men of the fist." Their purpose, Hitler insisted, was not military but rather to protect Nazis and their gatherings from attacks by similar "hall protection units" organized by the Communists and the Socialists. "Every German should have the right to stand up for the ideals he believes in and to use his fists to strike down others who use their fists to block him or prevent the truth from getting through." A mouthful, but an unashamed endorsement of the violent mayhem of 1920s politics and, in fact, an accurate prediction of years of street fighting to come. Reveling in his combative rhetoric, Hitler declared that the "race problem" was the "hardest and most profound issue" facing Germany and that solving "the Jewish question," which he conflated with "the Marxist problem," could be done "not by a government bureaucrat but only by a firebrand [*Feuerkopf*] who can ignite national passions." That hot-blooded character would, of course, be Hitler himself. "I refuse to be modest about something I know I am capable of," he said.

To make his radical solutions acceptable, Hitler had to make the problem radical. The problem was the illegitimacy of the existing German government, the "November criminals" who staged the "stab-in-the-back" 1918 revolution—and their current successors. The revolution itself, by Hitler's lights, was "an unspeakable crime"—mainly because it was Socialist-led. Though it had been affirmed in summer 1919, in a constitutional convention that wrote and adopted the Weimar constitution, and though it had been through numerous parliamentary elections in the past five years, the Weimar Republic, in Hitler's eyes, had never been legitimized by a simple up-or-down plebiscite on its right to exist. "To me," Hitler told the court, "the 1918 revolution does not exist." The current government, he said, had taken Germany "farther backwards in its development and greatness than the Thirty Years' War"—a harrowing image to Germans who all learned in school that one-third of their population was slaughtered (or killed by war-borne disease) during the period between 1618 and 1648. As proof of the illicit nature of the current regime, said Hitler, one only had to look at the failure of parliamentarianism—majority rule—to solve the country's many ills, from inflation to foreign occupation to hunger ("people were crying for bread!"). "Majority decisions are always weak decisions," he claimed.[33] That's why, he stated, he was determined to remove the existing system and replace it with "a nationalistic, absolutely antiparliamentarian national government"—about as clear an admission of treasonous intent as one could ask for.

Nonetheless, Hitler rejected the charge of high treason. For defense against it, he went on offense. Hitler accused his accusers, Kahr, Lossow, and Seisser, the state's crown witnesses, of being themselves guilty of treason. "If our whole undertaking was an act of high treason, then Kahr, Lossow and Seisser must have committed high treason with us. For months on end, we talked with them about nothing else, the very same thing for which we are now sitting in the dock."

Rather than deny his role in the putsch, Hitler embraced it and seized the opportunity to ridicule those who had been tentative. He mercilessly pummeled Kahr as a man "with no iron fist" who "will start a fight but never finish it.... The minute a fight begins, he will collapse in fright." The putsch was, Hitler argued, a joint exercise but with half the team ready to leap (Hitler and friends) and the other half paralyzed by qualms (Kahr, Lossow, and Seisser). "They were like a horse that loses heart just before the jump," argued Hitler. "We had to give them the will to make the leap."

Hitler ridiculed the triumvirate's hairsplitting on the question of using force as opposed to *just* applying political pressure as they attempted to impose a directorate in Berlin. "Some people try to explain [this situation]...by saying, 'Sure, [a takeover] was our intention but we didn't want to achieve it through *force* but rather through *pressure*, although through *pressure* that included *some force*, but not really applying *force*.... It was a *coup d'état*, to be sure, but not a *usual coup d'état*, as it has been historically understood up until now, but rather the way *we* mean it.'"

By now Hitler had everyone in the courtroom grinning; they could see where he was going. The triumvirate was well hoist and looking foolish. Hitler wrapped up: "Well, then I have only one regret: nobody told us at the time about this special Lossowian idea of a coup.... We took it for granted that if Seeckt or Lossow went today to see Mr. [President] Ebert and told him nicely: Mr. Ebert, here are our divisions. We won't use *force*, but the divisions will no longer obey you. The door is right over there. Then you could say: no *force* was used."

When the courtroom burst into laughter, Neithardt, in a rare moment of disciplinary zeal, shouted: "This is not a theater!" Oh, but it was, and Hitler was the chief protagonist in his own drama. He was turning his prosecution for treason into a political show trial, but with all the roles reversed.

Hitler also deployed a they-made-me-do-it defense. "Kahr, Lossow and Seisser had me believe they were ready to strike," he said.

"They discussed even the smallest details with us. Baron Aufsess [Kahr's representative] said to a small group that Kahr was sitting on a powder keg holding the fuse." Besides, added Hitler, everybody under the sun was expecting a coup. "People were shouting it from the rooftops.... The general mood was: a savior must finally appear." Hitler addressed the bench: "Esteemed Gentlemen, I ask you to put yourselves psychologically in our shoes. An incident was inevitable. [Our people] were asking, 'When do we move? When do we start throwing out that gang in Berlin?'" Hitler also asked rhetorically why, if the triumvirate had such clean hands, Kahr had not arrested Hitler on his first day in office as unofficial dictator (Hitler had posed exactly the same question during his five-hour conversation with Ehard in Landsberg Prison). "Of course he should have come to me, or sent a policeman, and said, 'Mr. Hitler, you are under arrest.' It would have been his bounden duty...to put all such people [who were planning a putsch] under lock and key."

Had Kahr, Lossow, and Seisser been playacting during the putsch when they shook Hitler's hand in the Bürgerbräukeller and joined in his "revolution"? Hitler painted a persuasive picture of sincere conviction on the part of his newly recruited co-conspirators. "Kahr held both my hands," he recalled. "I trusted him like a brother.... I would be as loyal as a dog to him." Lossow and Seisser "had tears in their eyes" when they pledged loyalty to Ludendorff, he said.

In his rambling rhetoric, Hitler sought to undermine the very legitimacy of the charge against him. "High treason is the only crime that is punishable only if it fails," he noted, stating a truism as though it somehow annulled the law. In a self-conscious display of manly courage, Hitler took "sole responsibility" for the putsch—thus emphasizing his role as the *soul* of the enterprise—but at the same time he denied the commission of a crime. Flatly rejecting his accomplice Colonel Kriebel's right to take any responsibility for events, Hitler hogged the self-sacrifice halo for himself, saying, in a typical twist of logic, "I confess to the deed but not to high treason, because there's no charge of high treason against the traitors of 1918."

With his histrionic style and careful forward spin, Hitler was laying the groundwork for his future martyrdom and that of his movement, should it come to that. "Our jail cells will become the beacon for the spirit of young Germany," he said.[34] In short, you may send us away, but we will be back. We're young. (Hitler was thirty-four.)

Finally, Hitler hedged carefully against the ever-worrisome threat of deportation. Having opened with his brief biography and a reference to his wartime years on the western front, he closed by returning to his youth and wrapping himself in the German flag, despite his Austrian nationality. "From my early years onwards, I've never felt myself to be Austrian.... I do not consider myself a traitor, but rather simply a German who only wanted the best for his people." Hitler sat down.

It had been a long, intense afternoon, and now evening was setting in. Nobody had left the jammed courtroom except journalistic messengers. No doubt tired but elated, Hitler could take satisfaction in his virtuoso performance. He had quickly found his rhythm, his pious certainties, his passion, and, where appropriate, his sarcastic tone. Though disorganized and laced with inconsistencies and non sequiturs, Hitler's argument sounded compelling to many by its very conviction. His relentless pounding of the complicity theme had its desired effect. "Much of what Hitler says about the lead-up to the coup...sounds at least subjectively convincing," wrote the

Frankfurter Zeitung. "One sees clearly how Hitler's plan grew out of the behavior of the men then ruling in Bavaria. The only thing dividing them were some personnel questions…and the courage to act."[35]

Kahr, Lossow, and Seisser had already lost their positions as ruling triumvirate in Bavaria, and now rumors circulated that they might, in fact, be arrested.[36] Within a day, a workman on a Munich street asked in a thick Bavarian accent, "Well, have they grabbed ol' Kahr yet?" After the sound courtroom thrashing by the brash Nazi, the hapless trio also had become the butt of more scorn and ridicule. In the Augustiner-Keller, one of Munich's downtown beer halls, students swayed with their beer mugs to a newly adapted tune, "Kahr is a li-ar, a li-ar, a liiii-aaaar!" A local comic named Weiss Ferdl entertained overflow crowds night after night in a little theater across from the Hofbräuhaus with a ditty praising the "German men" who only "want to save their German fatherland."[37]

Of course, not everyone was charmed by Hitler's performance. As had been true in assessments of Hitler before his putsch, the sachems of the high bourgeoisie—columnists for the most sophisticated newspapers—tended to dismiss Hitler after his speech as an untutored rustic. "Hitler is a proletarian natural—no doubt about it," wrote Dr. Carl Misch in Berlin's high-toned *Vossische Zeitung.* "He is an autodidact who has assembled elements of a modern education and knows how to deploy them with a certain god-given slyness and skill.…For him, everything is thesis and antithesis. His speech works in contrasts, pairs and triplets.…there are only two possibilities, or only three, sometimes more.…His vocabulary is minimal. Everything is fundamental, exclusive, without exception, in principle or absolute.…He is a political natural…but a man of character he is not."[38]

To less critical eyes, however, Hitler was a man with a vision and the willingness to act on it, a man of both fists and brains, with rapier language for his opponents' weak spots. He was thus perfectly suited to serve as the average suffering German's convenient alter ego. "What a tremendous guy, this Hitler!" one of the lay judges in the trial said within earshot of journalist Hans von Hülsen.[39] That was exactly the impression Hitler had wanted to make. He was back.

CHAPTER EIGHT

The Judgment of History

"The eternal court will... pronounce us not guilty."
—ADOLF HITLER, MARCH 27, 1924

Hitler's trial had lasted but one day and already it had reached a turning point. The chief defendant had turned the proceedings upside down, making the triumvirate his co-defendants in spirit if not in fact. Before a spellbound audience, he had already found them guilty—of co-thinking, co-planning, co-wishing.

He had scorched his enemies, trashed the parliamentary basis of the Weimar Republic, and made the case that his putsch practically *had to happen.* On the trial's first day, Hitler had set the parameters where he wanted them, establishing the purity of his movement's motives and casting himself as a selfless leader trying to be a hero, not a traitor. For the first time since his brief hour of triumph on that November night in the Bürgerbräukeller, Hitler must have felt the heady rush of performing on the high wire of public speaking.

This was a resurrection; he had shown the world—and especially himself—that he still had his chops.

Now the question of the triumvirate's culpability in the putsch began to dominate the trial. The proceeding also opened a window into the ambiguous military mission of the confused postwar Reichswehr and the bitter contempt in which far-right nationalists held the Weimar Republic, its leaders, and its parliament. In the coming weeks, the testimony would unmask a larger plot to overthrow Germany's democracy than had previously been known.

Hitler could now move into the role of cross-examiner, declaimer, and one-man Greek chorus. Without objection from Judge Neithardt, he behaved more like a lawyer than a defendant, hopping up with questions or interjecting statements when he wanted to augment someone else's testimony. Under the German procedural code, defendants were allowed to question witnesses almost at will, but with the questions controlled by the judge, who could rule anything out of bounds. Neithardt ruled very little out of bounds, except when Hitler used personal insults, and even then his admonitions were routinely ignored.

Over the next two days, Hitler and everyone in the court again relived the run-up to the events of November 8 and 9, 1923, as seen through the eyes of three key defendants: Dr. Weber, head of the well-armed Bund Oberland paramilitary; Ernst Pöhner, the former Munich police chief; and Colonel Kriebel, the military commander of the Kampfbund. In closed-door sessions, Weber and Kriebel for the first time explained the secret training and hand-in-glove cooperation among the Reichswehr, the Bavarian State Police, and the paramilitaries—in direct violation of the Treaty of Versailles. As an example, Weber cited "high priority" exercises for younger recruits "who had never before faced enemy fire." Live-ammunition and "sharpshooting" drills had been held at least three times per week "under the leadership of Reichswehr officers," he noted. Hitler joined in, neatly implying government involvement in his putsch by underlining the Reichswehr's and the Bavarian State Police's training of his Nazi Storm Troopers, thus implicating Kahr, Lossow, and Seisser. Since the previous October, Hitler said, "our troops were trained in the [Reichswehr] barracks at an intensified pace...not for the purpose of border defense but...absolutely only for *offensive* purposes, including...all the technical necessities for mobile warfare to the north." His men, who usually did their training at night or in their off hours from their jobs, often wore Reichswehr or Bavarian State Police uniforms, said Hitler. All this activity was in the context of the so-called Autumn Exercise that Lossow had ordered with a demand for the "highest state of readiness." That kind of pressure, Hitler said, was one of the key reasons he felt he had to stage the putsch: "It was no longer possible to hold back people who, day after day, night after night, had been coming to the barracks with only thoughts of war."[1]

Weber, Pöhner, and Kriebel each added a fillip of invective to the sometimes venomous atmosphere of the trial. Weber said he had ordered a detachment of his paramilitary to seize Munich's main train station once the putsch began "to prevent the racially foreign Eastern Jewish *vermin* from fleeing head over heels with all their foreign currency." That this order was never carried out—and nobody was reported trying to flee during the night of the putsch—was irrelevant. The order's very existence, like the putsch-night dragnet to round up hostages with Jewish-sounding names, revealed again the Nazis' and Kampfbunders' eagerness to implement their fanatical anti-Semitism.

Pöhner, a severe man with a fuzz haircut and rimless glasses, came on even stronger. In his testimony, he denounced the 1918 revolution as "an act of treason against the whole German people" that had been committed by "racially foreign people driven by international Jewish Freemasonry"—with the shameful result that high German officials were "suddenly crawling on their bellies before Jews and calling them 'Excellency.'" Pöhner's raw style was shocking and, to some, refreshing. He unhesitatingly admitted that the top political leadership, including himself, had long been plotting to overthrow Berlin. "If what you're accusing me of is high treason, then we've been in that business for the last five years," he said to an outburst of courtroom laughter.

Kriebel, too, the sharp-elbowed Kampfbund military leader, related his role in the putsch but also recalled the 1918 capitulation in World War I that started him down the nationalistic, right-wing path. As one of the German officers who had to serve at war's end in the Armistice Commission in Spa, Belgium, Kriebel was the object of the "most uncouth, lowest humiliations" imaginable, he said. Describing the German military delegation's final departure by train after the armistice was settled, he said a "drunken, worked-up crowd threw stones and cursed us without mercy." Kriebel, in response, leaned out of the train's window and shook his fist at his tormentors. Not knowing how prophetic his words would be, he shouted: "*Auf Wiedersehen!* We'll see you again in a few years."

Kriebel's feisty testimony became more emotionally laden as he recalled the events of the long night and morning of the putsch, especially the final march to Odeon Square. Kriebel had marched in the first row with Hitler, as well as with Scheubner-Richter, who had been killed. "There was deep breathing in the courtroom as Colonel Kriebel haltingly described the details," wrote one observer. "Nobody, not even the presiding judge or the prosecutor, made an objection when one of the defense attorneys rose and spoke the fearsome word, 'Murder!'"

The seemingly limitless range of Hitler's testimony, coupled with Kriebel's angry statements, had by the trial's third day led some observers to wonder what the whole affair was really all about, since nobody was boring in on the defendants' allegedly treasonous actions. "If the public sessions are to be merely devoted to anti-French and anti-Belgian speeches, as was the case today, there must be little reason why the proceeding should be continued at all," complained the London *Times*.[2]

Kriebel had, surprisingly, supplied one of the trial's most memorable emotional moments. Yet it was Hitler who once again seized an opening he could exploit to even greater advantage. Deputy Prosecutor Ehard asked him to "briefly explain" how he had planned to pull off a big march on Berlin. What about the logistics of food, accommodation, clothing, "and such things"? And what about a march's foreign policy implications?

In reply, the star defendant rose from his chair and launched into a classic Hitlerian disquisition on foreign policy, world history, and high treason. His "answer," which lasted for twenty-two minutes without interruption, began with a slash at England's historical balance-of-power politics and France's ambitions to dominate Europe. "France desires only the dismemberment of Germany so it can achieve hegemony for itself," he said. To Hitler, France was Germany's ultimate blood enemy.[3] In his opening-day rant, he had said, "I'd rather hang from a lamppost in a Bolshevized Germany than live happily under French domination."[4]

And his swipe at France was merely a springboard for a tour through national uprisings in Spain, Italy, Turkey, and the greatness of the Bismarckian "revolution" in late-nineteenth-century Germany. He painted a glorious vision of the "national uprising" that was supposed to flow from his planned march on Berlin. "In Munich, Nuremberg and Bayreuth there would have been indescribable joy, a wave of enthusiasm would have swept the Reich," he declaimed. People would have seen "that German suffering is coming to an end, that salvation comes through uprising." And again a derogation of majority rule: "I was asked if I thought I had a majority behind me.... Germany wasn't founded by the decisions of majorities, but through the willpower and resolution of individual personalities, often enough against the will of the majority. Germany is the product of a hero [Bismarck], not of a majority."

Hewing to his cardinal belief in the power of repetition, repetition, and repetition, Hitler pivoted to treason, reprising his earlier statement that "high treason is the only crime that is punished for failing." As a counter-example he took, once again, Bismarck. "In the opinion of people on the left wing, Bismarck committed treason and staged a coup," said Hitler. "The *Frankfurter Zeitung* called it high treason when Bismarck dissolved the Prussian parliament.... Bismarck's treason was later legalized because the German Reich was created from it. The [1918] act of high treason has never been legalized because all that's left of the German Reich is German suffering."

These assertions might not withstand careful historical scrutiny, but they made great polemics. Hitler was on his usual roll. He evoked his sense of the near-miss grandeur of his putsch attempt; he even began putting a positive spin on the coup's failure, seeding a legend he would later nurture. "I am convinced that we were on the verge of changing Germany's destiny, but then our effort foundered.... Sometimes fate intervenes in unexpected ways. When I look at today's developments, I conclude that it's perhaps a good thing that more time has passed." This was also an early hint of Hitler's shifting view of whether to pursue power in Germany by revolution or by politics.

But Hitler could not pass up the chance, during this impromptu speech, to invoke the judgment of the ages. "You should not think that this trial will destroy us," Hitler told the court. "You can certainly lock us up. But the German people will not destroy us. Our prisons will open and there will come a time when the accused become the accusers.... Future generations will acquit us and say that we were the only ones with the courage to stand up against the ongoing high treason [of 1918]." Closer to earth, Hitler for good measure lashed out at his nemesis, Kahr. "If he is in charge, it is a catastrophe," he concluded.

Hitler was ranting and perhaps even panting by now. When he finished, Deputy Prosecutor Ehard said: "I simply wanted to ask Mr. Hitler a calm and sober question."

"I didn't mean to offend you," said Hitler.

> EHARD: Excuse me — I don't even think of being offended. I just mean that it might not have been necessary to reply in such a polemical way.
>
> HITLER: Nothing of the sort. But my temperament is somewhat different from that of a state's attorney.
>
> EHARD: Probably a good thing in this case.[5]

Not a word about clothing, food, accommodation, or any of the logistics to which the question referred. Not a peep of objection from the chief prosecutor, Stenglein. Not a hint of a reprimand from the judge on the relevance of the testimony. Not a moment of doubt as to who was on stage and in charge. The trial had effectively become Hitler's political showcase. "Hitler presented his calling card as the next Bismarck," noted a German news service, "and gave Herr Kahr a few kicks."[6]

The defense attorneys, meanwhile, were not above using the proceedings for some lawyerly grandstanding that aroused prickly feelings among the trial's participants. Karl Kohl, a blustery lawyer, gratuitously insulted Stenglein, suggesting that the chief prosecutor was not "a respectable person" if he did not believe in the complicity of Kahr, Lossow, and Seisser. As mild as those words might sound to modern ears, such language came close to a serious personal offense in the Munich of the 1920s. Kohl was forced to retract, but Stenglein did not forget the slight.

Besides Hitler's testimony, no appearance was more keenly antici-pated than General Ludendorff's. Until Prosecutor Ehard had declared Hitler the "soul" of the putsch, Ludendorff had been regarded in some quarters as equal to Hitler in political and sym-bolic importance. Ludendorff was, after all, the former command-ing general (with Field Marshal Paul von Hindenburg) of all German forces in World War I. Though he had a nervous collapse and fled from the field at the war's end, Ludendorff was still widely regarded as the embodiment of Germany's onetime military great-ness. Some newspapers, like the *New York Times* and *Berliner Tage-blatt,* had often headlined the event as the "Ludendorff-Hitler trial." But Ludendorff's standing in the drama was already on shaky legs. Rumors circulated that a deal might have been cut at the highest levels to make sure the war hero was acquitted. Hitler had clearly established himself as the celebrity defendant and chief orchestrator of the offense in question. Now came the aging general's chance to show where he stood in the firmament of nationalist coup-makers. Though only fifty-eight, Ludendorff looked and seemed older.

Ludendorff's chauffeured car had gotten stuck in the snow on Thursday, so his testimony was moved to Friday—and took all afternoon. For nearly three hours, he spoke in the stern style of the soldier that he was.[7] But he was all over the map, reading from let-ters, quoting Bismarck, talking about separatist tendencies in the Rhineland, dwelling on his longed-for restoration of the monarchy, and becoming fixated on what he considered the near-betrayal of Germany by the Catholic Church. Ludendorff managed gratuitously to offend Catholic-dominated Bavaria and to prove himself the loosest of cannons on the witness stand. Bavarians who had always suspected Ludendorff of not having South Germany's interests at heart—he was a Prussian transplant from the North—felt confirmed in their doubts.[8]

Worse, some people wondered if Ludendorff was losing touch with reality; his ramblings seemed nearly senile. He denied any prior knowledge of the putsch on the night it happened, assigning himself an exceptionally passive role in the whole business, though most historians believe he was well informed.[9] (Later Ludendorff even claimed, "Hitler misled me and lied to me," and called the Nazi leader "only a sloganeer and an adventurer."[10]) "Ludendorff seemed like a man from another planet," wrote the *New York Times*. "Never did Ludendorff prove his political incompetence so conclusively.... [He is] an old man not only physically but mentally." *Vorwärts,* the Social Democratic Berlin newspaper, took the opportunity to excoriate the general as "totally lacking in political judgment" and "no better than what clear-sighted subordinates knew him to be during the war, an 'insane cadet.'"[11] Despite politically calculated warm words about Ludendorff in his opening oration ("I worshipped him"), Hitler would not have been bothered by these cutting remarks about the man. The "firebrand" was already trying to figure out how to distance himself from the unpredictable old general.

The trial had its share of odd moments. During the first week, several defense lawyers began a round of symbolic fisticuffs with the outside world, as represented by the press. The first attorney complained to Judge Neithardt that the *München-Augsburger*

Abendzeitung had misstated the attorneys' position on holding secret sessions. While the defendants seemed eager to avoid endangering state secrets through open sessions, wrote the newspaper, "the same cannot be said of the defense lawyers" since they had strongly resisted the idea of holding the entire trial in camera. "I object in the name of all the lawyers here," huffed the attorney. He also cited a report in the Nazi-friendly *Völkischer Kurier* based on an unnamed source. The article read:

> Someone told us the following story: "I was by chance sitting in a streetcar next to two sketch artists whom I had noticed in the courtroom because of their sneering grins. They were showing each other their drawings. One of them, apparently a Bulgarian or Hungarian, in any case a typical Slav, showed a triangular caricature of one of the lay judges. The other one, a Jew, triumphantly showed a really nasty cartoon of Ludendorff, looking crushed, gaunt and staring fearfully ahead like a shrew."

The attorney asked Judge Neithardt to ban "such people" from covering the trial, to which the judge readily agreed. "Necessary measures have already been taken to remove these kind of people," said the judge.

But the lawyer wasn't finished. He needed to have a go at the foreign press as well. One foreign newspaper reported that the defendants didn't seem to be taking the charges against them very seriously and were "putting on an act," said the attorney. He continued: "The accused are real German men who represent a holy idea with the purest of motives. Of course they don't come into court tearing their hair and rending their garments. In a German courtroom we should strictly prohibit such rough treatment by a foreign

publication." Ludendorff's attorney took great exception to an article in the *New York Herald,* which had called the general in its
headline the "Leader of the Beer Revolution." This lawyer, too,
asked the judge to prevent "such misuse of visitor's rights."

State's Attorney Stenglein couldn't stand it; he had to get his say,
too. "One newspaper claimed that during Herr Hitler's defense
statement, everyone was quite serious except the state's attorney,
who had a smile of condescension on his face the whole time. That
is completely untrue! I reject any suggestion that the state's attorney
behaved inappropriately during Hitler's speech."[12]

Such lawyerly ravings highlighted the politicized nature of the
Hitler trial as well as the crucial role of newspapers in the public and
national life of the 1920s.

Hitler's co-putschists offered varying versions of the same events,
but all fit neatly into the script Hitler had laid out on the first day.
Each emphasized the coup attempt's high-flung goals and struck
patriotic notes that echoed Hitler's claim of salvationist purpose.
They also picked up on Hitler's occasional dark hints at conducting
politics "with a sword." Wilhelm Brückner, leader of the Hitler
Shock Troop that had played a key role during the putsch, ranted on
the witness stand that "Germany needs men who have a burning
love of the fatherland and a sense of fanatical hate," including a
willingness to commit violence, like saboteurs in the Ruhr region
who had switched from passive to active resistance.[13]

The prosecution was outgunned. Hitler's side had ten defendants and eleven lawyers.[14] It also had the big names—Hitler and,
in theory, Ludendorff. The prosecution, by contrast, had exactly
two people, Stenglein and Ehard. Even though they had the power
of the state behind them, the two attorneys seemed singularly unag-
gressive, politically neutralized, and tame in their tactics. At no

point, for example, had Stenglein objected to either the length or the content of the tendentious testimony by the accused.

Having nine co-defendants and a roomful of mouthy lawyers was a considerable advantage for Hitler; he did not have to carry all the water. It was neither Hitler nor his attorney, Lorenz Roder, who threw down the first legal gauntlet in the trial—an official request for the arrest of Kahr, Lossow, and Seisser. Instead, it was Attorney Kohl, Brückner's lawyer, who struck first. Adding to growing tension over the triumvirate's role in fomenting a coup attempt, Kohl called for the "immediate arrest" of the trio. Kohl was one of the most aggressive figures in the trial and, given a newspaper's reference to his *embonpoint,* one of its weightiest.* Short and stolid, with drooping eyes and a drooping mustache, Kohl looked like a small cannon. "The defense brought its heavy guns into position," noted the *Münchener Post,* tongue only slightly in cheek.[15]

That Hitler and his Nazis had been working closely with the Bavarian State Police and Reichswehr was by now well established. That they were also being sheltered by the Munich City Police Department—the so-called blue police because of the color of their uniforms—was less well known until defendant Wilhelm Frick, Pöhner's former chief political adviser and now a defendant, stood to testify. Frick and Pöhner had run the police from 1919 to 1922. With its powerful political section, the police department had played a secret role in nurturing the infant Nazi movement. "We could have easily suppressed it in 1919 and 1920," said Frick. "But we realized that this little National Socialist movement should not be crushed" because they saw in the Nazis "the germ of a rebirth of Germany," said Frick, sounding like Hitler's speechwriter, if he had had one. Just like Hitler, the two bosses of the Munich police

---

* *Embonpoint* is generally translated from the French as "corpulent."

wanted to roll back the Marxist tide they saw washing over the labor movement, luring workers back into the nationalist camp. "We held a protective hand over the National Socialist German Workers' Party [Nazi Party] and Herr Hitler," confessed Frick.[16]

As the coup attempt unfolded, Frick and Pöhner had been assigned to seize control of the Munich police apparatus. Instead, they ended up being arrested at the police headquarters. Frick put on a pitiful display of ducking and dodging as Judge Neithardt confronted him with a stream of evidence about his prior knowledge and central role in the putsch. None of that seems to have bothered Hitler; he later appointed Frick the Third Reich's interior minister, where he played a central role in the crimes of the regime.

By the trial's second week, the mood in the converted Infantry School courtroom was turning tense. Judge Neithardt's unwillingness to cap the loose language and sometimes toxic insinuations was beginning to irritate. "One feels a thunderstorm brewing," noted a column in the *München-Augsburger Abendzeitung*. Even a Paris newspaper, *Le Temps*, described the courtroom temper as *"orageuse"* (stormy).[17] Supporters of the Weimar Republic "declare that the trial is the most scandalous ever conducted in Germany," wrote the *New York Times*.[18]

The political establishment was also beginning to feel uneasy. After Hitler's opening blast put them on the defensive, there was considerable wringing of hands on March 4 at a meeting of Bavaria's Council of Ministers—effectively the government cabinet. The chief target of their dismay was Neithardt's behavior on the bench; he became the object of derision and complaints. Dr. Franz Schweyer, the interior (police) minister, said he had received steady complaints from the Reichswehr and Bavarian State Police that courtroom slanders against them had gone unchallenged by the judge. One minister noted that Neithardt had said Ludendorff was the best thing Germany had—leading to the assumption that the judge wanted Ludendorff acquitted. It is obvious, said one minister, "that the judge is one-sided." The accused, it was noted, were being allowed excessive freedoms. Their rooms were always open, they dined in style, they had two hours per day in the courtyard, and they received visitors whenever they wished. Weber had even been granted a "Sunday vacation" and given the run of Munich for a day. Finally, the justice minister, Dr. Franz Gürtner, admitted that he had met several times with Neithardt and let him know people were uneasy about his allowing Hitler "to speak for four hours."[19] (Despite his reservations about the trial, Gürtner went on to become Hitler's justice minister in the Third Reich.)

Meanwhile, the trial was becoming an unpredictable adventure story. On Thursday of the second week, the *Vossische Zeitung* wrote: "The reports from the Hitler-Ludendorff trial read like installments in a serial novel."[20] Little did the newspaper know that within hours the proceedings would hit a dramatic new low when simmering emotions in the courtroom erupted. Again, the bellicose Attorney Kohl was the instigator. Complaining about arrest warrants issued by Prosecutor Stenglein's office in another case involving a different client,[21] Kohl accused Stenglein's office of indulging in an "arrest frenzy." That was too much for Stenglein. He jumped to his feet and, in effect, brought the trial to a standstill. "During this proceeding I have repeatedly been the subject of injurious attacks, some of them personal," he said with barely restrained fury. "I have curbed my reaction and tried to keep the proceedings on a serious plane. I've avoided every pointed response. But enough is enough! Today you have gone too far. . . . I will no longer participate in a trial in which such attacks on my honor continuously come my way. Mr. Ehard, please take over the prosecution."

White with anger, Stenglein stalked out. As Stenglein passed him, Kohl taunted: "There are plenty of men to take your places as states' attorneys."[22]

"That goes too far!" sputtered Judge Neithardt. The flustered presiding judge adjourned the trial until the next day.

Stenglein's drastic move made headlines. "Hitler Trial Session Blown Up," declared the *Vossische Zeitung* on its front page; "You've Gone Too Far," headlined its columnist. Foreign newspapers were taking notice. All regarded the prosecutor's stormy departure as a withering indictment of Neithardt's trial management and a scandalous day for the German justice system. Clearly the presiding judge did not have his trial under control; he lacked the confidence and competence to preside over strong personalities. The young deputy prosecutor Hans Ehard was taken aback by Stenglein's move, which he regarded as a tactical mistake. "He should have banged on the table instead and complained loudly to the judge," said Ehard. "But of course he would probably have lost out in that confrontation."[23]

By the next day, Attorney Kohl had apologized — sort of — and Prosecutor Stenglein was back on the job. People could return to focusing on what had become the central question of the trial: how deeply were Kahr, Lossow, and Seisser implicated in Hitler's plot? Originally scheduled to last two weeks, Hitler's trial would now enter a third week devoted solely to answering that question.

Hitler's best-defense-is-a-good-offense strategy was working. Watching from his small defense table at the front of the courtroom, reading every night the voluminous newspaper coverage of his trial in his spartan cadet's room, Hitler could see that things were moving in his direction. The two-week drumbeat of recrimination against Kahr, Lossow, and Seisser had built a large base of credibility in the press corps and in public opinion. Pressure was building on State's Attorney Stenglein to do something. Over the weekend, the dam of expectation finally burst; Stenglein announced an investigation of Kahr, Lossow, and Seisser on suspicion of high treason. The trial now officially had become what one Munich newspaper, retrospectively, would describe as "a competition between two forms of nationalism—the old nationalists around Kahr and the young *völkisch* types around the admired, God-sent Leader."[24] The three men who had played a central role in crushing Hitler's putsch, who were expected to deliver the most incriminating evidence against him, and who represented the existing order in terms of oath, uniform, and responsibilities now faced the possibility of treason charges.

This posed a strange dilemma for the prosecutor: he was calling as witnesses men whom he had just started investigating for a crime. But then, as one newspaper headline put it later in the week, this was "A Strange Trial."

On Monday, March 10—the first day of the critical third week—everyone was relieved to find Munich experiencing milder temperatures and melting snows.[25] Yet even as spring beckoned, the trial threatened to darken with the confrontational testimony of the triumvirs. Whatever they said or did would reflect well or badly on the authority of government, on the reputation of Bavaria in the larger German republic, and on the men themselves. Their performance was now shaped entirely by the man who would only be sitting and watching, waiting for openings to pounce and corner them. The trial had become a high-stakes game of "gotcha" whose political import was lost on no one: the deeper the triumvirs were drawn into Hitler's web of complicity, the higher his stock rose.

Lossow went first. A classic, straight-backed German officer, Lossow at fifty-six had a head of thinning hair and favored a pair of rimless eyeglasses. Though a born Bavarian, he was a pure Prussian officer in style and demeanor. Shorn of his army assignments in the fallout of the putsch, the former Reichswehr commander arrived in court wearing a simple black frock coat, not the resplendent bemedaled uniform with the wide shoulder sash shown in his official army portrait.

Although a lieutenant general, Lossow had in fact spent most of World War I far from the slaughter on the eastern and western fronts. He had been Germany's chief military representative to Turkey, where he helped organize the successful Turkish defense against the Allied landings in Gallipoli. Unlike a rough-edged, war-hardened officer like Kriebel, Lossow had experience and skills in the world of diplomacy and negotiating. He had no fear of the witness stand. He had no fear of Hitler.

Marching straight to the stand-up lectern he had requested—most witnesses sat at a small table in front of the judges' bench—Lossow plopped down a thick manuscript. He had come to do battle. The embodiment of the exquisitely mannered and perfectly disciplined officer class, Lossow had more cause than most to take offense at the upstart enlisted man. Lossow was on serious business: he had to keep himself out of jail, and keep Hitler in.

Lossow spoke for nearly six hours. "If a person had landed in the courtroom from another planet...he would have thought Lossow was Saint Michael with a gleaming sword," wrote the Ludendorff-friendly *Deutsche Presse*. "He slashed left and right....After a while we were surprised that the general's strident tone didn't get on the chief judge's nerves."[26] Other members of the press noted an arrogantly martial style. "His speech is edgy, loud and sometimes forceful. His testimony is very pointed," reported a newspaper. Plunging his left hand confidently into a pocket, turning slowly toward his audience like a skilled lecturer, he would underline a statement with a practiced wave of his right hand.[27] Another newspaper wrote: "As the counter-hero to Hitler, he was masterful!"[28]

Lossow hotly denied any interest in a march on Berlin—"childish stuff," he said, that could provoke an invasion by French and Czech forces. An unprepared military horde with insufficient logistical support—food, accommodation, clothing—could soon turn into a band of thieves trying to live off the local population, he predicted.[29]

Initially, Lossow said, his relationship with Hitler had been a good one. When they first met in early 1923, he recalled, the Nazi leader had "made a big impression on me." But that soon faded. "I noticed in all his big speeches he always said the same thing. Part of it was already well understood by all nationalistic people. Part of it simply showed he had lost all contact with reality and any sense of proportion for what was doable."[30] Hitler's "driving force was ambition," said the general; he suffered from "overheated patriotism"; attempts to reason with him failed. "In conversations, Hitler is the only one who speaks. Objections are hard to get in, and they don't do any good."

Hitler was also a liar, said Lossow, in so many words. For proof, he invoked Hitler's comments when Lossow had in 1923 defied orders to shut down the *Völkischer Beobachter* for defaming General Seeckt's wife. "Hitler told a newspaper that he saw my 'human side' for the first time," said Lossow. "Hitler claimed he had assured me that he stood behind me. He said he gave me—and no one else—his word of honor that he would not [stage a putsch] and that he would support me in the fight against Berlin." Lossow added: "There is not one true word in this report." As for the notion that Hitler would suddenly feel a sentiment of kinship with Lossow, the general scoffed: "Hitler...is obsessed with the word 'brutality.' I've never once heard him use the word 'sentimentality.' This entire story was made up after the fact."

Lossow vigorously disputed Hitler's assertion that he and the other triumvirs had broken their words of honor on the night of the putsch, claiming instead that it was "Hitler's breach of his own promise" that led to the current proceedings. At that point, "a hush came over the courtroom," wrote one reporter. "Even the defendants' claque, which fills most of the audience seats, was quiet. Hitler sat there with a reddening face, and General Ludendorff lifted his horn-rimmed glasses from his eyes to his forehead for the umpteenth time."[31]

General Lossow didn't exactly emerge victorious (he was now the subject of a criminal investigation), but his testimony dealt a blow to Hitler's credibility. Belittling Hitler as a "swashbuckler" and "political drummer," Lossow said that if he were to correct all the false statements of the past two weeks, "I would be speaking here for days on end."

Throughout, Hitler could barely contain himself. Leaping to his feet as soon as Lossow finished, at 6:15 in the evening, he said flatly that Lossow's portrayal was "untrue and incorrect," but that he would withhold his questioning of the witness until after Lossow's partner in crime, Gustav von Kahr, had appeared.

Gustav Ritter von Kahr, sixty-one, was a beaten man almost before he started. Following in the footsteps of the tall, aggressive Lossow, the short, turtlelike Kahr, with his meaty face and walrus mustache, seemed the anti-hero. Though he had been Bavaria's strongman twice—mainly because of his bureaucratic skills and monarchical conservatism—Kahr came across as wishy-washy, uncooperative, indecisive, and defensive. He spoke in a low monotone that half the courtroom could not hear. "In contrast to Lossow's speech in the sharp key, today was in the flat key," wrote one musically minded observer. With his dull responses, alleged memory lapses, and tendency to duck behind the fig leaf of "official secrecy," the stubborn if wily Kahr exasperated Hitler and his lawyers. Yet during Kahr's three days, off and on, in the witness chair, they pounded him mercilessly. Unlike Lossow, who had gone on the counterattack, Kahr acted like what he was: an accused man who might be guilty. "One could hardly imagine a greater contrast than that between Kahr's speech and that of Hitler at the beginning of the trial," wrote the *München-Augsburger Abendzeitung*. "Hitler was bursting with passion and temper, while Kahr was steadily quiet [with] a certain note of melancholy and resignation."[32]

After Kahr's long opening speech, Hitler pounced. Starting like any good lawyer, he tried first to establish exactly when and through whom Kahr had first been offered his sweeping powers as state commissioner general in fall 1923. Hitler posed the question: "When did you first hear about the creation of a state commissioner general's office?"

KAHR: That is naturally hard to say.
HITLER: It's not a question of the day, but of the time.
KAHR: I can't answer for sure.
HITLER: End of August? Beginning of September?
KAHR: I can't say with certainty.

Taking a different tack, Hitler asked: "Did the initiative come from the Council of Ministers or from someone who later had a job in the state commissioner general's office?"

KAHR: I can give no information on that.

Hitler also tried to corner Kahr on the question of the Autumn Exercises, the cover name for the proposed melding of paramilitaries with the Reichswehr in the weeks before the putsch. *What did*

Kahr know and when did he know it? Kahr stonewalled Hitler at every turn.

And so it went, hour after hour, until it turned dark outside the Infantry School. Kahr's "hedgehog tactic" (as one German newspaper called it[33]) was compounded by his refusal to look directly at Hitler or any other questioner. He resolutely sat at the witness table facing the judges, showing the rest of the room his back.

Slowly, the lawyers were able to squeeze out of Kahr more details on his planned directorate for Germany. Trial observers were surprised to learn that Friedrich Minoux, a leading Ruhr region businessman; Baron Wilhelm von Gayl, an East Prussian aristocrat and politician; Heinrich Class, head of the right-wing Pan-German League; and two of Germany's most famous military men — Grand Admiral Alfred von Tirpitz and Admiral Reinhard Scheer — had been in discussions with Kahr, or with each other, about regime change. It became increasingly obvious that, if Hitler had not jumped the gun with his rushed and bumbling putsch, some other form of coup d'état would quite likely have been unleashed in Germany in fall 1923. Whether it would have been a directorate attempt by the Bavarian triumvirate or a business- and army-led conspiracy formed in Berlin by General Seeckt, the pressures for an overthrow of Germany's parliamentary system were strong and widespread.[34] "A far more serious scheme to alter the existing constitution of Germany was being planned, and presumably still meets with the approval of the extreme nationalists," wrote the London *Times*.[35]

On Kahr's final day in the witness chair Hitler could not contain his frustrations with his evasive responses. He repeatedly pressed the former commissioner general on the matter of their heartfelt handshake in the beer hall on the night of the putsch, painting a moving scene of Kahr's left hand on top of the two men's joined right hands. "You gave me your hand for the third time!" insisted Hitler, standing only a yard away from Kahr, his voice rising. "You shook both my hands for the third time!"

Now Hitler was shouting: "Am I a liar here or am I not?"

JUDGE NEITHARDT: Don't get worked up, please. The witness will answer.

HITLER [SCREAMING, WAVING HIS HANDS IN THE AIR]: Am I now a liar or am I not one?

KAHR: I can only say again that I absolutely do not remember putting my hand on top of Hitler's.[36]

Though Kahr had obstinately resisted Hitler's baiting and bullying and had steadily snubbed him in the courtroom, he seemed by the end of his testimony a broken soul. The short man had sunk deeper and deeper into his chair, his head bent between his shoulders. One reporter called it a "scene of misery like one seldom sees."[37]

Before he could go after General Lossow, Hitler had to sit through the testimony of Colonel Hans Ritter von Seisser, head of the military-style Bavarian State Police during the putsch. Seisser, forty-nine, was like Lossow a perfect military specimen, slim and shaven-headed, and he also stuck to the party line. Yet his testimony was refreshingly free of posturing and fireworks, and without a long political preamble. As had Lossow, Seisser said he had found Hitler a compelling person at first, but less so as he saw the Nazi "drummer" give in to his own "megalomania" and finally commit what amounted to an "outlaw gang attack"—the putsch. Like his partners in running Bavaria, Seisser said he had rejected Hitler's idea of a march on Berlin out of hand. "We have no heavy artillery, no airplanes, no gas protection equipment, nothing but willing patriotic men who would only have been sacrificed to the enemy gas attacks," he testified. A military march would have "immediately mobilized France, Poland, and Czechoslovakia" against Germany, he said.

Seisser took frequent issue with the testimony of Hitler and other defendants, calling it "invented and untrue." In a style that was sharp but not contemptuous, Seisser's performance strengthened the triumvirate's credibility and slowed Hitler's juggernaut in the court of public opinion. "He speaks from the soul," noted one commentator. Seisser directly contradicted Hitler's version of events, but managed to do it without provoking a Hitlerian tantrum or duels with the lawyers. Again the Nazi leader had lost ground.

On Friday, General Lossow returned for questioning. It had been a frustrating week for Hitler; he had not scored many points. Except for briefly screaming at Kahr on Thursday, he had been a background presence while the triumvirate made the news. "My whole life can be summed up as this ceaseless effort of mine to persuade other people," he once said.[38] Now it was time to start persuading again. He needed to regain the offensive. Friday promised to be the hottest day of the week.

From the beginning, Lossow assumed a belligerent posture and commanding tone. He paced up and down — three steps one way, three steps back — in front of the stand-up lectern, to the rising irritation of the defense lawyers. "He flung his answers out, so to speak, while taking a walk," said one reporter. "His voice was like a megaphone." Lossow confused the courtroom with a military parade ground, said another.[39]

For more than three hours, Lossow, the retired lieutenant general, did battle with the defense attorneys. Behind every lawyer's question he saw — and avoided — trapdoors and pitfalls.[40] Each side, it seemed, was moving back and forth between the roles of accused and accuser, alternately on the attack and on the defensive.[41] For a long time, Hitler only watched and listened. Finally, having heard enough, he jumped up and joined the fray. He wanted to know, who was "the father of the idea" of a directorate in Berlin?

> LOSSOW: I object to the question! I don't even know the answer. I learned about this in confidential conversations. I have no right to violate that confidence.

That got Hitler's color up. He began yelling at Judge Neithardt to compel Lossow to break confidence and answer his question.

> JUDGE NEITHARDT: Mr. Hitler, may I ask you to moderate your voice, please?

Hitler did not moderate his voice, and before long Neithardt admonished him again. Finally, Hitler turned to the ever-sensitive topic of one's "word of honor." Much had already been made of Hitler's promise in January 1923 "not to make a putsch." But nobody had raised the word-of-honor issue with reference to another incident: the Reichswehr's refusal, despite Lossow's earlier promise, to let Hitler's Storm Troopers keep their weapons on May 1, 1923, for a confrontation with Communists. The stand-down had led to considerable loss of face for Hitler.

Lossow now reminded Hitler of the confrontation in the side room of the Bürgerbräukeller on the night of the uprising. Accused of breaking his word by staging a putsch, Hitler had replied: "Forgive me, I did it in the interest of the fatherland."

Hitler snapped, raising his voice: "Was that the 'brutal Hitler' or the 'sentimental Hitler' who was asking for forgiveness, as you say?"

LOSSOW: That was neither the sentimental nor the brutal Hitler! That was the Hitler with a guilty conscience!

HITLER: Lieutenant General! I have a lot less need of a guilty conscience for breaking a word of honor...because the only one here who broke his word of honor is the lieutenant general—on May 1![42]

The courtroom went into a shocked silence. The foot soldier had just accused the general, in open court, of breaking his word of honor. There was no greater insult in German life.

For seconds the courtroom was still. Knocked back as if by a blow to the face, Lossow finally gathered his papers and strode toward the door. Turning, he bowed to the court, then disappeared. He never returned.

Neithardt fumbled for words. "That's an affront, a gross impropriety!" he gasped, but his words were mostly lost in the tumult.

HITLER: I accept the reprimand.

NEITHARDT: An impropriety without precedent!

HITLER: It was a response to the statement of the witness.

The court was in an uproar. Nobody had ever seen anything like this before. Judge Neithardt adjourned for lunch.

Hitler was criticized in some media for his brusque, out-of-control tactics. Still, he had chased Lossow from the playground. He had humiliated the old general and gotten away with it. To the little man on the street looking at the newspaper headlines, Hitler was now indeed a "tremendous guy."

Eighteen days of argumentation, hairsplitting, word-parsing, voice-raising, and mutual recriminations now seemed to have ended in a legal draw. It was impossible to assign sole guilt for conspiring to overthrow the government. Clearly both sides had been bent on regime change. Whether or not the establishment enabled the rebels—Hitler's putschists—was never really proven. But neither was the triumvirate's claim that they never, ever would have considered a march on Berlin. Somewhere in all the harrumphing the accused had admitted they carried out the crime as charged. But what did that mean in terms of guilt, conviction, and punishment? The convoluted and ambivalent nature of the whole affair was adroitly captured by a caricature on the cover of *Simplicissimus,* a leading satire magazine. Sitting atop the shoulders of General Lossow is Hitler himself, holding a torch to the edifice of government. But Lossow is atop the shoulders of his own enabler, Commissioner Kahr. Kahr, while boosting the two men, is also summoning the police to take down these two malefactors who are committing the crime of revolution. Meanwhile, high in the sky, Hitler's swastika has become a shooting star.

One week after General Lossow's startling departure from the courtroom (for which the judge later fined him sixty marks), Prosecutor Stenglein made his final plea. It was time to quantify the crime and, if any, the punishment. If the verdict were guilty, a sentence could run from the minimum of five years to the maximum of life imprisonment—or anywhere in between.

For the crime of high treason against the "Free State of Bavaria," as it is called, and against the German Reich, the prosecutor asked for eight years "fortress imprisonment" (honorable arrest) for Adolf Hitler, three years over the minimum. For Colonel Kriebel, Dr. Weber, and Ernst Pöhner, Stenglein asked for six years. For General Erich Ludendorff, co-leader of the putsch, Stenglein requested only two years as an accessory to treason. For other defendants, he suggested from fifteen months to two years.

In his plea, Stenglein granted Hitler his essential historical point: that high treason is considered a crime only when it fails, dryly pointing out that Hitler's and his confederates' undertaking manifestly fulfilled the definition: "Their act didn't work and therefore is punishable." For form's sake, the state's attorney spent an hour and a half recounting, once again, the full details of the putsch, beating the dead horse of proof. Then, suddenly, he woke everyone up.

Perhaps sensing that he might someday need to be in Hitler's good books, Stenglein launched into an unexpected paean to the man whom he wanted to send to prison for eight years. His words stunned the courtroom. "Raised in modest circumstances, Hitler proved his German patriotism as a brave soldier in the Great War," he began. "Filled with glowing, honest enthusiasm for his great German fatherland, he created, with tireless labor after the war and from the tiniest beginnings, a great party, the National Socialist German Workers' Party. Its essential program is fighting international Marxism and Judaism, settling accounts with the November criminals...and spreading German nationalism."

As the audience listened agog, Stenglein went on to note that while it was not his place to make a judgment about Hitler's party politics, the Nazi leader's "honest effort to re-arouse belief in a German destiny" was, in the end, "his great service." If Hitler's intense point of view and the aggressive spirit of his followers sometimes turned into excesses, continued Stenglein, it would still be "unjust to call him a demagogue in the negative sense of that word." As for Hitler's personal virtues, Stenglein said, "he deserves respect for the way he has kept his private life pristine, given the temptations that naturally come his way as a celebrated party leader."

Only after this song of praise did the prosecutor finally return to prosecuting the defendant, but with an almost apologetic tone. Hitler had unfortunately let himself be "drawn beyond the bounds of his own natural inclinations" by overzealous supporters, said Stenglein. Lionized by his mass following and the toadies in his party, Hitler had developed an exaggerated understanding of himself as the savior of Germany, a view all too gladly reinforced by the men around him. And in this one cardinal error, said Stenglein, lies "his tragic guilt."

If there were any doubt that Hitler's was a political trial as much as a legal one, Stenglein had cleared that up. He had set a new standard for prosecutorial ambivalence.

What really counted was the final act on the final day: the closing statements of the defendants. One month and one day after the trial began, the accused could have "the last word," as it is called in German court procedure. The minor figures among the defendants— Röhm, Brückner, Wagner, and Pernet—relinquished their right to speak in favor of their betters. For the other six—Kriebel, Pöhner, Frick, Weber, Ludendorff, and Hitler—the attorneys decided on a slowly rising crescendo, beginning with the lesser lights but ending, in a final flourish, with Ludendorff's self-defense and then with Hitler's oration.

As the morning session opened, the courtroom was filled to bursting. Reporters noticed more women than usual, more flowers, more gifts. "Hitler's feminine following baked their loyalty into the cakes and snacks that form little mountains in Hitler's open cell," noted the *Münchener Post*.[43]

The testimony began with an unrepentant Colonel Kriebel confessing once again "to the deed" but adding defiantly, "Given the same situation, I would do the same thing again."[44] Frick, when his turn came, echoed the sentiment. Former police chief Pöhner delivered another nasty jibe at Germany's Socialist president, Friedrich Ebert, calling him "Ebert Fritze," a derisive nickname. ("The trial didn't teach Pöhner any manners," wrote a newspaper.)[45] The tone of this day of high pleading and high whining was finally lifted by Ludendorff, who was surprisingly eloquent, dignified in manner, and "lacking in his previous laborious attempts to whitewash himself and blacken everybody else," reported the *New York Times*.[46] He became again the Ludendorff everyone remembered—before the 1918 capitulation, before the armistice, before his departure in the war's waning days. He invoked "the cry of the German soul for freedom." If the *völkisch* movement—Hitler and his allies—"does not succeed, we are lost," he said. "[Germany] will be condemned to continual slavery to France and be stricken from the roll of nations."[47] Tipping into grandiloquence, Ludendorff invoked the judgment of history and assigned himself a place in Valhalla, the mythic hall of the noble dead in Nordic mythology ("Ludendorff Exalts Himself with Gods," headlined the *New York Times* the following day).

Ludendorff's broad-brush political speech unleashed a storm of applause in the courtroom. But all the speeches were just the prelude for what everyone had come to see. Taking the stand at mid-morning, Hitler plunged directly into his full beer hall manner. "If lung power were an argument, by God, then Hitler would have won a brilliant victory in the Infantry School," commented one newspaper.[48]

Hitler's putsch attempt, his months behind bars, his weeks in the courtroom—they had all crystallized on this cold Thursday morning, in this Munich courtroom, in this speech. Natively adroit at legend-building and propaganda, he now painted the putsch's bloody failure as a long-term success. In his ninety-minute declamation, Hitler brazenly claimed that the young people who had been killed in his reckless undertaking "went joyfully to their deaths" on Odeon Square and would someday be commemorated as having "died for the liberation of the fatherland"—a prediction that came true during the Third

Reich. The success of the putsch would be evident, continued Hitler, in a "storm surge of young Germans who will rise up and express their will in massive organizations.... The hour will come when the masses who carry our flag...will join with those who fought against them. The blood that flowed then will not forever divide them.... The army that we are building grows from day to day and hour to hour." Hitler's aim, he insisted, was not simply taking power. "My goal was a thousand times greater than becoming a cabinet minister. I wanted to be the destroyer of Marxism. That is my task, and I will accomplish it."

He then moved the fight out of the human court and into a higher one, donning the martyr's mantle. "From our graves and from our bones will arise the court which will have final judgment over us," Hitler told the judges in a typically twisted metaphor. "For it is not you who will speak that final judgment...but the goddess of the final court...called 'history.'...She will not ask: did you commit high treason? In her eyes [we] are those who wanted the best for our country. Even if you pronounce us guilty a thousand times over, the eternal goddess of the eternal court will laughingly tear up the prosecutor's indictment and the judgment of this court. *She* will pronounce us not guilty!"

To some it was pure kitsch. ("Hitler has the secret of the common touch, an instinctive feel for what people want who don't think much," wrote the *Vossische Zeitung*, revealing again the condescension that, in years to come, would cause many in the intelligentsia to underestimate Hitler.) But to others, including to some journalists, it was so moving that they had tears in their eyes. ("This speech should be publicly posted," said one newspaperman.) In the end, the *Vossische Zeitung* reporter had it right; Hitler knew what people wanted. His speech, with its cunning invocation of "the final court," offered his impassioned followers something to envision and strive for. The disaster of the Odeon Square would become a unifying Nazi Party narrative in the future.

Hitler had won the political fight. It only remained to be seen if he had won the legal fight. Neithardt promised a verdict on April 1, four days hence. In the meantime, the city and the press were loudly divided. It would be "a crime against the nation to take Hitler and these men away for years [to prison] from the task they have set for themselves," wrote the Nazi-friendly *Völkischer Kurier.* The Socialist *Münchener Post,* naturally, saw things differently, recommending a state-sponsored "vacation for this traveling troupe."[49] Many agreed with the *Münchener Post* that the conduct of the trial by Judge Neithardt had deeply tarnished the reputation of the Bavarian justice system. "The last remnant of respect for the Bavarian judiciary hangs on the verdict," the paper editorialized.[50]

Munichers grabbed up newspapers as fast as they could be printed, in press runs of thirty thousand to fifty thousand, "an enormous sale for a city the size of Munich," reported the *New York Times.* Even the banned Hitlerite publications organized a "highly efficient news and courier service," keeping their followers up to date.[51]

Tensions mounted over the weekend. Rumors swirled of possible violence. One far-right newspaper darkly hinted at nasty deeds if Hitler were convicted. "A conviction of German patriots who put their lives on the line for Germany's honor should unleash the most terrible outrage in our people," it thundered. Judge Neithardt received a threatening telegram from a Nazi named Karl Brassler in the nearby town of Augsburg, informing him that "the Augsburg National Socialists and *völkisch* activists offer a warning voice: they are determined to reject, with strength and passion, a guilty verdict against our leader." (Brassler was later hauled into court for the threat.[52])

The police and the Reichswehr reverted to a siege mentality and began strengthening defenses around the Infantry School. A unit of mounted police, an effective crowd control tool, was put on standby. Troops were kept in the barracks over the weekend for possible riot duty.[53] Gatherings of three or more people were prohibited in the immediate vicinity of the Infantry School. "Policemen everywhere on the alert... beer halls denouncing the German Republic—that is Munich this weekend as the turbulent Bavarian capital, its nerves strung taut with excitement, awaits the verdict," the *New York Times* reported.[54]

Into this unpredictable atmosphere fell a mini-bombshell: Kahr, Lossow, and Seisser had skipped town. According to semi-confirmed reports—carried in every newspaper in Munich—the triumvirate had made a speedy getaway from the scene of the recent unpleasantness. They had gone to Italy, said one story, or to the island of Corfu in Greece, said another.[55] In any case, they had gone for *Erholung*— a German word for rest and recovery from arduous times.[56] Of course, the trio had nothing to flee from, even though they were technically under investigation for high treason. They were free men. But their absconding from Munich heightened the appearance of their guilt and added to Hitler's aura of victory. "Can there be any stronger guilty conscience?" asked the *Völkischer Kurier* in a breathless editorial denouncing the "flight" of the triumvirate. "What an end for the almighty [Kahr]!" wrote the newspaper. (Kahr's real end would come ten years later. On Hitler's orders, he would be hacked to death in a swamp near Dachau concentration camp during the 1934 Night of the Long Knives.)

On Tuesday morning, April 1, with the mounted police out in force, the Infantry School again looked like an armed camp. A crowd gathered near the barbed-wire cordon; nobody chased them away.

They were there, as usual, to greet Ludendorff when his chauffeured car arrived from his villa on the edge of Munich. Hitler and the other prisoners, in their open-door "cells" on the school's second floor, could tell by the cheering that the war hero had arrived. For the first time during the trial, Ludendorff's car flew a black, white, and red pennant, a sign of his loyalty to the *völkisch* cause.[57]

Today, also for the first time, General Ludendorff appeared in full uniform, wearing his *Pickelhaube* and a lifetime of medals on his chest. He was the old quartermaster general of World War I again. Except for Hitler and Frick, the other defendants wore their military raiment. Hitler wore his frock coat and Iron Cross medals; Frick wore a high collar and cutaway, as though going to a wedding. Before entering the courtroom, the entire defense team gathered at nine thirty on the back steps of the Infantry School. Heinrich Hoffmann, by now Hitler's personal photographer, had persuaded the men to pose for a picture. The shot shows only nine defendants— Pöhner was absent. Ludendorff, his double chins neatly tucked over his high collar, holds his dress sword in front of him in a formal pose, like a cane.[58] Hitler, in his ubiquitous brown raincoat for the outdoor photo, clutches his slouch hat in one hand and stands with one foot slightly in front of the other, a typical pose of the era. Also in the style of the times, no one is smiling, though on this day the news would be good.

The scene in the courtroom was one of anxious anticipation and barely restrained jubilation. The space was packed so tightly with spectators that journalists had to fight their way to their seats. Many women carried enormous flower bouquets for the defendants. As Ludendorff entered the old officers' mess, the "entire assemblage rose as one in a gesture of deference," wrote one reporter.[59]

Judge Neithardt, wearing his tall beret, led the judges to the bench and got right down to business. Adolf Hitler, he read, was guilty of high treason. Apparently undaunted by rumblings and threats, Judge Neithardt sentenced Hitler to five years of "fortress imprisonment," the same kind of "honorable imprisonment" that he had already experienced at Landsberg. He was also fined two hundred gold marks. Kriebel, Weber, and Pöhner received the same sentences.

The lesser malefactors—Röhm, Brückner, Pernet, Wagner, and Frick—were pronounced guilty of abetting treason, not treason itself. They received fifteen months of imprisonment, immediately paroled, plus a fine of one hundred gold marks.

"Outrageous!" shouted some members of the audience. "A scandal!" But Neithardt soon silenced them with Ludendorff's verdict. The man who had fully supported the putsch and co-led the fatal march to the Odeon Square was acquitted. He was a free man. Among general murmurs of approval, several spectators shouted, "Long live Ludendorff!"

Judge Neithardt then added his next surprise: Hitler and his confederates would be eligible for parole in six months.

Like Prosecutor Stenglein, the judge felt the need to sing a song of praise to the men he was sending to prison for a high crime. What they did was wrong, to be sure, but they meant the best. Because they had acted out of the "most noble, unselfish motives" and "in a purely patriotic spirit," he was issuing the minimum sentences allowed by the law for their acts.

As this amazing justification was sinking in, there was another delicate matter to address: what about Article 9 of the Law for the Protection of the Republic? It stipulated that "foreigners [who commit treason] are to be deported."[60] The law was so plain and so clearly applicable that in his final declamation four days earlier, Hitler the Austrian had explicitly pleaded: "Don't apply Article 9!" He had pointedly reminded the court of his four years as a soldier on

French soil, where "with glowing love I counted the hours until I could return" to the fatherland. Hitler had argued that only "inferior peoples" would expel "an iron man" who happened to offend public opinion. Deporting him, claimed Hitler, would force future schoolboys to read "with shame burning in their cheeks" the story of this disgraceful moment in German history.

Neithardt heard and heeded Hitler's message. "Hitler sees himself as a German," the judge concluded. "Article Nine cannot be applied to a man who thinks and feels as German as Hitler does, who served four and a half years in the German army during the war, who won high honors for bravery in the face of the enemy, who was wounded and otherwise suffered damage to his health."[61]

No deportation for Hitler. No long prison time. And no appeal. The People's Courts, originally founded as summary courts during the bloody chaos of 1919, had no provision for appeal. Besides, they were now going out of business.

The trial was finished. Suddenly, the courtroom fell silent as Ludendorff rose to his full military stature and, with chest out, back straight, and lips quivering with indignation, proceeded to condemn his own acquittal: "I consider this judgment a disgrace and an insult to my uniform and my medals!" The courtroom burst into cheers and *"Heils!"*

News of the verdicts snapped through Munich like a whip. Some heard only the first part—five years for Hitler!—and were outraged. But as soon as the second part arrived—only six months!—the mood flipped. Extra editions of the newspapers were grabbed out of newsboys' hands. An eleven-year-old Municher, Otto Gritschneder, noticed joy and laughter as he ran errands to the bakery and the milk store that day. "I can still hear the outbursts of joy with which people greeted Hitler's 'conviction,' even though I did not understand what it was about," he wrote many years later.[62]

Hitler at his window in "cell" number seven of Landsberg Prison. (National Archives)

This famous photograph shows Hitler in a pro-war crowd at Odeon Square in Munich on August 2, 1914. The photograph may have been doctored years later for propaganda purposes. (Fotoarchiv Heinrich Hoffmann, Bayerische Staatsbibliothek)

Hitler, far left, with other German army field messengers in World War I. He usually positioned himself on the edge of the group. (National Archives)

Hitler at Munich's Café Heck, on the edge of the Royal Gardens, with his walk-around buddy, Ernst Hanfstaengl. (Fotoarchiv Heinrich Hoffmann, Bayerische Staatsbibliothek)

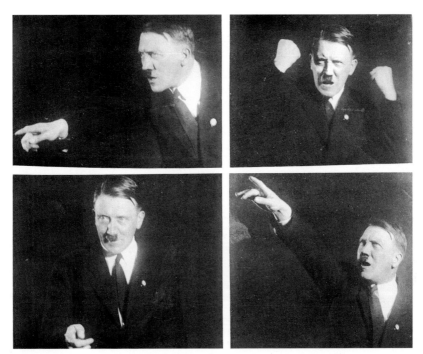

Hitler practicing his speaking poses for photographer Heinrich Hoffmann's camera. (Bundesarchiv)

A Nazi rally at the Bürgerbräukeller beer hall, where Hitler staged his 1923 putsch—and his 1925 comeback rally. In 1939, he barely escaped an assassination attempt in the hall. (Bundesarchiv)

Hitler and Gen. Erich Ludendorff, the hero of World War I. They led the putsch's final march together but later became bitterly estranged. (Fotoarchiv Heinrich Hoffmann, Bayerische Staatsbibliothek)

Putschists patrolling Munich by truck. (Fotoarchiv Heinrich Hoffmann, Bayerische Staatsbibliothek)

Putschists plastered proclamations around Munich
declaring a new provisional
government. (Historisches
Lexikon Bayerns)

Proklamation
an das deutsche Volk!
Die Regierung der November-
verbrecher in Berlin ist heute für
abgesetzt erklärt worden.
Eine
provisorische deutsche
Nationalregierung
ist gebildet worden, diese besteht aus
Gen. Ludendorff
Ad. Hitler, Gen. v. Lossow
Obst. v. Seisser

Putschists kidnapped Socialist and Communist city councilmen. Hans Kallenbach is
on the far right. (Fotoarchiv Heinrich Hoffmann, Bayerische Staatsbibliothek)

During the putsch, a Nazi speaker exhorts a dense crowd in front of Munich City Hall. (Fotoarchiv Heinrich Hoffmann, Bayerische Staatsbibliothek)

Heinrich Himmler, a new convert to the Nazi cause and future head of the SS killing machine, holds a flag as putschists take over a district military headquarters—their only success. (Fotoarchiv Heinrich Hoffmann, Bayerische Staatsbibliothek)

Hitler and his fellow defendants on the last day of their treason trial at the Infantry School. (Pöhner is absent.) (Fotoarchiv Heinrich Hoffmann, Bayerische Staatsbibliothek)

A secret photograph taken at Hitler's treason trial. Judge Neithardt, wearing a judicial beret, sits at the center of the bench. (Fotoarchiv Heinrich Hoffmann, Bayerische Staatsbibliothek)

Hitler's argument before the court depicted by a sketch artist. (Otto D. Franz, Library of Congress)

During Hitler's trial, a leading satire magazine showed Hitler torching a government edifice while sitting atop the shoulders of General Lossow, who is sitting atop Commissioner Kahr, who is summoning the police. Nazi fortunes soar as the swastika becomes a shooting star. (Library of Congress)

Behind its faux-fortress entrance, Landsberg Prison was a thoroughly modern facility in 1923. (Landsberg Prison)

Hitler's sunny cell in Landsberg Prison. The upright typewriter was added for effect in the 1930s when the Nazis turned the cell into a shrine. (Archiv Manfred Deiler)

Hitler wrote *Mein Kampf* on this small Remington portable typewriter. (Hermann Historica)

Festooned with a plaque and laurel leaves, Hitler's cell became a place of pilgrimage in the 1930s. "Hitler tourism" boomed as 100,000 visitors passed by the room in 1938. (Archiv Manfred Deiler)

The "fortress" at Landsberg Prison was a modern building, not an old castle. After Hitler's cell became a shrine, the Nazi banner was hung from his windows on holidays. (Archiv Manfred Deiler)

Hitler lived well in Landsberg Prison, where he had a wicker chair for drinking tea while he read the newspapers. The wreath was a gift from an admirer. (Yad Vashem)

Hitler bought a beer for 18 pfennigs every day from April 20 to May 5, 1924. His signature is in the middle of the page. (Archiv Manfred Deiler)

In prison Hitler lived with four other putsch participants on the second floor of the "fortress" building. Left to right: Hitler, Emil Maurice, Col. Hermann Kriebel, Rudolf Hess, Dr. Friedrich Weber. (Landsberg Prison)

Hitler and Emil Maurice walk and talk in the prison garden. Steadily supplied with sweets and pastries from his admirers, Hitler gained weight. He looks stuffed into his lederhosen. (Fotoarchiv Heinrich Hoffmann, Bayerische Staatsbibliothek)

After leaving prison, Hitler poses at the Landsberg city gate. He loved fancy touring cars like the one that took him back to Munich. (Yad Vashem)

"Hitler Free!" proclaims a Nazi newspaper on Hitler's release. (Fotoarchiv Heinrich Hoffmann, Bayerische Staatsbibliothek)

An early edition of *Mein Kampf*, first published in 1925, had a simple look and included on its cover the subtitle *Eine Abrechnung* (A Reckoning). (Hermann Historica)

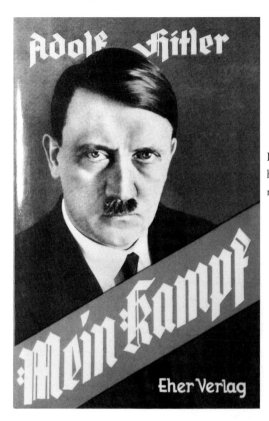

Later editions of *Mein Kampf* had a dramatic book jacket and no subtitle. (Author's copy)

Hitler revisits his cell in Landsberg Prison in 1934, ten years after he lived there and wrote *Mein Kampf.* He was now dictator of Germany. (Yad Vashem)

After World War II, Landsberg Prison became U.S. Army War Criminal Prison No. 1. Two hundred fifty-nine Germans convicted of crimes against humanity were hanged just fifty feet from the building where Hitler lived in 1924. (National Archives)

Outside the courtroom there was pandemonium. Crowds that gathered a block away from the Infantry School were attacked by the mounted police, with several injuries. But enough people were able to send up their cheers in front of the building that they could be heard inside the school, even with all the windows closed. Hitler's political instincts fired up and he quickly found a window that he could open and he waved, smiling to his admirers on the street. They waved back with flowers. It was a moment of triumph.

But Bavaria and Germany had lost. Except on the far right, most commentators denounced the wrist-slap verdicts of Hitler and the other leaders as a scandal—"equal to an acquittal," argued one newspaper. Neithardt's conduct was considered an extreme embarrassment to the German judiciary. "It was a trial in name only," wrote the strongly pro-Bavarian and nationalist daily, *Bayerischer Kurier.* "In fact it was more like a *völkisch* mass agitation gathering."[63] The *Berliner Tageblatt* pronounced the Bavarian justice system "bankrupt."[64] "All Munich is chuckling over the verdict," reported the *New York Times,* "which is regarded as an excellent joke for All Fools' Day."[65] One critic, years later, called Judge Neithardt "a reverse Pontius Pilate" for having found a guilty man innocent.[66]

Ludendorff's exoneration drew as much dismay as Hitler's easy sentence. After all, the old general was far better known abroad, especially among former adversaries like France, where the reaction was strong. *Le Temps* suggested the acquittal was proof of Germany's lingering revanchist longings.[67] Even Judge Neithardt seemed to have some regrets about the Ludendorff acquittal. When a junior state's attorney, Martin Dreese, ran into the judge in a hallway soon after the trial, he asked the judge why he freed Ludendorff. "I thought he was guilty of high treason," Neithardt said (according to Dreese). "But the lay jurors were all for acquittal, so I joined them."

The lay jurors, enamored of Hitler and convinced that Kahr, Lossow, and Seisser were in fact guilty, had almost blocked the Nazi leader's conviction even to a sentence of five years. But Neithardt warned them that an acquittal of Hitler would raise such a public ruckus that Kahr, Lossow, and Seisser would be dragged before the Leipzig State Court that the Bavarians had tried so hard to avoid. To persuade the lay jurors to accept even a five-year sentence for Hitler—Neithardt needed four out of five votes for a conviction—he had to promise he would offer him parole in six months.

Throughout Germany, Hitler was now known as the man who had turned the tables in his trial, chased Bavaria's top general out of the courtroom, rhetorically destroyed his adversaries in the Bavarian political establishment, and put the Nazi brand into nationwide circulation. Whether the party could survive Hitler's six-month absence in prison was another question. But not many people could say they had never heard of him anymore. He had used the platform of the court like the podium of a beer hall, but with a national (and international) audience.

Thanks to Hitler's new presence on the national political map, many formerly fence-sitting people were seeing the far-right message in a new light. His notoriety also acted as a recruitment force in the competitive swirl of *völkisch*, nationalistic, right-wing political groups—of which there were at least fifty in Bavaria. Many a German right-winger had views different from the Nazis on certain issues—such as socialism in Russia or the role of Christianity in politics. But one thing most of them shared was anti-Semitism—plus a fervent sense of Germanness.

In the Ruhr region town of Rheydt, four hundred miles northwest of Munich, one young, university-educated nationalist had been reading newspaper reports on Hitler's trial every day. His enthusiasm fired, he began making entries into his diary: "I am busying myself with Hitler and the national socialist movement," he wrote. "Communism, the Jewish question, Christianity, the Germany of the future.... Hitler touches on many questions. But he makes the solution very simple." From Hitler's trial speeches, the young man began envisioning what the leader must be like. "What is liberating about Hitler is the involvement of a really upright and truthful personality," he noted in his journal. "Hitler is an idealist...who is bringing new belief to the German people. I am reading his speeches, I am allowing myself to be inspired by him and carried to the stars.... Only Hitler continually concerns me. The man is indeed no intellectual. But his wonderful *élan,* his verve, his enthusiasm, his German feeling."[68]

Thanks to the trial and the newspaper reports, this young man was swiftly moving into Hitler's hypnotic ideological and political orbit. His name was Joseph Goebbels.

CHAPTER NINE

Rearranging the World

*"From Hitler's barely legible handwriting, we could tell it
was something political."*

—FRANZ HEMMRICH, LANDSBERG PRISON GUARD

Hitler left Munich on a high. After waving to a cheering crowd
from the Infantry School window, Hitler did not mind being
returned to Landsberg Prison that same day. He was on top of the
world that mattered to him. The favorable outcome of the trial had
given him new energy. Hemmrich noted that Hitler "seemed notice-
ably refreshed and relaxed" when he returned to the prison.[1] With
the prospect of parole only six months away, Hitler entered one of
the most productive periods of his life.

For Hitler, life behind bars was, in many ways, a blessing. For
almost the first time in his political life, he had no gatherings to
attend, no speeches to give, no office to go to. "He can't race from
meeting to meeting until late at night in constant turmoil," wrote a
fellow prisoner. Now ensconced in room number seven on the

second floor of Landsberg's fortress building, Hitler was, in a sense, a free man. "Increasingly I had the feeling that he didn't mind the involuntary stay since it gave him the chance to think about his future in the peace and quiet of the prison," wrote Hemmrich.

After living for five weeks in a cadet's room in the Infantry School in Munich, returning to Landsberg may have seemed to Hitler like coming home. Prison guards Lurker and Hemmrich, Warden Leybold—the familiar faces were all waiting as the police van opened its doors beside the fortress building. And many more familiar faces, including forty members of the Hitler Shock Troop, would be coming soon, after their trial and conviction as accessories to treason in the putsch. In May and June, they too would arrive at Landsberg Prison.

For now, however, only bumptious Colonel Kriebel and the bookish Dr. Weber were with Hitler in the thick-walled fortress building. The two fellow prisoners had moved into room numbers eight and nine, just to the right of Hitler's. These rooms in the recently remodeled structure—"it still smelled of plaster and fresh paint," noted Hemmrich—were nearly identical to the one Hitler had occupied during his first days at Landsberg, before his hunger strike. They were small but functional, with high windows and a pleasing view of outlying fields and the distant mountains beyond the tall prison wall (one inmate called the scene "friendly silence"[2]). The prisoners' rooms all gave onto a spacious dayroom. It was furnished with a table for six, spread with a white tablecloth, and had a sitting corner with comfortable wicker chairs surrounded by flowerpots. Along with a laurel wreath sent by an admirer, Hitler had hung two pictures of Frederick the Great on the wall (Hitler would still have Frederick the Great on his wall in the Berlin bunker at the moment of his demise in 1945). Alongside another wall stood a cast-iron stove—for heat and for warming food—beside double sinks with a high mirror. Behind that lay a bathroom containing a bath-tub "just for us," marveled one inmate.

With their doors open as much as they wanted and no obliga-tion to labor, the "honorable" prisoners could easily congregate or take their meals together. Spring was in the air and Hitler often wore his favorite prison outfit, Bavarian lederhosen (leather shorts) with suspenders and a white shirt, sometimes with a tie and cuff links, along with the customary kneesocks. He liked to read news-papers in the wicker chairs.[3] The men could spend up to six hours per day outdoors in the adjacent garden.

But Hitler's peace and quiet did not come immediately. He was flooded from the beginning with visitors, mail, and gifts. Landsberg Prison had never had such a celebrity on its hands. On his first day in Landsberg, Hitler received eleven callers in the visiting room of the fortress building. On the second day, thirteen came, including Hanf-staengl and Alfred Rosenberg, Hitler's designee as acting head of the Nazi Party. The now-banned party, functioning under various dis-guises, was already showing signs of splintering or making alliances Hitler did not want. He spent much of the next two months meeting with party functionaries who were trying to hold the party to Hitler's line.[4] During his first months in prison, Hitler had visitors almost every day. Nearly everyone brought gifts of food or flowers. Knowing Hitler's notorious sweet tooth, the edibles ran to pastries and cakes, regarded in Germany almost as a basic food group.

Settling into prison life, Hitler was at a crossroads. At a classic midpoint in life—his thirty-fifth birthday was just days away—he faced six months of empty time and an uncertain future. Triumphant in his trial but with his political movement still banned and crum-bling, Hitler confronted the challenge of whether and how to reinvent himself for a new political reality. Germany was in economic and political recovery and the Nazi Party was in disarray and disrepute.

Would there be life after political death? How would Hitler position himself for a comeback? Beyond his hard-core adherents, did the Hitler idea—National Socialism, dictatorship, the Führer principle of infallible leadership, and especially anti-Semitism—have appeal? Was Adolf Hitler still a marketable brand? Hitler seemed to think so, or at least he put a good face on his prospects. "Our struggle must and will end in victory," he wrote to an admirer.

On April 20, Easter Sunday, Hitler also received a positive answer from those who cared the most about him. It was his thirty-fifth birthday. His stream of well-wishers at Landsberg Prison peaked at twenty-one, the most he received in a single day. His mail over this weekend, reported Hemmrich, was delivered "in laundry baskets" and took several days to get through the prison censors. His room was "overflowing with flowers like in a greenhouse." Hitler stood among the greenery to accept birthday greetings from Kriebel and Weber.[5]

In Munich, three thousand true believers gathered to celebrate his birthday at the Bürgerbräukeller, the beer hall where his disastrous coup attempt had begun. The hard core of Hitler's following was holding strong. It did not take long for Hitler to choose his course. His trial success and the support of his devotees persuaded him of his continuing mission to save Germany. He would continue promoting his message. But since he could not mount the podium at the Circus Krone or the Hofbräuhaus, Hitler would now need to reach the masses through his pen rather than his voice. Always one to struggle more with writing than with speaking—he had said as much to Deputy Prosecutor Ehard in their first meeting—Hitler had recently undergone the longest writing exercise of his life, composing the sixty-plus-page defense memorandum, which had guided him to his courtroom speeches. That experience had increased his confidence.

For one thing, Hitler wanted revenge; he wanted to expose "the lies and deceit" of his tormentors—Kahr, Lossow, and Seisser—who had slipped through the net he had thrown over them at the trial, then slipped out of town. He wanted to unmask the perfidy of the "November criminals," as he labeled everyone associated with creating and running the Weimar Republic. He wanted a "reckoning," as he called it—a settling of accounts.

Now that he had gotten people's attention, Hitler was ready to preach to Germany. His mountaintop pronouncements from inside the Infantry School had been a mere prelude to what would grow into his massive, 782-page statement of what he believed, what he wanted to do, and how he wanted to do it. That statement would set forth Hitler's worldview and his "road map" to Germany's future, as some later described it.[6] It would be titled *Mein Kampf.*

But the title would come later. In his first days back at Landsberg Prison, Hitler's first challenge was simply to produce an article. The right-wing publisher, Julius Lehmann, had asked Hitler to write an essay for his magazine, *Deutschlands Erneuerung* (Germany's Renewal), Germany's leading monthly journal of *völkisch* thought.[7] Lehmann was also the book publisher of such famous racist writers as Houston Stewart Chamberlain, Hans F. K. Günther, Paul de Lagarde, and Arthur de Gobineau. The publisher's political sympathies were clearly with the Nazis; he had allowed his villa on the outskirts of Munich to be used to hold hostages during the putsch. For *Deutschlands Erneuerung,* Lehmann wanted not a rehash of the trial or even a score-settler, but a think piece on Hitler's politics pegged to the November 8, 1923, putsch attempt.

"Why Did November 8th Have to Happen?" ran in the April 1924 issue of *Deutschlands Erneuerung.*[8] This often overlooked essay, which contained numerous passages and concepts that would later appear in *Mein Kampf,* openly presented Hitler's aggressive expansionist dreams and his utterly race-driven view of the world. Though he had written numerous editorials for the *Völkischer Beobachter*, Hitler's five-thousand-word article for Lehmann's journal was an unusually detailed and concentrated summation of his thinking, especially on foreign policy. To read it now is to encounter a preview of the Third Reich.

In his very first sentence, the always apocalyptic Hitler cast his argument in grandiose terms, evoking the existential "being or nonbeing" (*Sein oder Nichtsein*) of Germany. Playing for the highest stakes, he argued that World War I had started a process—still unfinished—that would decide the continued existence of "the German nation for centuries into the future, maybe forever." Germany's enemies were bent on Germany's obliteration. Their "battle cry is not, 'Victory!' but rather, 'Destruction and annihilation!'" wrote Hitler.

The highest goal of national government was not simply "preserving the peace for its own sake," Hitler claimed, but "preserving and expanding one's own people." Hitler was highlighting a central element of his political philosophy: the standing of one's people, one's *Volk*, is everything, and any means—including war—should be used to augment its strength. To Hitler, race was at the heart of the concept of nation; he considered not only Jews but Germans, as the perfect Aryans, to be a race. The "fundamental pillar" of the German nation, its "race and culture," was under threat and must be protected in a "battle to the death," he wrote. Marxism was the "mortal enemy," and Marxism was a Jewish creation.

Beyond the focus on "nation and race"—the title of what would become the key chapter of *Mein Kampf*—Hitler was preoccupied with Germany's international alliances. His essay sketched out what would, after 1939, become his policy of conquest toward Eastern Europe and Russia. To Hitler, war was already coming; that was the natural state of relations among nations. It was just a question of who against whom. That's why he had to work out the question of alliances. Hitler posited that France was Germany's implacable "hereditary enemy" and was single-mindedly focused on the "Balkanization" of Germany into its weak component parts (Germany had consisted of three hundred independent states, municipalities, and principalities before Bismarck united them in 1870). Therefore, Germany had to choose Russia or England as its ally. The choice was a macroeconomic one: did Germany want "sea power and international trade," or land power with greater "agrarian space"? If the former, then Germany should ally itself with Russia against the great colonial power, Britain. If the latter — forsaking overseas ambitions for "continental expansion" to the east — then Germany should seek an alliance with England against Russia. Though he had often talked of Germany's need for "land and soil," he left open for the moment the matter of which alliance he would choose.

But for the first time, Hitler linked acquisition of land for "continental expansion" to the fierceness and the threat of "the sword." Trying to improve a nation's economic position "without power-political thinking and actions" could lead only to disaster — "a Carthaginian end," as Hitler liked to put it. Hitler also connected power politics to his racial doctrines in a foreshadowing of what would be called, in *Mein Kampf*, his policy of "living space" for the "Germanic race."

All these dire conditions and harrowing possibilities, Hitler offhandedly noted at the end of his essay, convinced him that, on November 8, 1923, "the moment had arrived" for his putsch. And he reprised a favorite dramatic conclusion: "Whether or not we were right will be decided not by any state's attorney or court but, someday, by German history." He had, in a way, answered the question posed by the article's title. More important, by writing the essay

Hitler had exercised the muscles that would help him draft one of the world's best-known and most notorious books. "In structure, language and themes, and taken as a whole, the article can be seen as precursor to *Mein Kampf*," wrote historian Plöckinger.

For a former trench runner sitting in a simple prison room in a sleepy town in the Bavarian countryside, this was big thinking. It was also radical thinking, and a sign of the special treatment given to Hitler as a prisoner, since inmates were theoretically not allowed to engage in political activities. The man who dropped out of school at age sixteen, never earned a diploma in anything, and got all his understanding of international relations from random though intensive reading could now rant at will in the public print without censure. And he obviously had no qualms about rearranging the world to his liking; he was moving nations about the global chessboard with the confidence of a seasoned statesman or, better, of a world conqueror.

The fact that he had jammed a number of bold ideas and complex international analyses into a relatively tight article showed Hitler that he could discuss big ideas that were not (this time) overfreighted with polemics. To be sure, he'd taken half a dozen ugly swings at Jews (a "racial tuberculosis") and at the weakling politicians of prewar Germany ("world pacifists"). But mostly he'd argued a tightly woven if extreme case. His argumentation still had, of course, its contradictions and gaps, and Hitler may have had professional editorial help in getting it in shape for publication. Yet writing for a journal of ideas in the *völkisch* movement must have convinced Hitler that he could be taken seriously by the intellectual heavyweights who were published by Lehmann. From there, it was a fairly short leap to the idea of writing a full book.

Hitler may have had more mundane reasons for deciding to

proceed with a book-length treatment of the avalanche of ideas in his head. One is pecuniary; he needed money to pay his expensive lawyer's bills. A fellow prisoner, Julius Schaub, later claimed that Hitler wrote *Mein Kampf* "only as a propaganda piece to earn money."[9] Another impetus to write was later attributed to fellow prisoner Gregor Strasser, who was said (in his own brother's not always reliable memoir) to have grown tired of Hitler's after-dinner perorations and suggested that, instead of talking ad infinitum, the party leader should be writing his wonderful thoughts down—in a book. In this unconfirmable version, *Mein Kampf* came about as a way of getting Hitler to shut up so the other inmates could relax, chat, and play cards.

Yet Hitler's need to pontificate and persuade may have been enough, on its own, to motivate him to write. Upon returning to prison, he had already begun making autobiographical notations in a notebook.[10] At his trial in Munich, his slightly exaggerated version of his youthful slide into hard times in Vienna had been a crowd-pleaser and easily framed the transition into politics. Two months later, sitting in room number seven in Landsberg Prison, Hitler apparently decided to try the same approach to a book.

Sometime in April or early May, he began typing on the same old typewriter he had used before his trial:

"It seems to me a felicitous omen that my cradle...."

Hitler stopped. Throwing the carriage back, he started over:

"Today it seems to me a happy omen that my cradle...stood in Braunau [Hitler's birthplace]. This little town lies on the border of the two German states whose reunification we of the younger generation have made into a truly noble life's goal." In something close to that form, those words would become the opening paragraph of Hitler's famous, infamous book, *Mein Kampf.*

Hitler wrote at least five pages in this first stab at his book. The original typescripts disappeared at the end of World War II from his Berchtesgaden retreat, taken by invading French soldiers. Decades later, they were found in a private U.S. collection. Carefully analyzed by scholars and certified by forensic experts for handwriting, typescript, and paper, the pages were described in detail in a 2009 article in the Munich-based *Vierteljahrshefte für Zeitgeschichte* (Quarterly Journal of Contemporary History) by Florian Beierl and Othmar Plöckinger.[11] Those first five pages turned out to be Hitler's original typescripts of what appeared in *Mein Kampf*'s opening chapter, entitled "Im Elternhaus" ("In the House of My Parents").

Hitler by now knew he was on a track he liked. He was convinced that he had a book in him—at least one, maybe more. He also thought he could write a book quickly. By early May, just five weeks after returning to prison, he was talking about the work as if it already existed. In a May 5 letter to Siegfried Wagner (son of Richard), Hitler noted that he was "finally writing a thorough reckoning with the men who enthusiastically shouted 'Hurray!' on November 9 [1923]"—but who had then turned coat and denounced the putsch as "an insane undertaking." Hitler was, of course, still obsessed with settling scores with Kahr, Lossow, and Seisser. His book's working title was a vindictive mouthful: *Four-and-a-Half Years of Struggle Against Lies, Stupidity, and Cowardice: A Reckoning.*

With the book still mostly a gleam in Hitler's eye, a small bidding war broke out. Clearly, a tell-all from the triumphant convict of the high treason trial, who knew so much about the questionable dealings of the Bavarian triumvirate and the Bavarian Reichswehr, could be a hot property. Max Amann, Hitler's former sergeant and now business manager of the temporarily banned *Völkischer Beobachter,* had major publishing ambitions (he would later control more than half of all German publishing interests). As the head of Eher Verlag— essentially the Nazi Party publishing house—he commissioned market research on the viability of a Hitler book. The response he received was astonishing: "If the publisher issues a limited collector's edition of only 500 copies of a work by Hitler with special treatment [laid paper and semi-leather binding], each numbered and signed by Mr. Hitler, it would have a collector's value of at least 500 marks each," wrote the assessor.[12]

Amann wanted Hitler's book, but he was short of funds — the book market was very weak, he said. And Hitler seemed interested in the possibilities of reaching beyond the Nazi-leaning market. He entertained overtures from another *völkisch* publisher, the Gross-deutscher Ringverlag. The Ringverlag (Ring Publishers) seems to have made a serious run at acquiring Hitler's book. Its editor, its business manager, and one of its co-owners paid Hitler a series of five visits beginning in April. Ernst Hanfstaengl also visited five times that month; he wanted to publish Hitler's book, he claimed, but could not persuade his brother, who controlled the family publishing company. In the end, for reasons unknown, Hitler spurned Ring Publishers and instead gave his book to Amann. While there were later claims of other publishers — such as Ernst Boepple's Deutscher Volksverlag — and even foreign publishers making serious offers to Hitler, no evidence has been found to support these statements.[13] Nor is there any known indication of interest by Hitler's conservative publishing friends — Julius Lehmann or Hugo Bruckmann. In any case, no matter what counter-offers may have materialized, Hitler clearly made the right choice: by keeping his book in the Nazi family, he and Amann both became very rich. *Mein Kampf* became the foundation of Amann's vast publishing enterprise and of Hitler's personal fortune. All the royalties from the book went into his personal account, not that of the Nazi Party.

Hitler had a publisher. By mid-May, he was telling visitors from Salzburg (Austria) that his book "would appear soon."[14] Signaling his intention to settle into a writing routine, Hitler had ordered a custom-made worktable from a Landsberg carpenter, Sebastian Springer. On May 8, Springer tendered a bill for fifteen marks for a "small typing table, stained brown and varnished."[15] A room, a table, peace and quiet, and lots of time. The only other thing a writer could want was a new typewriter. In yet another of the turns of fortune that seemed to befall Hitler just when he needed them, a guardian angel again descended into his life. It was Helene Bechstein, the wife of the famed Berlin piano builder, who arrived for a visit "in a big car with a liveried chauffeur" on May 15 with her husband and daughter in tow.[16] All that is known about that first visit is that the *grande dame* with the private suite at Munich's Four Seasons Hotel got into a high snit with the prison guards. She was upset that her gift package for Hitler had to be inspected for security in the customary way. Angrily ripping open the package, Frau Bechstein sent "pralines of the finest sort" flying all over the room, screaming: "There! See if you can find a machine gun in there!"[17]

Helene Bechstein returned five more times in the next two weeks. Already enamored of Hitler and a contributor to Nazi Party coffers at that time, she is considered to have been the probable donor of the next felicitous addition to Hitler's writing setup, a brand-new, American-made Remington portable typewriter, black with white keys,[18] built just one month before in New York, according to its serial number.[19] The shiny little Remington was an appropriate complement to Hitler's narrow room with its small, new typing table. Whatever its provenance, the Remington portable is the machine on which Hitler wrote almost the entire first volume of *Mein Kampf* (in the beginning, he planned only one volume).

Hitler began using his new machine in a surprisingly systematic way, given his generally unsystematic and chaotic style. Having already drafted the autobiographical opener to his book on the older

German typewriter, Hitler now set about writing an outline for the rest of the book on his Remington. He was using a new, higher quality paper at this point, apparently Nazi Party letterhead; each page had a swastika emblazoned on the upper left-hand corner. (Researchers Beierl and Plöckinger suggest that Helene Bechstein may have also brought the paper to Hitler, implying that the Bechsteins stopped by the Munich party headquarters on their way to Landsberg or were visited in their hotel by a party representative.)

The resulting outline, an eighteen-page document, bristled with such lines as "settlement policy can only happen in Europe... demands immediate war" and "renounce international trade and colonies, renounce a naval war fleet." Another attention grabber: "I was never a pacifist." The outline was logical and structured, built around an autobiographical approach to telling his political story and selling his ideological message. Most surprisingly, Hitler actually followed the outline, with many digressions, while writing his book.

By late May and early June Hitler was filling the fortress building with the clackety-clack of his new typewriter, often starting as early as five in the morning, reported a new prison inmate, Rudolf Hess. "At five o'clock, I make a cup of tea for Hitler (who is working on his book) and for me," reported Hess in a letter home.[20] Hitler also frequently paid an extra fee to keep his room lights on for two hours after the 10 p.m. curfew. Making notes and drafting sections in pencil, Hitler threw rejected pages into his trash can, which guards dutifully retrieved each morning. "From Hitler's barely legible handwriting, we could tell it was something political," wrote Hemmrich. "At first, we took the loose sheets to the censor. But since he would have to present the finished work to the censors when leaving the prison, we were ordered just to destroy the [rejected] pages. I had the contents of the trash can thrown into the stove."[21]

Though Hitler was still in the drafting stage, in mid-June Amann went so far as to produce a four-page brochure announcing a book "of approximately four hundred pages," still including Hitler's long, vengeful title about "lies, stupidity, and cowardice." A formal photo of Hitler, mustache prominent, hair slicked back, nearly filled the first page. Stories about the brochure, along with ads for the coming book ("in July") began appearing in some *völkisch* newspapers. One of them, the Nuremberg *Völkisches Echo,* ran a large front-page story headlined, "Hitler's Sacrifice!" Two days later the newspaper breathlessly reported rumors of a press run of fifty thousand copies of Hitler's (still unwritten) book, which the paper was already calling "the bible" of the *völkisch* movement.[22]

Amann had certainly succeeded in firing up interest. But, so far, there was no book.

CHAPTER TEN

The Boss

"No throwing cigarettes into the flowerpots."

—HANS KALLENBACH, "TEN COMMANDMENTS
FOR DECENCY AND ORDER"

"In the evenings, Hitler frequently read to his fellow prisoners from his work in progress. They gathered around him like apostles on the Mount of Olives and hung on his words." Prison guard Hemmrich could report this scene because he, along with some of the other prison personnel, had begun eavesdropping on Hitler's unofficial lecture series in the fortress dayrooms. As Hitler was plunging ahead with his book, Landsberg Prison had come to life.

After a month of living as a threesome, Hitler, Kriebel, and Weber now had some company. Forty members of the Hitler Shock Troop—those arrested for violence and hostage-taking during Hitler's putsch—had been tried in Munich. Despite its forty defendants, the proceeding against them was called "the little Hitler trial" by the newspapers to distinguish it from the "big" one that had tried the leader himself. The "little" trial took only five days; all the Shock Troops were convicted on May 3 of being accessories to high treason and sentenced to an average of fifteen months in fortress arrest—honorable imprisonment, just like Hitler's. Yet they, too, enjoyed the prospect of early parole if they exhibited good behavior.

In the first week of May, the convicted men began filtering into the prison, filling rooms on the fortress building's first floor and overflowing into specially segregated quarters in the main prison. Though the rooms in the main prison were darker and cut off from the social atmosphere of the fortress building, each prisoner sent into the main building received two cells, one as his "sitting room" and the other for sleeping. Still, some prisoners—like Hermann Fobke, the law student—opted to move into a crowded, large room in the fortress building ("with five other guys," he wrote to a friend) rather than live in the main prison.[1] Others had to double up in the single rooms—it was "like being inside a submarine," noted one prisoner.[2]

There was one exception to this arrangement. Emil Maurice, Hitler's sometime chauffeur and close companion, was given space on the second floor—in room number six, just to the left of Hitler's. Maurice, the tall, dark-featured former watchmaker, was the first of the Shock Troops to arrive and was regarded as a hard case: recall that he had been especially aggressive during the ransacking of the *Münchener Post* and was accused of manhandling the wife of one of its editors. Yet it was Maurice's special relationship with Hitler—and the leader's need for a kind of manservant—that had earned Maurice a coveted spot on the second floor. "My room is large, bright, and spacious," he wrote to a friend.[3] Maurice initially took on both secretarial and everyday menial chores for Hitler, such as procuring milk and eggs.[4] Soon, however, he was relieved of the secretarial assignment by the arrival, on May 15, of Rudolf Hess.

Hess was a very special case. The former World War I pilot and university student, quiet but devoted to Hitler, had become one of the leader's closest co-workers in everyday Nazi Party activities. With his bourgeois upbringing and higher education, Hess was more than a scheduling secretary—he was also a sounding board for Hitler's intellectual meanderings. During the putsch, Hess's most serious crime had been the kidnapping of two Bavarian government ministers, and he had been on the lam ever since. He finally turned himself in and was convicted on the very last day of the People's Court's existence. Arriving at Landsberg, he was given the last remaining room on the second floor, room number five, right next to Maurice's.

Some of Hitler's most revealing conversations during the writing of *Mein Kampf* would take place in that room, as Hess would disclose in the roughly thirty letters he wrote over the next few months, most to his future wife, Ilse Pröhl. But in his very first letter, written to his mother on his first night in Landsberg, Hess captured another aspect of prison life with World War I veterans led by a man whose greatest formative experience had been at the combat front. "I can hear [Hitler's] voice coming from the common room right now," wrote Hess. "He seems to be reliving his war experiences—he is imitating the sounds of grenades and machine guns, jumping wildly around the room, carried away by his fantasies."[5]

When Hess arrived in mid-May, Hitler was drawing and sketching constantly in pencil and pen. "This afternoon he brought me really splendid designs of individual museums for the land, sea, air, and colonial wars," noted Hess, "along with designs for theaters, a national library, and a university...plus set designs for [the operas] *Tristan, Lohengrin, Turandot, Julius Caesar,* etc. Since I had seen only the wildest caricatures by him before now, I was quite surprised to see this side."

THE BOSS

*   *   *

In early June, Hans Kallenbach arrived. Short, sandy-haired, and
handsome, Kallenbach had commanded a machine-gun unit during
the putsch. An army lieutenant during World War I, the twenty-six-
year-old Kallenbach identified passionately with the "frontline generation" that supplied so many of Hitler's supporters and street fighters.
The young ex-soldier moved into room number eleven on the first
floor, the same jammed space that housed Hermännchen ("Hermie")
Fobke, as his roommates were calling the ambitious law student. Consciously or unconsciously, new arrival Kallenbach began gathering
string for what would become his post-prison memoir, *Mit Adolf Hitler
auf Festung Landsberg* (With Adolf Hitler at the Landsberg Fortress).

With a large contingent of his followers on hand, Hitler was
once again the master of his immediate universe, the much-
worshipped leader of his little team. Just as the Nazi Party had militaristic overtones — uniforms, marching boots, flags, martial
music — and included both Storm Troopers and Shock Troops, the
gathering in the prison now acquired a certain military structure
and feel. This appealed not only to the military-minded Hitler but
to tough old officers like Colonel Kriebel and former frontline fighters like Kallenbach. Every new arrival — the convicted men began
their sentences on different dates — was told to report immediately
to *"der Chef"* ("the boss"), just like reporting to a commanding
officer in a new military unit. (Hitler was not yet called Führer —
leader — but simply, "boss," or "chief."[6]) "My heart was pounding,"
remembered Kallenbach as he marched up the stairs to Hitler's
second-floor room on the day of his arrival. "I was in such awe of his
personal magnetism and the drama of the moment that I can no
longer recall his exact words. [Hitler] questioned me in great detail
about myself and my loved ones, about our personal and financial
situations....A strong handshake accompanied words spoken from

201

the heart and taken to heart." (Kallenbach's book is filled with hero worship.[7]) Then, thoroughly enamored of Hitler and initiated into life at Landsberg, Kallenbach glided back down to room number eleven, where his new comrades were preparing grain-based ersatz coffee and slices of bread with marmalade.

The Landsberg fortress building had never held more than a handful of prisoners. Now it housed more than forty. Conditions were generally cushy. Like the inmates on the second floor, the crew on the first floor had a large dayroom for taking meals and lounging about. They could read, nap, smoke, write letters, or do nothing. They could wear their own clothes—not the usual prison garb— and were allowed to keep most personal items, including pocket knives. Only money had to be turned over to the prison guards, who deposited each man's funds into his prison account, which was kept on a ledger updated weekly. As "honorable prisoners," the men did not have to work or even make their own beds. Room cleaning and bed making—along with all household chores, including emp- tying trash, polishing shoes, and serving the food—was done by trustees. These were lucky lads from the main Landsberg Prison who had won the position of *Kalfaktor*, or special servants, in the fortress building.[8] Not allowed to speak with the putsch-makers, the trustees nonetheless considered it a bonus to work in their building and, after serving meals to Hitler and his men, to eat whatever food was left over. Fortress meals were taken at the common tables in the dayrooms on the first and second floors.

Life in Landsberg Prison was good for the former putschists (who were also kidnappers, thieves, house-breakers, vandals, and— if one attributes the deaths of four policemen to them—accomplices to homicide). Their routines were comfortable and afforded enough variety to avert tedium, at least during the warm months. "I can't complain of boredom," wrote Hess to his father.[9] "I am a 'worker of the brain' until 7:30 a.m. After breakfast, from 8 until 11, I am a 'worker of the fist [hand].' I chop wood. A very healthy activity, since I can hack at roots. Also it earns me 20 pfennigs per hour! Hitler says he might do this when he's finished with his book. Afterwards, a hot bath. At 11:35 a plentiful midday dinner. Then a nap, tea and more 'work of the brain.' After our evening meal from 7:45 to 8, we are allowed outside again, play games, or I chat with Hitler while walking up and down. After that, we gather inside again—Hitler, Colonel Kriebel, Dr. Weber, Maurice and I—for tea and pastries, which never cease to arrive."

Life in Landsberg has been compared to hotel living or being at a spa. Given the crowded living conditions and doubling up in smaller rooms on the first floor, it might be better called a boys' camp. Any way it was labeled, imprisonment at the Landsberg fortress was the easiest prison time any convict could do in Bavaria. Among Socialists and Communists, this was taken as further proof of the rightward bias of the Bavarian judiciary; left-wingers convicted of political crimes had almost all been sent to Niederschönenfeld Prison, a much harsher institution fifty-seven miles north of Landsberg.

The five "honorable prisoners" on the second floor—Hitler, Kriebel, Weber, Maurice, and Hess—led a near-monkish life, with reading, writing, and chatting as their chief activities. The first-floor inmates were a rowdier bunch. With few officers or professionals in their midst, they referred to themselves as *raue Landsknechte,* or rough country boys, and behaved accordingly. "It was loud and boisterous, and we always had a steady stream of men coming in and out of room number eleven," wrote Kallenbach. They played pranks, hazed newcomers, thought up plays and poems, and reinvented songs to old rhythms. In room number eleven, Kallenbach came up with the "Ten Commandments for Decency and Order," including "No throwing cigarettes into the flowerpots…this is not a slum or a bar"; "Don't throw your clothes on the chairs, that's why you have a wardrobe"; and, with casual nastiness, "Don't shout and scream…this is not a Jew school."

For entertainment, they even created their own "Landsberg Prison Band" with a violin, a lute, and a homemade "Turkish crescent" with jingling bells. Josef Gerum, a Munich policeman who was secretly a Nazi and was caught during the putsch, was the violinist. The Landsberg fortress had become a downright lively place. "Our treatment here is impeccable," Hess wrote home, "exactly as befits the term 'honorable.'"

On special occasions—like birthdays, holidays, and many Saturday evenings—the five men on the second floor, now dubbed the Field Marshals' Hill by those on the first floor, would descend for a common dinner with the foot soldiers. Hitler, as king of the castle, sat at the head of a long table. In keeping with the strict military mood, everyone stood at attention until Hitler arrived and shook each man's hand. Then the group tucked in with a will. Meals tended to be eaten swiftly and in silence until, finally, Hitler issued the traditional German mealtime greeting, *"Mahlzeit!"* That ended the meal and opened the table to a period of relaxed conversation. Out came the cigarettes, cigars, and pipes. Predictably, these after-dinner klatches often turned into monologues by Hitler, who never minded the sound of his own voice. Since the men around the table represented the closest thing he could find to a beer hall audience, he often began reading from draft chapters of his book. As Hemmrich noted, at such times the men were mesmerized by his pronouncements. "We hung dumbstruck on his words and the hours passed like minutes," recalled Kallenbach.

Sometimes, especially on rainy days when it was impossible to walk in the garden, Hitler would hold talks in the dayroom at 10 a.m., lecturing his men on politics and world history. Like a good teacher, he even used the easel-mounted school blackboard that stood conveniently in the room. According to Kallenbach, Hitler gave his rapt listeners his full journeyman's tale of living in Viennese poverty and of drawing critical lessons from the flawed multinational parliament and the great deeds of the (deeply anti-Semitic) mayor, Karl Lueger. Hitler "hammered into our heads" the concepts of "nation and race, blood and soil... nationalism and socialism," wrote Kallenbach. Preservation of one's own race was the highest value in Hitler's belief system. It was not hard to sell to Germans filled with a deep sense of grievance.

But Hitler was already moving from his fully confrontational, blow-up-the-ship politics of force to the notion of political maneuvering and reconciliation among rivals to create a new, united society in Germany—what Hitler called a *Volksgemeinschaft,* or national community. In his closing argument at his trial, Hitler had forecast the day when those who shed each other's blood on the Odeon Square would march arm-in-arm to form "regiments" and "divisions." In Landsberg, he said, he came to realize "that we could no longer win power by force; the state had had time to consolidate itself and it had the weapons." The shift from a politics of force— overthrowing the state by revolution—to one of electioneering and embracing one's former enemy was, for many a hardened Nazi, difficult to take. While he was still at Landsberg, said Hitler, "many of my supporters never understood" the transformation.

That certainly seems to have been true of the band of radicals in prison with Hitler. "For hours we debated our master teacher's concept of a comprehensive German 'national community,'" recalled Kallenbach. "We couldn't grasp it.... We just wanted to replace the 'dictatorship of the proletariat' so loudly proclaimed by the other side with a 'dictatorship of the frontline veterans' [of World War I].

We wanted to deal with our opponents...an eye for an eye and a tooth for a tooth. We did not want to offer the hand of friendship, as our leader was advising us to do."

Political debates and lectures were, of course, easier to take in the comfy confines of the men's cosseted imprisonment. Food and drink, always the chief complaint of soldiers and prisoners, were both good and abundant at Landsberg. Besides the usual beverages, the men enjoyed a huge bonus at dinner time: unlike the five hundred poor souls serving time in the main prison, the fortress inmates had access to alcohol. Officially, they were allowed to purchase a half-liter of beer or a large glass (a *Schoppen*) of wine per day if they had money in their accounts. Hitler, who later quit drinking altogether, drank one beer per day, at least in April and early May. The prison records from that period show eighteen pfennigs deducted every day from his account for beer.

For many of the men a half-liter beer ration seemed stingy indeed. Born Bavarians, they were used to imbibing their region's renowned brew like water. "We approached the Mufti [their secret nickname for Warden Leybold] with a request for more," reported prisoner Karl Fiehler, a Shock Trooper who went on to become mayor of Munich during the Third Reich. Leybold cited regulations and turned the men down — until the next day, when he found a way. The rules allowed him, he told the inmates, to pay them up to twenty pfennigs (cents) per hour for work in the garden. In view of the summer heat, he felt justified in providing another half-liter of beer to anyone who put in six hours of work per day. The men got their extra ration and the garden began to look a lot better under the guiding hand of Colonel Kriebel, who had a green thumb and a commanding style as he directed digging, planting, and the widening of the gravel walk. In a broad straw hat against the summer sun, Kriebel looked, noted Lurker, like a "Brazilian coffee planter."

In addition to beer and wine, hard liquor was somehow allowed in or smuggled past guards. Maurice said he had "spirits" in his nightstand and reported the schnapps holdings of the rowdies on the first floor: "A bottle of Steinhäger arrived, a bottle of Enzian arrived, a slew of bottles of schnapps and liqueur arrived...our guards' mouths started watering when they saw what we had in our liquor cabinet." How all this contraband slipped through security inspections is not entirely clear—except in one case: Kallenbach's case, specifically, his case of malaria.

During World War I, Kallenbach had picked up malaria while serving in swampland in Macedonia. Even years later, he sometimes fell into a fever on hot days. Somewhere it was written that if quinine could not quell the fever, "the daily intake of the strongest possible dose of alcohol would increase its effectiveness," claimed the patient.[10] With records to prove his illness and a prison rule allowing alcohol for medicinal purposes, Kallenbach obtained permission to receive booze. If his story is to be believed, he ordered a bottle of cognac from home and it arrived quickly, to the general excitement of the fortress gang.

The rules read that the patient could receive a single glass per day of the liquor, and that a guard had to pour the liquor into the glass. Lacking a cognac snifter, Kallenbach grabbed a water glass and proceeded to the guard station, where the bottle with his name on it was now under lock and key. Kallenbach's self-appointed legal adviser, Hermie Fobke, went along. The fast-talking law student was able to convince the guard that the water glass fell legally under the rules' definition of "glass" and should be filled to the top, which it was. The two slipped hurriedly back into the main dayroom, where everyone awaited the outcome of the malaria gambit. All the other prisoners entreated Kallenbach to let them pass the golden liquid around so they could at least "get a close look" and maybe even "inhale a whiff" of its heady fragrance. The end of this game is easy to predict: by the time the glass made the rounds and returned to its owner, it was empty. "Fobke and I didn't get anything!" recalled Kallenbach. "I could barely wet my lips with what was left of the much sought-after firewater."[11]

The next night, however, Kallenbach and his unlicensed lawyer became even more creative. They arrived at the guard station not with a water glass but with a half-liter beer mug. Fobke argued that it was not the size or measure of the container that fulfilled the legal definition of "glass," but the basic materials of its construction. Surprisingly, the twisted logic worked and the two sly foxes walked away with all the cognac left in the bottle. According to Kallenbach, numerous other prisoners suddenly recalled deadly diseases they had contracted, and high-proof hooch began filling up the guards' cabinets. One "insatiable inmate" had himself sent a goldfish bowl that he wanted to have legally declared a "glass." Even Fobke balked at that.

Among their subterfuges, the Landsberg inmates also flouted the prison's prohibition on political symbols by getting their hands on a Nazi Party flag—the swastika. When unsupervised, they hung it on the dayroom wall. How the banned banner made it into the prison is uncertain, though one suspects an inside job, especially in light of numerous claims that the guards and prison staff were gradually being won over to Hitler's cause and even wept when he was released. But the mischievous malefactors had to avoid detection. The moment anyone heard a guard approaching—one guard had the habit of jangling his bundle of keys as he walked—the inmates swiftly rolled up their flag and stashed it beneath the claw-foot bathtub. It seems they were never caught.

In addition to importing hard drink and an illegal flag, the men of the fortress could order in everyday necessities like shoe polish or writing paper—or even food items such as butter or a tin of herring—if they had funds in their accounts. A prison guard took orders every afternoon between 1 and 2 p.m. Hemmrich even purchased a large water glass for Hitler who said he needed it for the daily gargling of his throat, still irritated from the World War I gas attack, wrote Hemmrich.[12] Since there were no specific limitations on what the inmates might order, the legalistic Fobke decided once again to test the limits of the system. He ordered strawberry ice cream with whipped cream on top.

Nobody was ready for this. Fobke had already prepared a complex legal argument under which he would no longer be medically "fit for imprisonment" if he did not get his cold treat. Rather than telling Fobke to take a hike, the Bavarian judicial system—which ran not only the courts but also the prisons—convulsed. Calls, letters, and memos. The buck was passed around. Everybody knew the Hitler gang could make trouble, and nobody wanted to run afoul of its members. Finally from on high came a finding that "in the interest of the health and fitness for imprisonment of Inmate Fobke," a one-time exception would be made. Hermie could have his ice cream. By then, of course, he had had his fun. He told them to forget about it.[13]

One of the greatest perks of Club Landsberg was access to the long garden that ran alongside the outer wall near the fortress building. A rectangle of grass nearly two hundred yards long was lined on one side by trees and shrubs, with a small vegetable garden at the far end. By early spring crocuses and amaryllis were blossoming, and fruit trees had popped into bloom. "We were out there without watchers, at least not that we could see," noted Maurice. (In fact, the men were well watched through slits in a small tower behind a high hedge. At one end of the garden stood a sign announcing BORDER! which meant what it said.)

The garden had two gravel walkways. One ran alongside a row of fruit trees, wide enough for several people to walk abreast. Here Hitler often strolled back and forth with Hess, Maurice, or other inmates, usually in animated conversation. One photo shows both Hitler and Maurice in shorts, Hitler wearing his slouch hat and looking slightly porky in his lederhosen, their heads bent in what appears to be intense discussion as they pass the blooming fruit trees.[14] Another narrow gravel strip ran hard by the outer prison wall. It became known as the "Hitler Path," because Hitler so often walked there alone, absorbed in his own thoughts. The two paths—and a bench in the garden—became new venues for Hitler's out-loud thinking, convenient platforms for expounding his views and working out his political convictions and rehearsing the ways he liked to say—and write—them. "Large parts of *Mein Kampf* may have been composed on these paths," speculated Hemmrich.[15]

The younger men spent much of their time in the garden play-ing soccer or *Schlagball*—a game similar to baseball—or doing gymnastics on equipment sent to them by the local gym club: paral-lel bars, a horizontal bar, a high jump, and a vaulting horse. The prisoners were allowed six hours per day in the garden. At the stroke of 8 a.m., the doors from the fortress building to the outside were unlocked, and the men hurried into the fresh air. Early mornings, Dr. Weber—commander of the Bund Oberland and a veterinarian who seemed to know a lot about human health as well—held a strict roll call and led exercises in a program of steadily increasing demands and challenges. "Only long after we were free did we grasp the absolute necessity of these early morning exercises, which seemed to us too tough at the time," wrote Kallenbach. "They were the only effective antidote to the onset of mind-numbing indifference and 'prison psychosis.'"[16]

Hitler initially participated in gymnastics but soon dropped the activity, focusing almost entirely on his book, wrote Hess. Kallenbach said Hitler's still-healing dislocated shoulder excused him from physical activity. But Hanfstaengl told a slightly different story. During one of his visits to Hitler, Putzi was struck by the Nazi leader's weight gain—Hitler had added eleven pounds since coming to prison, hitting 170 pounds.[17] After all, Hanfstaengl wrote, Hitler's room "looked like a delicatessen" with all the fruit, wine, and gifts of food. "You really must take part in some of the gymnastic exercises and prison sports," urged Hanfstaengl. "No," replied Hitler. "It would be bad for discipline if I took part in physical training. A leader cannot afford to be beaten at games."[18]

During competitive sports, Hitler's role was that of sideline spectator or referee. He refereed soccer matches among his men and, on one occasion, attended a boxing match that got out of hand. A punching bag had come with the gym equipment, and one inmate, Edmund Schneider, gave boxing lessons. "Hitler showed great interest in this especially hard, masculine sport," Kallenbach wrote. So an exhibition match was organized. The short but game Fobke challenged the much taller Maurice to a friendly fight. The match escalated quickly, however, when both men became overeager and began whaling wildly at each other. Fobke concentrated on Maurice's midsection while the taller boxer let loose on Maurice's head. Finally, other men jumped in to pull apart the bleeding fighters. Fobke's left eye was closed and turning purple; Maurice could barely breathe. Hitler, meanwhile, loved it. "I rarely saw him laugh as heartily as he did when the two separated boxers were presented to him," wrote Kallenbach.[19]

Nonetheless, following the bloody match, boxing was dropped from the outdoor curriculum and wrestling was added, followed later by jujitsu, both leading to frequent pulled muscles and tendons.

While Hitler was clearly the most serious and studious of the fortress inmates, he still occasionally participated in the fun and games of the younger prisoners. He was drawn in to a long evening of surprise entertainment on June 17, his "name day"—an occasion celebrated in Germany with all the ceremony of a birthday. Secretly decorating the first floor dayroom, the fortress men prepared a series of sketches, songs, poems, and miming that, according to Kallenbach, had Hitler laughing and applauding for hours (one poem "sentenced" Hitler to travel throughout Germany "beating up Jews and Reds"). By the end of the evening, the men decided to stage such jolly diversions every Saturday night—and to create a house newspaper.

The *Landsberger Ehrenbürger* (Landsberg Honorary Citizen) became, for a while, the weekly newspaper of the Hitler crew. It was somehow copied by hectograph and, according to several sources, kept secret from prison officials. Typically it contained three or four pages of tongue-in-cheek commentary on the oddities of life in prison and the prospect of the Nazis someday reviving their cause. Like the entertainment on Hitler's name day, creative doggerel and feisty jokes laced the pages. And there was usually an essay, often of a historical nature, by Hitler, sometimes including drawings by him.

Alas, all but one copy of the *Honorary Citizen* was lost. Because the newspaper was supposedly secret, copies were limited and hidden. But when one inmate carelessly referred to it in a letter home (which was of course read by the censors), the guards executed a raid. Hearing the approaching guards, the fortress rowdies quickly threw all copies of their little newspaper into the burning stove in their dayroom. All but one copy went up in smoke.

The rescued "newspaper" was issue number six; it celebrated on August 1 the tenth anniversary of the beginning of World War I. The issue, which Kallenbach reprinted in his book, contained eighteen articles and poems filled with war remembrances. Kriebel wrote about the "Mobilization of the Second Company." Fobke penned a poem called "The Dead." Dr. Weber related the successful attack by the First Bavarian Snowshoe Battalion on a snowed-in French position in the Vosges Mountains of Alsace. Hess wrote a 140-line poem called "Facing Verdun," the story of the famous battle in northern France where he had been wounded.[20] He read it aloud, stirring an emotional response from the assembled Landsberg crew at a special dinner on the war's anniversary.

But Hitler wrote nothing for this issue of the *Honorary Citizen*. He was busy preparing his longer work to share with the outside world.

CHAPTER ELEVEN

The Holy Book

"Without my imprisonment, Mein Kampf *would never have been written."*

—ADOLF HITLER, 1942[1]

"I've decided to withdraw from politics."

Those stunning words came at the end of a long letter Hitler sent on June 16, 1924, to Ludolf Haase, a young Nazi in the small university town of Göttingen. Haase was a friend of Fobke's and one of the activists in the restless northern German wing of the party. Disgusted with the backbiting and disarray in the Nazi Party, Hitler had decided to quit the whole mess, he said, until his release from prison would give him the chance to be "a *real* leader again." From now on, wrote Hitler, "no one has the right to speak in my name."

Hitler's unexpected exit reverberated throughout the banned Nazi Party and the *völkisch* movement across Germany. His letter was fervently discussed in such faraway places as Hamburg and Greifswald on the Baltic coast, where splinter groups were sprouting. Even with all the party upheaval, people asked, How could Hitler just quit politics?

Their answer came soon enough. Hitler sent a resignation statement to the *Völkischer Kurier*,[2] a Munich newspaper that was partially filling the void of the Nazi Party's now-banned *Völkischer Beobachter*. The newspaper ran a front-page box reporting Hitler's decision to step down from Nazi Party leadership, noting that he "asks that his former followers please refrain from visiting Landsberg.... The reason for this decision is the current impossibility of exercising political leadership.... Also, Herr Hitler needs time for his work on a comprehensive book."[3]

There it was—Hitler was writing a book. He not only wanted the disputatious party squabblers out of his life, he wanted time and peace for writing. He now had something else to do besides referee quarrels among his would-be rivals and successors. "He's showing everybody on the outside that they can't function without him," wrote Hess.[4] The party that Hitler was quitting was broken, no longer healthy. While his rivals depleted their energies with infighting, he withdrew from the field to consolidate his own strength. Staying out of the mud fights would help clear the way for an unchallenged comeback later on. "[Hitler] considers the cart hopelessly off track," wrote Fobke in a subsequent letter to Haase. "He knows that he's going to have to start from scratch once he's free."[5]

With Nazi Party problems now someone else's to solve, Hitler was free to write. Whether he was conscious of entering the long lineage of prison memoirists—from Marco Polo to Martin Luther to Sir Walter Raleigh—is impossible to know. Yet somehow he sensed it was time to turn himself into one, cranking out a classic of the genre, a message-driven outpouring of pent-up passions and beliefs that had been percolating for several years and needed to be channeled between two covers.

In taking over the Nazi Party in 1920, Hitler had cavalierly elbowed aside its founders and demanded unlimited executive power. In following his dream of a triple-bank-shot putsch and a Mussolini-like march on Berlin, he had stuck with his grandiose idea until it left him injured, jailed, and with a banned political party. In taking on the weight of German justice in a Bavarian courtroom, he had rolled all his dice—and won, at least symbolically. Hitler always went for the big play.

So it was with *Mein Kampf.* Hitler plunged into his writing project with the same "brutal fanaticism" that he had invoked during his trial as a necessity for his movement. He was not writing a simple political tract, or an entertaining memoir, or a typical party program: he was writing his version of a bible (though he never called it that), an ideological guide for the sum of life, the catechism for a new secular religion. His new creed was National Socialism, and *Mein Kampf* (*My Struggle*) would be its scripture.

In two volumes and nearly eight hundred pages, Hitler would not only present a vision of Germany's political future, but declaim, with a dilettante's fluency, on any subject that occurred to him, be it the "sole" purpose of marriage ("increase and preservation of the species and the race"), the "art of proper reading" ("to fit into one's existing picture"), and the importance of combating syphilis ("*the* task of the nation"). Except for the overwrought syphilis part, he said years later, he would not change a thing in *Mein Kampf.* He would also carefully craft an image of himself, through an autobiographical structure, as a man uniquely endowed to remake the world in Germany's favor—a politician-philosopher chosen by fate to lead the nation (and eventually the world) in its darkest hour.

Though he claimed that he was addressing his work "not to strangers" but to heart-and-blood "adherents of the movement," Hitler said he decided to set down the basic elements of his political doctrine "for all time"—hardly the description of an internal party document.[6] On the contrary, it was as though Hitler were carving his words into stone. Even as he was hammering it out in his room at Landsberg, Hitler's writing had, to him, the gravitas of a holy book. Like a divine voice from on high delivering final wisdom to his messenger—God to Moses—Hitler was channeling his chaotic years of reading and speaking onto the written page. He was both god and messenger. With almost no bows to the sources of his mostly derivative thinking, Hitler's book does indeed have a biblical tone of oracular truth.

In biblical terms, Hitler's four months at the typewriter were his forty days in the wilderness. Just as Jesus (according to the Gospels) came out of the desert and its satanic temptations with a clarified sense of self and dedication, Hitler came out of his moment of internal exile—and the trials of failure and scorn—with a heightened and hardened sense of his destiny and of his capability to lift Germany out of the valley of misery. Whether he anticipated that the months of removal from the churn of politics and a forced period of thinking and writing would have such a clarifying effect on him is unknown. But they did.

Even as he transformed the raw clay of his political instincts into a coherent if exceedingly broad-gauged doctrine, Hitler was transforming himself into his own truest believer. Hitler's "ruthless systematizing power" grew from the "crystallizing experiences"[7] of his time in Landsberg, wrote historian Hugh R. Trevor-Roper in his renowned 1953 essay, "The Mind of Adolf Hitler."[8] Much of the crystallizing took place in Hitler's room in the fortress building as he poured forth the pages of *Mein Kampf* (then still known only as "my book" or "my work"). "I gained clarity about a lot of things that I had previously understood only instinctively," said Hitler.

During this time, he later said, he acquired enough knowledge and understanding "to provide my philosophy with a natural, historical foundation." In short, he found the "facts" to support his prejudices and to convince himself that he was right about everything; his self-belief no longer "could be shaken by anything." This completed Hitler's conversion, in his own mind, from "drummer"—chief propagandist—to leader. This is the period that can be said to have made Hitler into the man who would not rest until he had Germany in his grip. This was the final step toward self-legitimization, the intellectual certification that was missing from Hitler's résumé.

Hitler was also busily creating a Great Man persona, with himself as the unnamed candidate for that job. He emphasized the paramount importance of "personality" in political change. "Personality cannot be replaced," he wrote. "It is not mechanically trained, but inborn by God's grace." The right personality was required for what Hitler called "Germanic democracy" in which "the leader is elected but then enjoys unconditional authority." This is the *Führerprinzip*— the Führer principle that would lead to Hitler's unchallenged control once he achieved power.

At the outset of his project, Hitler's focus had been on revenge. With more than four years of grievances to redress against all manner of adversaries, Hitler wanted to attack every establishment figure, left-wing political force, or national government official who'd ever crossed him. But by late May, Hitler had begun sliding away from his revenge theme and into an autobiographical structure. He began conflating ideology and autobiography. Hitler was now at the "interface between rabid party leader and ideological theorist," noted Beierl and Plöckinger, and he was moving increasingly toward the theorist.[9] To rationalize his standing as political philosopher, Hitler had to polish, and sometimes seriously embellish, his personal story to fit the new image that he was creating. His very birth in a small Austrian town smack on the German border served in *Mein Kampf*'s opening line as his first claim to be a child of Providence. In language almost identical to the words he had typed in his earlier five-page beginning, Hitler wrote: "Today it seems to me providential that Fate should have chosen Braunau on the Inn as my birthplace. For this little town lies on the boundary between two German states which we of the younger generation have made it our life's work to reunite by every means at our disposal." Historian Kershaw noted, "His almost mystical faith in himself as walking with destiny...dates from this time."[10]

As he wrote the tale of his early years in Vienna, Hitler created a mini-bildungsroman* of hard luck and hard lessons, which led inevitably to his hatred for polyglot legislatures ("a wild, gesticulating mass...screaming in every key"), mongrel nations, Marxism, and Jews; the autobiography was already fitting the politics that were yet to come. There is an "innocent abroad" quality to Hitler's alleged discovery of his anti-Semitism through his first sighting of an Eastern Jew in a caftan ("Is this a Jew?...Is this a German?"), followed by his scales-fell-from-my-eyes realization that the Social Democratic Party (synonymous with Marxists in Hitler's view) "was run by Jews."[11] His bitter disagreements with fellow workers on a construction site exposed, in Hitler's telling, the tyranny of the Socialists, who "made use of...terror and violence" by forcing him "to leave the building at once or be thrown off the scaffolding."[12] Whether true or not, this version of events makes for better story-

---

* Even Hitler's title for his Vienna chapter, "*Wiener Lehr- und Leidensjahre*" ("Apprenticeship Years and Suffering in Vienna"), echoes the title of the original bildungsroman, *Wilhelm Meisters Lehrjahre* (*Wilhelm Meister's Apprenticeship*), written by Germany's greatest man of letters, Johann Wolfgang von Goethe (1749–1832). Hitler's chapter title also neatly brings in Goethe's most popular novel, *Die Leiden des jungen Werther* (*The Sorrows of Young Werther*). If intentional, this subtle choice of words was a clever piece of self-marketing.

telling than admitting he gathered his ideas from the political tracts and free newspapers he found in Vienna's grungy slum cafés, which, to some historians, seems more likely the case.[13] Equally suspect is Hitler's claim that he fell on his knees "with an overflowing heart"[14] when Germany declared war in 1914 since it gave him a chance to fight for his fatherland (Germany, not Austria). Similarly, Hitler's alleged road-to-Damascus decision to take on the Jews, which he describes in a way that makes it sound fated, comes as the perfect end to his war story and Germany's 1918 revolution. A novelist could hardly have done better.

In the prison, Hitler had now near-perfect conditions to achieve the task he had set for himself. With his Nazi Party duties shed and the visitor stream diminished, he could set as a goal the completion of his book before his expected parole date of October 1. He was burrowing deeper into his own head, into the small world of his little room in the fortress building, and into the airy constructs of world history that derived from the autodidact's sprawling reading habits. He was fitting together the "mosaic stones," as he liked to call them, that he had gathered along the way from the diverse material that passed through his brain. He culled nuggets from a body of ideas that included, according to political scientist Barbara Zehnpfennig, a dizzying array of sources: Schopenhauer's and Nietzsche's metaphysics of will; Karl Haushofer's and Friedrich Ratzel's geopolitics; Arthur de Gobineau's, Houston Stewart Chamberlain's, and Paul de Lagarde's anti-Semitism and racism; Thomas Malthus's population theories; Charles Darwin's theories of survival; Gustave Le Bon's teachings on mob psychology; and, of course, Karl Marx. Hitler also leaned on conspiracy theories like *The Protocols of the Elders of Zion;* borrowed from post-Spenglerian theories of history such as anti-modernism, anti-liberalism, and anti-capitalism; dabbled in obscure and occult explanations of the universe; and absorbed ideas about a "conservative revolution." Hitler was, in his way, a scatterbrained renaissance man who believed that when he reassembled the booty of his intellectual piracy, the new version possessed an internal consistency that gave it the strength of religious belief. "He adopted almost nothing in its original form," wrote Zehnpfennig. "He simply took the parts he could use and fitted them to the frame that he had already created."[15]

And he attributed almost nothing to anyone. Giving credit to the sources of his thinking would have vitiated the godlike sound of his own voice. Hitler was used to speaking in the omniscient tone before masses of people; why change that in a book? As he explained in *Mein Kampf,* "the magical power of the spoken word" has its greatest impact when kept simple: one enemy, one idea, one solution (Hitler's enemy was the Jews and his solution was their removal.)[16] Likewise in a book: offering complex explanations or comparative versions of one's ideas would only undermine them and distract readers.

For all its strewn writing and wandering anecdotes, Hitler's book offered clear clues to his future actions. The book was dismissed for decades by postwar critics as a mishmash of "grubby jargon,"[17] a "chaos of banalities,"[18] and "superficial and triumphalist accounts"[19] of his life story, and it was all of these things. Yet Hitler's work presented, for those willing to put together its scattered pieces, a worldview that gave meaning and understanding to all that followed later. "Rarely in history — if ever — has a ruler so precisely described in writing before coming to power what he did after coming to power as did Adolf Hitler," wrote historian Eberhard Jäckel.[20] In the space of four months — and drawing on four years of speechmaking as well as his lengthy statements at his trial — Hitler was able to lay out most of a political dogma that had at least some structure and logic. The degree to which this scheme led directly to Auschwitz, however, has been hotly debated by historians.*

Hitler's intellectual starting point was apocalyptic: Western civilization, and especially Germany, he believed, faced downfall. In an atmosphere shaped by the pessimistic thesis of Oswald Spengler's 1918 runaway bestseller, *The Decline of the West,* Hitler was playing the "politics of cultural despair," as historian Fritz Stern described the prevailing mood. Fueled by writer Arthur Moeller van den Bruck's proposals for a German "special path" between eastern Communism and western capitalism under a newly invented label — the "Third Reich" — this unsettled political climate was ideal for Hitler's portentous predictions and offers of salvation. He proferred an instant "leap from despair to utopia," wrote Stern.[21] In this Hitlerian vision, only radical measures could halt the collapse. World War I had left Europe reeling and the entire existing order threatened by the sole winner of the horrible conflagration: Marxism. The Russian revolution had exposed itself as a murderous perversion and declared itself a world revolution. Germany was its next target. Both Lenin and Trotsky had spoken openly of Germany as the coming prize: "Without the victory of the revolution in Germany we are doomed," Trotsky quoted Lenin as having said in 1918.[22] This Marxist threat, Hitler wrote in *Mein Kampf,* was controlled by Bolsheviks who were "a band of Jewish writers and stock market thieves."[23] The Marxist virus had already infected Germany in the

---

* One school of thought, the intentionalists, has argued that Hitler foretold and directly ordered the Holocaust — the top-down theory. The other, called functionalists, has contended that the killing began at much lower levels through local officials or small-unit military commanders and expanded into mass murder — the bottom-up theory. Today there is growing consensus that ideology drove action and that *Mein Kampf* was the blueprint.

form of Social Democrats, the largest political party, and by Communists as well (much smaller but still able to poll 10 percent in national elections). The enemy was inside the gates.

The only antidote to these destructive forces, in Hitler's eyes and in his book, was the nation—united, pure-blooded, ready to fight. Fighting, in fact, was nature's imperative for cleansing, growth, and survival. "Struggle is always a means for improving a species' health and power of resistance and, therefore, a cause of its higher development," he wrote in *Mein Kampf*.[24] The strength of the nation lay in the concept of race; only a pure race, not degraded by outside elements, could fight and win. Thus, one must raise national (racial) consciousness and expel any impure elements, which meant Jews. No matter how hard they tried, claimed Hitler, Jews could never be Germans (or any other nationality). Their claim to be only a "religious community," he wrote, was "the first great lie." They were, instead, a separate race—a condition that could not be overcome by geography (living for generations in Germany), language (speaking only German), or even religious affiliation (converting to Christianity). As a race, a Jew was always a Jew (and a German was always a German). And fighting the Jews, for Hitler, was a veritable religious calling. "In resisting the Jew, I am doing the work of the Lord," he wrote.[25]

Much of this analysis in *Mein Kampf* was based on simplistic interpretations of serious science—as when Hitler equated human races to animal species and their undiluted mating habits. He also created specious categories of races that are "culture-creating" (Aryans), "culture-bearing" (Japanese), or "culture-destroying" (Jews). This typology provided a handy ranking system with no serious grounding in science but with a convincing pseudo-scientific sound to a mass audience. Still, the basics of Hitler's worldview added up to a political system that would justify three massive undertakings:

war on the West, war on Russia, and the Holocaust. He stuck with this scheme until the very end.

For his worldview to have credibility, wrote Zehnpfennig, Hitler felt he had to make it an ideological antipode to Marxism that was just as complex and detailed as Marx's. Against Marx's emphasis on man's ability to overcome nature for his own purposes, for instance, Hitler offers the power of natural law, which dictates racial division and, ultimately, race war. Against the Marxian goal of perpetual peace, National Socialism dictates eternal struggle. Marxism rests on the concept of class warfare, Hitlerism on eliminating class divisions through a single-minded "national community." Marxists believe that turning from community to the creation of private property was the original sin; Hitler claims that turning from the naturally dictated racial separation was the original sin, leading to race mixing and degeneration. Marx posits economic determinism; *Mein Kampf* elevates *der Wille*—human willpower—to determinative power.[26]

This swirl of ideas animated Hitler's long periods of seclusion in the relative quiet of the fortress building's second floor. During what became a very warm summer, he began spending less time in the garden and with the other inmates. He also stopped reading to his followers from his book drafts after the evening meal. Kriebel and Weber complained, but Hitler gave them the excuse that "the link to the previous chapters had been broken." Hess offered a more mundane explanation: "He just doesn't feel like reading in the evening because he wants to go to bed at nine o'clock [and] reading aloud will cost him several hours of not being able to get to sleep."[27]

Contrary to legend, Hess did not take dictation; Hitler wrote the book himself "with two fingers" on his little typewriter, noted Ilse Pröhl Hess years later (she had married Hess).[28] But having Hess as his tea-bringer and sounding board was a huge advantage for Hitler. Hess became Hitler's first reader or, more frequently, first listener, as Hitler worked his way through his ideas. Hitler always wrote like he spoke, say the critics of his prose, so it must have helped the writer to hear himself delivering his text to Hess's willing ears. That may not have made for graceful writing, as his literary detractors are quick to note, but it gave Hitler his rhythm, balance, and perspective. And it was a long perspective. With his little Remington, Hitler was cranking out the pages. Always verbose, he could hold audiences in mass gatherings for an uncommonly long time; he must have thought the same principle applied to his writing. People, he thought, could take Hitler in large doses.

While he was no longer reading to the after-dinner assemblage, Hitler was now reading often to Hess. "When he finishes a chapter, he comes directly to me," Hess wrote. A relatively educated man with an upper-bourgeois background, Hess was the best Boswell Hitler could have wanted. Slim, tallish, with wavy dark hair and deep-set eyes, Hess was both handsome and thoughtful, though some found him to be oddly silent, obsessively neat, and jealously protective of his closeness to Hitler. Hess was one of the very few of Hitler's inner circle to share in private the familiar *Du* greeting, the intimate form of "you" then reserved in German for family, children, and very close friends.[29] As Hitler's Praetorian guard, Hess helped to keep the curious away, a role that would only grow in coming years, leading to Hess's appointment in 1933 as deputy Führer of the Nazi Party and Hitler's right-hand man. Hess's self-appointed role in prison naturally led to frictions with other prisoners who found him neurotic and distant. When Hanfstaengl visited Landsberg, he noticed that Hess "only grudgingly left Hitler's side while I was talking with him....He could not bear to see Hitler exposed to any views other than his own and was always trying to distract attention."[30]

As a Hitler devotee, Hess was occasionally swept away by Hitler's drafts. After one reading, Hess wrote to Pröhl that he was so taken by the "logic, liveliness, colorful and beautiful language" that he had to "exhale when the tension was released at the end, just like after one of his best speeches." Hitler apparently heightened the effect of his words with his typically energetic presentation — "his constant facial expressions and hand gestures underline it," recalled Hess, who considered such verbal playacting one of Hitler's charms. "No matter what he does or says, he remains completely himself — he can't escape it!" Even Hitler was quite pleased with himself, "beaming like a little boy, sitting in the wicker chair in [Hess's] room." Hess called it an odd "mixture of cold-blooded, mature superiority and uninhibited childishness!"[31]

Hitler's writing reflected the dramatic role World War I had played in his life. His emotional core still rested to a large degree on the brutal and disillusioning experience of World War I. He and many of his followers — especially those in prison with him — were, after all, the lost soldiers of a lost war. Bound together by their grim frontline years, they took political energy from their belief that the left-wing traitors at home had stabbed the soldiery in the back; their common training in combat and arms gave their politics its militaristic and violent cast. With World War I as his formative period, Hitler's fundamental experience of the public arena was the battlefield. This can only have fed his later view of politics as a theater of war, not as an arena of compromise and parliamentary debate, which he scorned.[32]

To Hitler, politics was the continuation of war by other means. Struggle and warfare were to him the natural, not the exceptional, state. "Man has grown great in eternal struggle and will go under in eternal peace," he wrote in *Mein Kampf*.[33] If he had a wish for the

German people, Hitler later said, it was that they would "experience a war every fifteen to twenty years."[34]

As he typed away, Hitler was often reliving his battlefield experience. He recaptured the intensity of conflict with a vivid recollection of marching off to battle in 1914. Reading from his draft to Hess, he evoked the euphoria experienced by many German soldiers during the first heady days of the conflict. In Hitler's case, the passage into war took place on a train that was carrying the Sixteenth Bavarian Reserve Infantry Regiment up the Rhine River and westward into the already blood-soaked fields of Flanders. Hitler had written and then rewritten all or parts of the chapter when he asked Hess to listen to what he had drafted. Hess recalled the moment in a letter to Pröhl:

> *He tells about…the journey along the Rhine…the train filled with a regiment of young volunteers passing the Niederwald German Reich Memorial lit up by the sun rising over a gentle fog, the guys beginning to sing "The Watch on the Rhine"—not long afterwards the first greetings of death sing and whistle at them. Regiment after regiment of young Germans storms ahead. Suddenly far down the right flank come the distant sounds of* "Deutschland, Deutschland über alles," *growing stronger and stronger. More and more men pick up the song and pass it on until the entire front is lustily singing it. But the first pellets begin whipping through the singing men, mowing down the flower of Germany. Still, the singing does not stop. The young soldiers perhaps did not know how to fight as well as the others, but they certainly knew how to die. The Tribune* [Hess's nickname for Hitler] *had begun reading slower, more haltingly.… he was pausing longer and longer until finally he just lowered the page, put his head in his hand and sobbed—*

"I hardly need tell you that at that point I had also lost my composure!" wrote Hess.[35]

In almost exactly the same words and tone as it appears in Hess's letter, and with the same emotional impact, Hitler's story of going to war appeared in *Mein Kampf*. Clearly the ex-soldier was willing to risk being maudlin in order to capture a mood and a moment that, he rightly believed, would strike a chord with readers—even if he had to butcher the truth, combining events that stretched over nine days and included no singing of *"Deutschland, Deutschland über alles."*[36] Nor was Hitler afraid, in this part of his increasingly autobiographical draft, to be self-revealing. Shortly after the scene on the battlefield, Hitler admitted to fears of injury or death that almost broke his will to run messages to the battlefront. "It was all just cowardice," he confessed, according to Hess. "I admit openly and with no shame that I have more sensitive nerves than some people." The man of extremes also transitioned easily from the vulnerable to the vicious. In the same conversation with Hess, Hitler suddenly began speaking bitterly of war wounds and "treason on the home front." He then lashed out: "Oh, I will take merciless and frightful revenge on the first day that I can."*

Sometimes Hitler used Hess's seemingly endless patience just to ramble on about the broad variety of topics that interested him— cars, road-building, mass construction of row houses, the technology of skyscrapers, even the details of armoring warships and the World War I mistakes of the former German navy commander, Grand Admiral Alfred von Tirpitz. "You can always tell that he has

---

* The frightful day came on June 30, 1934, when Hitler used the excuse of a purported putsch attempt by Ernst Röhm to unleash a bloodbath that saw more than one hundred of his presumed enemies, including former chancellor General Kurt von Schleicher, Gustav von Kahr, and Röhm himself cold-bloodedly murdered in the Night of the Long Knives.

studied these things in detail," noted Hess,[37] who said he was convinced that Hitler still had another political life coming. "My conviction comes from daily contact with his teeming brain,"[38] he told Pröhl.

Hitler's concentration could easily have been broken by the constant stream of visitors (150 in April, 154 in May, and 94 in June) and the well-wishers' gifts, not to mention the comradeship and comforts of his special imprisonment. Among those who came to give Hitler succor were Hitler's brother-in-law, Leo Raubal, and Leo's beautiful daughter, Geli. The sixteen-year-old Geli was the daughter of Hitler's half-sister, Angela, and thus his half-niece. Yet when she arrived for a July visit, Hemmrich claims to have seen Hitler kiss her "heartily" on the mouth—she was the only woman to whom he had shown the slightest attraction, wrote Hemmrich.[39] Hitler was years later said to be in love with Geli, who died under mysterious circumstances by a shot from Hitler's pistol in his apartment, where she lived. It was ruled suicide.

Intellectually, Hess sometimes served as more than just Hitler's obedient servant. He was a close disciple of Haushofer, the quirky former Bavarian army general who as a University of Munich professor had developed an elaborate construct of nationalism and geopolitics that few could understand—"clothing simple geography with political mysticism," an American geography professor wrote.[40] But Haushofer's simplest and best-known concept was, at its core, easily grasped: *Lebensraum,* or "living space." Used earlier by another German political geographer, Friedrich Ratzel, and batted around by various nineteenth-century theorists, *Lebensraum* had not yet been widely popularized.

For years, Hitler had been promoting the idea that Germany needed "land and soil" for its future survival. The demand was even part of the little-noticed twenty-five-point Nazi Party program that Hitler had announced in his first Hofbräuhaus speech in 1920. That Germany's new geographic acquisitions would almost certainly come "at the expense of Russia," as Hitler soon wrote in *Mein Kampf,* was hardly a secret. The idea of a *Drang nach Osten*—a push to the east—was an old German refrain, partly a nostalgic revival of historic German expansions six hundred years earlier by the Teutonic knights. But Hitler had never used so elegant and simple a concept as *Lebensraum.*

Through Hess, Hitler had met Haushofer before, but the men had never really trusted each other. Since his teenaged days of rejecting formal education, and his soldier's belief that hard knocks and a few years on a battlefield were "worth thirty years of university education,"[41] Hitler had made no secret of his disdain for "the university parsons," as he liked to call the professoriate. Haushofer, in turn, regarded Hitler as a "half-educated man" and wanted little to do with him directly. "I think he [Haushofer] hates the Tribune," Hess had once written to Ilse Pröhl.[42] When Hess brought the two together in Landsberg, they met only briefly, always in the presence of Hess.[43] Later, however, Haushofer would lend scientific legitimacy to Hitler's expansionist policies during the Third Reich and World War II. (After the war, he came within a hair of being prosecuted as a major war criminal and later committed suicide.)

In early July 1924 Haushofer's intriguing phrase—"living space" (also translatable as "habitat")—was suddenly much talked about at Landsberg, but not fully understood. Heated discussions had broken out among the Hitler crew. "Kriebel and a few others teased me in the garden about the geopolitical *Lebensraum,*" wrote Hess to Ilse Pröhl. "I said, 'Living space is a more or less well-defined piece of the earth with all its life forms and influences.' But Kriebel claimed to be too dumb to understand that.... When the general

[Haushofer] was here on Tuesday, I asked him to write for us a more precise definition."[44] The result that Haushofer delivered was—according to Hess's letter—almost exactly the same thing Hess had said, dressed up in more opaque language.

But that did not matter. What mattered was that, through Hess, the term *Lebensraum* had now gotten into Hitler's slogan-minded brain, where it must have gone off like a flashbulb. This single and singular word encompassed all he had been thinking about German overpopulation, German expansion, and Russian land. The word was a propagandist's dream: positive, clear, self-explanatory, goal-oriented, and tilted toward the future—much more appealing than the inanimate phrase "land and soil" (*Grund und Boden*). Who, in densely populated Germany, would not want more *Lebensraum*? And "living space" was a much nicer way to describe future land-holdings than to call them what they were—targets of conquest. Military invasion was now elevated to a law of nature, and Hitler had a shiny new name for one of his fundamental principles.

Hitler began using *Lebensraum* right away. In July, drafting a chapter called "Munich," he laid out "four paths" by which German foreign policy could solve the country's problem of an alleged net population growth of nine hundred thousand per year without enough land to feed such a rapidly expanding nation. Veiling his intentions in a hypothetical discussion of what German colonial policy should have been before World War I, Hitler clearly chose the same solution he had hinted at in many speeches and in his earlier journal article: a massive land grab in the East. A great deal of land was available only in western Russia, he claimed, which was under-populated (Hitler asserted that Russia had eighteen times more land per capita than did Germany).[45] The region was later called by the Nazis a *Raum ohne Volk,* a space without people. This was a dubious claim but it paired perfectly with the other side of their coin—that the Germans were a *Volk ohne Raum,* a people without space. Thus, the obvious answer: *Lebensraum* for the Germans. It was a classic Hitlerian oversimplification of the facts to fit the theory. But there it was: Germany would conquer and settle the vast semi-empty spaces between the Russian border and the Ural Mountains, filling them with German agricultural settlers. The hapless and hopeless Russians—incapable of turning their land into highly productive modern agriculture—would become an underclass or die out, helped into serfdom or extinction by the merciless German rulers, the new *Herrenvolk,* or master race.

Thus *Lebensraum* became a powerful new concept in Hitler's book, and later became a central pillar of Nazi territorial ambitions and justification for war. Thanks to Hess and Haushofer, Hitler now had an easily digestible term with scientific gloss and positive overtones to add to his expansionist arsenal. Having appeared nowhere in Hitler's eighteen-page outline or in the previously written sections of his book, *Lebensraum* now sprang up repeatedly in Hitler's manuscript, beginning in July.[46] That marked a turning point in the writing of *Mein Kampf* and in the framing of Hitler's future policies.

The *Lebensraum* formulation was also a handy fulcrum for Hitler's corollary argument: that a nation without *Lebensraum* was not a true "culture-creating people," as Hitler liked to call the nations he approved of. The Aryans, of course, and especially the Germans, were culture-creating. The Jews, of course, were not; they were parasites "on the body of other nations." Part of their problem was that they had no *Lebensraum,* he argued. Alleging ahistorically that Jews had never had a country of their own, he dismissed Jews as a wandering band "always searching for new nourishment for [their] race."[47] When Jews settled, they created a state within a state. Since they lived everywhere, they had no well-defined *Lebensraum* anywhere. Even nomads, wrote Hitler in his book, "have a clearly delimited *Lebensraum* which they cultivate with their herds, just not as settled farmers." The Aryans, Hitler claimed, "probably started as nomads."[48]

By August, Hitler was in the midst of a writing marathon. Trying to stave off interruptions, he sent another statement to the *Völkischer Kurier:* "In spite of my previous plea in the press to refrain from visiting me in Landsberg-on-Lech, I still receive numerous outside visitors....I must emphatically repeat my request and will only accept visits that are agreed to in advance."[49] Maurice wrote to a contact asking for understanding that Hitler was not answering his mail; he was under a "colossal mountain of work."[50] In early August, Hess wrote that "the Tribune thinks he'll have his book finished by next week—I don't believe it."[51] Two weeks later, Fobke—who by now was acting as Hitler's link to the North German Nazis and the liaison between the Field Marshal's Hill and the foot soldiers— noted in a letter to a friend in his hometown of Stettin that "it's hard to catch H. now for a conversation, he's working non-stop on his book and doesn't like to be disturbed."[52]

Yet during this August writing rush, Hitler did find time for a detailed conversation with Fobke about a key topic that he was almost certainly just then writing into the book: the melding of the "programmatist" (*Programmatiker*) with the "politician" (*Politiker*).[53] The words can better be translated, without the convenient alliteration, as theorist (or political philosopher) and practical politician. The terms are more or less self-explanatory, but as usual Hitler took several pages to explain them. "The theorist must set the goals for a movement, the politician must implement them," he wrote. "One is guided by eternal truths, the other by current practical realities." The theorist should be the "polar star of curious humanity," insists Hitler.[54] As examples of such great men, Hitler mentions Frederick the Great, Martin Luther, Richard Wagner, and the "founders of religions," which could include Jesus Christ and Muhammad. Without saying it, of course, Hitler was elevating himself into their company.

More important, Hitler saw his appearance on the world stage as something like a millennial coming. "At long intervals of human history," he wrote, "it may occasionally happen that the practical politician and the political philosopher are one. The more intimate the union, the greater are the political difficulties. Such a man does not labor to satisfy demands that are obvious to every small-minded person; he reaches for goals that only a few can see." Such a moment, Hitler implied, had now arrived.

Fobke could not know it—maybe even Hitler did not know it in mid-August—but one of the most revealing sections of *Mein Kampf* had just been composed and discussed. Nowhere else in the book does Hitler more blatantly display his exponentially growing "self-belief," sense of divine calling, and hardening infallibility. His gifts as a politician are manifest, he believes. Nobody else has his combination of practical and philosophical talents.

If there were a single month, a critical pivot point, a precise moment that can be said to be the one that made Hitler in 1924, this was it. It was from this point forward that Hitler "acquired that fearless faith, that optimism and confidence in our destiny that absolutely nothing could shake afterwards," as he put it.[55]

With his claim to the mantle of philosopher-politician—a latter-day "philosopher-king"—Hitler had inserted the keystone into the psychological arch he was building. Like one of his heroes, Napoleon, crowning himself emperor in 1804, Hitler had effectively anointed himself as the great man of his age. Having touched the sword to his own shoulders, Hitler could now make himself the undisputed and unchallengeable leader of his movement—a one-man show uniquely unfettered by advisers' inputs and restraints. From that model grew the Führer myth, the unique form of non-collegial dictatorship with which he later ruled and ruined Germany.

In August, Hitler was rushing to finish his book. Chapter eleven, Hitler's long disquisition on race and Jews—entitled "Nation and Race"—may have been put together out of three different pieces produced at different times.[56] His high-handed description of the "Path of the Jews," for example, had appeared in earlier speeches—but now it went from three basic steps ("court Jew," "people's Jew," "blood Jew") to eleven developmental stages covering eighteen printed pages. This chapter was a critical one in *Mein Kampf,* forming a cornerstone of Hitler's race theories and what eventually led to the Holocaust. With this chapter, Hitler was trying to pull off a massive subterfuge, according to analysts Beierl and Plöckinger. Having first come to rabid anti-Semitism, Hitler was now inventing an elaborate race theory in which to embed his hatred of Jews. Even though the anti-Semitism preceded the generalized theories, "he tried in *Mein Kampf* to make it look the other way around," they write.[57]

In "Nation and Race," Hitler bared for all to see his conviction that "the stronger must dominate and not blend with the weaker." Combined with his belief in perpetual struggle as the route to national and racial health, Hitler had his fundamental justifications for war, a renewing and cleansing force that sorted the wheat from the chaff. "Those who want to live, let them fight, and those who do not want to fight in this world of eternal struggle do not deserve to live," he wrote.[58] Foreshadowing his future eliminationist eugenics policies, Hitler added: "All who are not of good race in this world are chaff."[59]

Such brutal racial judgments—and worse—can be found all over *Mein Kampf.* At least six hundred words, lines, or sections of the book are driven by hatred of Jews.[60] Yet Hitler also claimed, in his Vienna chapter, that he arrived at his anti-Semitism only after long "inner soul struggles." He even talked about it with Hess, who described the conversation in a letter to his friend, Professor Haushofer. "I had no idea that [Hitler] wrestled his way to his present position on the Jewish question only after a hard inner battle," wrote Hess. "He kept having doubts about whether or not he was doing the right thing, and he said that even today he expresses himself differently in small groups of educated people than in front of a mass audience, where he has to take the most radical position."

If Hitler at this point was still willing to moderate his anti-Semitism "in small groups of educated people," that would certainly change soon. When a Czech Nazi named Kugler came to visit Hitler a few weeks later, the Czech asked the leader if being in prison and writing a book had in any way affected his position on fighting the Jewish threat. "Oh, yes," replied Hitler. "I have in fact changed my view on how to combat Jews. I've seen that so far I've been too mild!" Working on his book, he said, had shown him that in future "the harshest weapons" must be used to fight the Jews, because, after all, "Judaism is the pestilence of the world!"[61]

Hitler's transformation from hotheaded revolutionary to long-view political player was a work in progress. Earlier that spring he had told Kurt Ludecke, a Nazi supporter and world-traveled fund-raiser who visited Hitler in Landsberg, "We must follow a new line of action....Instead of working to achieve power by an armed coup, we shall have to hold our noses and enter the Reichstag against the Catholics and Marxist deputies. If out-voting them takes longer than out-shooting them, at least the results will be guaranteed by their own constitution."[62] Ludecke called Hitler's change of direction a shifting "from the true north of idealism to the magnetic north of realism."[63] This moment "truly marked the turning point for the Party," wrote Ludecke in 1938.[64]

These developments were a toxic shift to some of Hitler's followers. Hitler soon assured Hermie Fobke that he was "still fighting against participation in elections but that he had learned a lot from events."[65] The dutiful Fobke communicated this muddled and ambiguous sentiment to his contacts among the North German Nazis. By the autumn, Hitler was becoming more explicit, writing into the final pages of the first volume of *Mein Kampf* his new dictum: parliament is a terrible thing, but we must join it to kill it. "Our movement is antiparliamentary, and even our participation in a parliamentary institution can only serve the purpose of destroying and removing it."[66] In the 1930s, Hitler was true to his word.

As he completed volume one of *Mein Kampf,* Hitler's confidence was soaring. He extolled the power of the skilled propagandist to sway both the intelligentsia and the "lower strata" with "primitiveness of expression." "Among a thousand speakers there is perhaps only a single one who can manage to speak to locksmiths and university professors at the same time in a form which...actually lashes them into a wild storm of applause."[67] It is obvious whom Hitler had in mind.

His belief in himself as the one and only person capable of reviving Germany was catching—at least in Landsberg Prison. The men, some of them young, were caught up in his persuasive power on the occasions when Hitler joined in group dinners and garden walks. "You can't believe what huge strength and thrilling passion emanates from Adolf Hitler, and the glowing love and respect we all have for him,"[68] wrote prisoner Paul Hirschberg after spending two hours over tea and conversation with Hitler on the young man's twenty-third birthday. Even Hess, who had worked closely with Hitler long before the putsch, admitted that "I've only really gotten to know him here" in prison. "I now have the unique feeling that I'm walking side by side with Germany's 'coming man,'" he wrote.[69] Not everyone, of course, thought Hitler's messianic style and influence on the young men was such a great thing. Prisoner Hans Krüger received an admonishing letter from his father, warning him against the Hitlerian gospel. "You'll see things differently, once you get out and can listen to some other people. It's unbelievable that the court incarcerates you guys with a type like Hitler. He ought to be cooped up somewhere all by himself."[70]

By the end of August, Hitler thought he was moving into the final stages of his book. "He formally asked me to help him with proofing and corrections," Hess wrote at the beginning of the month.[71] As Hitler was becoming excited about the look of a book with his name on it, he told Hess the pages would have gilt edges and he even asked Hess to help him examine leather samples for the book's spine and colors for its covers. Hitler was seeing the finished product before his eyes.

In early September, Hitler was looking a month ahead. On October 1, he would be eligible for parole. He was hoping for release from prison and worried about legal complications, especially the danger that he might be deported to Austria. For his book, he wanted immediate publication. Hitler knew he would need money right away, and not just for his lawyer. He already had his heart set on something else.

CHAPTER TWELVE

A Second Chance

"It is essential that Hitler, as the soul of the völkisch
movement, be deported."

—MUNICH DEPUTY POLICE CHIEF

If Adolf Hitler had a personal weakness for worldly pleasures—
besides his Austrian sweet tooth—it was his love of luxury cars.
From his earliest days in politics, he had craved fine automobiles to
drive him around Munich, giving him comfort and prestige at a
time when both were in short supply. Status derived from the newly
arrived monster machines with their bulging headlights and fold-
back cabriolet roofs. For all of his sometimes backward-looking
politics and anti-modernist attitudes—Hitler denounced the "financial tyranny" of big cities and loathed contemporary art—the Nazi
leader was a high-tech junkie who loved the smooth calibration of a
sumptuous touring car.[1] His fascination with automobiles inspired
his interest in building grand *Autobahnen* and, someday, a "people's
car" that would be called a Volkswagen.

Hitler did not drive. He said he had learned but never put the skill into practice for fear that his enemies would stage a street accident to embarrass him. But Hitler was a happy passenger who loved being chauffeured around the city or into his beloved Alps. He was, by his own accounts, a pesky backseat driver, constantly telling his drivers to speed up or slow down, constantly showing off his knowledge of technical details. Hitler was especially fond of well-engineered machines produced by entrepreneurs like Karl Benz, who called his cars Benz, and Gottlieb Daimler, who named his cars after a rich customer's daughter—Mercedes. (In 1927, Benz and Daimler would join forces to build Mercedes-Benz.) On the biggest night of his political career—the 1923 putsch—Hitler had arrived in a big red Mercedes at the Bürgerbräukeller. But since the day the putsch failed, and he was driven to Putzi Hanfstaengl's villa outside Munich in a doctor's car, Hitler had not even sat in an automobile—only in police vans.

In mid-September 1924 Hitler was still languishing in Landsberg Prison, hoping for parole on October 1. But his release was by no means certain. Pressures were building to hold him behind bars—or to deport him to Austria. Both police and prosecutors were keenly aware of Hitler's potential for repeat mischief, and wanted to keep him off the streets and out of the beer halls. They would soon mount a campaign to annul his parole chances. Knowing his situation could be precarious, Hitler had for months fastidiously maintained good relations with Warden Leybold and his guards, hoping for a perfect "good behavior" report. Yet his lust for a new car led him to a rare lapse that could derail his hopes and plans.

On Friday, September 12, Hitler summoned to the prison Jakob Werlin, the Benz dealer in Munich. Werlin's Benz Garages, as his dealership was called, was conveniently situated near the *Völkischer Beobachter* office in the Schellingstrasse. One can only imagine the sight of Hitler and Werlin in the Landsberg Prison visitors' room, the slick Benz car brochure spread out before them. It is a scene straight out of all the car showrooms in the modern world—with the slight difference that the windows had bars and the customer had no money. What Hitler did have was a book manuscript, a reservoir of hope, and a lot of chutzpah. His only problem, he told car salesman Werlin, was deciding between the forty-horsepower and the fifty-horsepower models. In his wavering, Hitler made a decision that would soon come to haunt him.

Werlin was barely out of the prison when Hitler sat down and banged out a letter to him. The typewriter that wrote *Mein Kampf* now wrote a customer's plea for a better deal on a luxury car. Hitler was haggling by mail with a car salesman. The Benz that had become the car of Hitler's dreams was priced at twenty-six thousand marks.[2] Hitler began by mulling the choices: "Actually I think the 11/40 would meet my needs at the moment. The only thing that concerns me...is the fact that it runs 300 rpm's faster than the 16/50." Hitler feared that the lower-powered vehicle might run hot and need replacing too often. "I won't be able to afford a new car every two or three years," he whined. Like car buyers everywhere, Hitler tried to poormouth his way into a lower price: "Even if I am released on October 1, I can't expect significant income from my work [book] until the middle of December. I'll be forced to get a loan or an advance from somewhere. That's why a couple thousand marks make a big difference. In addition I have to pay my court and trial expenses which already make my hair stand on end....I would be grateful if...you could inquire as to whether I could get a discount."

Hitler wanted Werlin to go to the top—the Benz headquarters in Mannheim, an industrial city on the Rhine. Hitler knew that Werlin had plans to call or to travel there on Monday. A cut rate for Hitler, the famous Nazi, could be granted or denied only by the main office. Hitler wanted to get his supplicating plea into Werlin's hands before that Monday meeting. In his mad rush to procure a car, he took an expedient step: he passed his letter to a prison visitor, Wolfram Kriebel, the young son of Colonel Kriebel. If mailed in Munich on Monday morning, Hitler's letter would reach Werlin on the same day.

It was a reckless error. Giving a letter to a departing prison visitor was blatant smuggling. The act violated censorship rules that required every piece of mail entering or leaving the prison to be examined and read (many letters *to* Hitler had already been confiscated by the censors, including one that contained a poem with the line, "We will break down the slammer's bars"). By skirting the rules, Hitler was jeopardizing a year's worth of model behavior and months of hard labor at his typewriter. If forced to stay at Landsberg and serve his full five-year sentence, Hitler as a political force could dissipate, remembered only as a spasm of extremism in a country still finding its way out of the disaster of world war. With the Nazi movement outside the prison already in a whorl of self-destruction, Hitler's continued absence would almost certainly have doomed his party's players to walk-on, walk-off roles in a Germany that, at that very moment, was beginning to halt inflation and find its political legs.

At first, Hitler's letter traveled under the radar. On the very day that it was mailed — September 15 — Warden Leybold was sending the Bavarian court a status report on his star inmate's time in Landsberg Prison. "He is a man of order and discipline," Leybold wrote, who "makes every effort to adhere to the rules of the institution." With Hitler's earlier hunger strike and shouting matches in mind, Leybold noted that Hitler had "without doubt become more mature and calm than he was." And not only that: Hitler could be expected to behave peaceably upon his release because he had no "ideas of revenge towards officials from the opposite [political] camp who foiled his plans in November 1923." Hitler's face-to-face meetings with the warden over the months had obviously paid off; Leybold, like so many others before him, had been swept off his feet by the Hitlerian force field.

But not everyone was so impressed with Hitler's political behavior and his political intentions. Outside the prison a drumbeat to thwart Hitler's parole was rising. On September 23, the Munich deputy police chief submitted to the court a scathing warning that, if released, Hitler could be expected soon to be up to his old tricks. His very presence on the political playing field could save the now foundering, still-banned Nazi Party and the *völkisch* groups. "He represents a permanent danger to the internal and external security of the state," read the statement. "There should be no discussion of releasing [Hitler]." In the unfortunate event that the Nazi leader were paroled, argued the police, "then it is essential that Hitler, as the soul of the *völkisch* movement, be deported."

With the police report on the table, and with Hitler's possible parole only one week away, there came another blast against releasing Hitler. This one came from State's Attorney Stenglein, the man who had prosecuted Hitler at his trial. Stenglein ominously objected to parole not only for Hitler but also for Weber and Kriebel. "There can be no discussion of the defendants turning away from criminal intentions," Stenglein wrote. He cited violence, kidnapping, and theft during their putsch attempt. The prosecutor's statement even revisited Hitler's 1922 conviction for assaulting political leader Otto Ballerstedt; paroled after serving only one month of a three-month sentence, Hitler had clearly violated his probation by staging a coup attempt. In addition, argued the prosecutor, Hitler was linked to recent illegal efforts by Captain Röhm to reestablish his outlawed paramilitary under a new name, the Frontbann.

In the midst of this barrage, Stenglein learned about Hitler's smuggled letter and others by Weber and Kriebel. He indignantly demanded an explanation from Warden Leybold, who quickly investigated and produced a report showing a history of letter-smuggling by Kriebel and Weber over recent months but only one violation by Hitler. Despite the unsettled state of their case, the court on September 25 ignored both the police and the prosecutor, approving parole for Hitler, Kriebel, and Weber, effective October 1.

Stenglein's office flew into action to try to block the parole. Working over the weekend, Stenglein's lawyers—almost certainly led by Deputy Prosecutor Hans Ehard—generated a long appeal to the court. It began with the smuggled letters (nine examples in all)[3] but also seized on Hitler's clandestine participation in efforts to restart Röhm's new Frontbann. Documents seized in his apartment showed Röhm to be acting in his outside political activities "on assignment from Adolf Hitler," and that Hitler had helped draft the new organization's charter. Even Leybold, madly scrambling to get out of the hole he had dug for himself, began backing and filling. "If my office had been made aware... of the police department's suspicions about efforts by our prisoners to promote a banned organization, our oversight of the letters would have been much stricter," he stated.[4] Yet Stenglein's appeal had its intended effect: it stopped Hitler's hoped-for release on October 1 while the Bavarian Supreme Court pondered the matter.

Meanwhile, the plot surrounding Hitler's possible deportation had thickened. A Bavarian envoy was sent to Vienna to request that Austria agree to Hitler's repatriation. But Austrian chancellor Ignaz Seipel said no; he would not accept Hitler even if he were shoved across the border. Since Hitler had fought in the German army, went the chancellor's reasoning, he was no longer an Austrian. Legally dubious though this argument was, it brought to a halt any hopes of deporting Hitler. The canny Austrians had stolen a march on the Bavarians, effectively deporting Hitler from his native land before their Bavarian cousins could deport him back into it. When this news reached Landsberg Prison, Hitler was "overjoyed," wrote Hess. The two men celebrated that night with a glass of wine.

On October 6, the Bavarian Supreme Court denied Stenglein's appeal, remanding Hitler's case to the lower court. Summarily dismissing the chilling (and subsequently vindicated) warnings of the police and the prosecutors, the Supreme Court tossed the ball back to the court that had once already ruled in Hitler's favor. It would take another two months for the judicial wheels to turn. Hitler was left temporarily in limbo.

A funk had fallen over the prison. Early autumn rain and fog had blanketed Landsberg, turning the cells and hallways cold, damp, and drafty. Gone were the outdoor walks and gardening adventures, the rowdy spirit of brothers in arms, the hopes of some of the men for an early release, and the renewal of the holy Nazi mission. Hitler's mostly young Shock Troops were finally confronting reality: Landsberg had walls and bars that couldn't be moved, even though some of the men occasionally tried rattling the iron staves that kept them penned up. "Gray melancholy, nerve-wracking boredom and a dull tedium set in among us and pressed on the hearts of the inmates," wrote Kallenbach.

A kind of "prison psychosis" was taking hold, Kallenbach reported. "We began to feel empty and burned out." Some men fell into long silences; others argued loudly and got into near-fights until they were separated by other inmates. Hemmrich, the prison guard, also wrote of "a noticeable and edgy stillness" among the prisoners. An inmate named Frosch—which means frog, so his nickname was Fröschl, or Froggie—began behaving oddly, sleepwalking and splashing like a child in the bathtub; there was speculation that he was going crazy.

Even gung-ho troopers began wondering about the purpose of their whole undertaking. Many were receiving bad news from home, since their families had lost their breadwinners to prison; in some cases, they also suffered from the men's now-sullied reputations as foolish radicals who had been thrown in jail. Some wives had been forced to take jobs as housemaids to make ends meet. They could hardly afford train fare to visit their husbands in Landsberg. A few of Hitler's foot soldiers perhaps shared the feelings of one inmate who had written upon arriving at Landsberg Prison: "'Hitler this, Hitler that,' and 'I got this for us,' and 'I got that' — that's what I hear all day from some of the comrades here.... I'm fed up.... That's the last time I'll ever have anything to do with politics. Those on the outside who shout 'Heil!' all day can run their heads against the wall, for all I care. When I get out of here, it's just going to be job and wife and family for me." Other inmates began expressing misgivings even about the grand man himself. "I don't have any doubts," protested one prisoner in a story told by Kallenbach. "But hey, even the Boss could make mistakes, couldn't he? What then?" To these young men, the future looked decidedly bleak and uncertain.

Even Hess's letters no longer rang with admiration for Hitler or mentioned any private readings from the book manuscript. Something had gone sour between the two men. Hess reported "terrible scenes" with Hitler, made worse by the fact that "Maurice naturally takes the side of the lord and master. And W[eber] and K[riebel] don't have a clue about the issue, but that doesn't stop them from jumping to the defense of the 'practitioner' (he may be a good architect and builder but doesn't know squat about technology, even though he's always throwing it into my face)." These were tough words from the man who up until recently had fawned over Hitler more than anyone, and who would later become Hitler's virtual alter ego in running the Third Reich. It is not clear what had caused the rift between the two men, but it was apparently more than momentary. Hess wrote: "It's getting worse and worse between us."

While awaiting further judicial action on his parole, Hitler faced another uncertainty: the publishing status of his book. By October 16, Hitler had written and "signed" the book's dedication to his sixteen followers who had died during the putsch on November 9, 1923. They were all listed by name, including the sole bystander who had been killed but was appropriated by Hitler into a list of "martyrs" and would go down in history as a Nazi supporter. Signing the dedication page suggests that Hitler had completed his manuscript of about 370 pages, and he was already planning a second volume. Parts of the manuscript had made their way to Max Amann, Hitler's publisher. But Amann was in a bind: he had no money.

"It appeared impossible to raise the necessary funds" to publish the book, wrote Amann later.[5] The book market had collapsed during the hyperinflation and had not yet fully recovered. In addition, politically tendentious publishers, especially on the right wing, were heavily dependent on mass meetings to move their products and highlight their writings. Since the putsch, the Nazis and other *völkisch* groups had been banned; there were no mass meetings. "Countless publishing businesses [and] a large number of newspapers went out of business and *völkisch* literature fizzled out because there were no gatherings where these books could be sold," wrote publisher Julius Lehmann.[6]

On the second floor of the fortress building, the only relief from the autumnal blues was once again provided by Hitler's watchful angel, Helene Bechstein. This time it was a gramophone that she provided, along with what appears to be a broad selection of records.

"Something soft, then military marches to wake you up!" Hess wrote to Pröhl. "Waltzes that go round and round, a delightful voice singing Schubert's 'Du bist die Ruh,' and Richard Wagner's 'Schmerzen.' If you close your eyes, you can forget for a few minutes where you are."[7]

As everyone in Landsberg eagerly waited for the court's parole decision, word of the inmates' easy lifestyle and possible illegal political activities in the prison leaked out to the socialist *Münchener Post*. The newspaper blasted the prison and its warden for a "scandalous scene" of the "state-owned Landsberg Prison being run as an outright political stronghold of Nazi desperados."[8] The newspaper attack threw Leybold into a defensive crouch; he responded with yet another panegyric to Hitler's good behavior. The prosecutors, Stenglein and Ehard, quickly fought back with another statement, citing Hitler's smuggled letter to car dealer Werlin as proof that his supposed "good behavior" was a hollow pose. Again, Leybold attested to Hitler's "good self-control and comportment," calling him a "model for his fellow inmates."[9]

Then, suddenly, Hitler's political violations and his risky act of letter-smuggling were brushed aside. On December 19, the Bavarian Supreme Court made a final ruling: Hitler was to receive parole immediately; he was getting a free pass back into political life. The court's decision was transmitted to State's Attorney Stenglein, whose job it was to execute the order. No doubt with great chagrin, Stenglein composed a telegram to Leybold in Landsberg: "Supreme Court threw out the objection of the State's Attorney.... Request Hitler... be notified and immediately released."[10]

It was nearly ten o'clock in the evening when Leybold showed up at room number seven in the fortress building. Hitler recalled later: "After some beating around the bush and hesitation, he told me,

'You are free!' I could hardly believe it."[11] He was to be released the next day, December 20, 1924, five days before Christmas. Hitler's year in prison was over.

By morning, word of his release had not only shot through the fortress but had reached Hitler's supporters in Munich. Before he could do anything about it, Gregor Strasser and Anton Drexler had driven to the prison to pick Hitler up, arriving mid-morning. Meeting Hitler in the visitors' room, they announced their plan to take their leader straight to visit Ludendorff to begin discussing political business. Hitler blew them off. Hitler "wouldn't even consider going," Hess related in a letter. "He was very angry! He wants first his rest and nothing else."

Despite his ire, Hitler must have taken wicked pleasure in seeing that his followers, and even a potential leadership rival like Ludendorff, were pushing and shoving to be the first to greet the returning hero. "The competition for him is beginning sooner than I expected," noted Hess.[12] Hitler wanted nothing of it. As for Ludendorff, he had told Hess, "I would like his name to disappear if possible from the movement because he makes it harder for me to win the workers."[13]

Instead of falling into the arms of his self-appointed drivers, Strasser and Drexler, Hitler called upon a non-political friend, Adolf Müller, to pick him up. Müller was the printer who produced the *Völkischer Beobachter;* his shop was also in the Schellingstrasse. Along with Müller came the one man who now always seemed welcome around Hitler, photographer Heinrich Hoffmann. His long-ago clash with Hitler's bodyguards a distant memory, Hoffmann was fast becoming the Boss's court photographer.

At noon, Hitler made his farewells among his men, all deeply moved in Kallenbach's telling, of course. Hitler even made the claim that much of the prison staff lined up with tears in their eyes to bid him good-bye at the castle-like front gate of the prison. "When I left, everybody wept, including the Mufti, the doctor, the guards—but not me!" said Hitler. "We had won them all to our cause!"[14]

In the prison records, Leybold had noted the remainder of Hitler's sentence: "3 years, 333 days, 21 hours and 50 minutes. Paroled until October 1, 1928." Had Hitler been forced to serve those remaining days in prison, he would have returned in 1928 to a Germany that was on far firmer political and economic footing.

Hitler was officially free at 12:15 p.m. While it is not known if he ever received a discount offer from dealer Jakob Werlin for the sleek Benz automobile he had craved in his smuggled letter, Hitler was picked up on this day by something almost as good. Müller and Hoffmann had arrived in a shiny black car with a convertible top, spoked wheels, and white sidewall tires—the very kind of vehicle Hitler had been hoping to buy (except that he wanted it in gray). As they climbed into the comfortable touring car, Hoffmann insisted on finding an appropriate spot for a departure photo (Leybold had forbidden pictures in front of the prison). The three men stopped just outside an old Landsberg city gate with a massive archway that looked like the entrance to a castle—or even to a prison. Hitler stood on the street beside the shiny black car with one hand on its door frame. His face serious and purposeful-looking, Hitler must have known this was the moment that his life was beginning again. Having dodged a barrage of bullets—including at least one real one—over thirteen months, he was now getting a second chance.

Even in this historic moment, however, Hitler looked a touch odd. From beneath his belted trench coat, his legs protruded like sticks. On the day of his release from a year in exile, Adolf Hitler was not wearing pants but kneesocks. Under his trench coat, he must have been wearing his Bavarian lederhosen, even in December. The photo session did not last long.

"Get a move on, Hoffmann," said Hitler. "It's bloody cold."

CHAPTER THIRTEEN

Starting Over

"No one can say I am unknown now, and that gives us a basis to start on again."

—ADOLF HITLER, CHRISTMAS EVE, 1924[1]

Munich was plastered with fire-red posters announcing Hitler's Friday night speech at the Bürgerbräukeller—the same beer hall where he had staged his putsch sixteen months earlier. For the first time since his release from prison, Hitler was ready to speak to the faithful. He had kept them waiting for two months after leaving Landsberg, refusing to be drawn into party quarrels or conjecture about his intentions. Finally, he was staging his coming-out, his return to the political lists. People were burning to know what Hitler would be like after more than a year behind bars. Was he, as the *New York Times* headline had claimed when he departed Landsberg, "Tamed by Prison"? Or was he the old firebrand who could rouse the crowds and hurl thunderbolts at his tormentors, at the Communists, and at "the system," as he called it? Most of all, they wanted to know, what was Hitler going to do about the fractured Nazi Party and the *völkisch* movement? How would he lead a wounded cause?

It had taken Hitler weeks to answer those questions in his own mind. After being greeted with garlands and wreaths on December 20 at his Thierschstrasse apartment by a small welcoming committee—and nearly knocked down the stairs by his exuberant German shepherd[2]—Hitler had kept his profile low and quiet. Speculation bubbled all about him. Whom had Hitler called on first—Ludendorff or someone else? Had Hitler disappeared to a rural retreat on the Baltic Sea coast for rest and restoration— *Erholung?* Hermann Esser's newspaper, *Nationalsozialist,* responded angrily that when asked about this claim, Hitler said: "I have neither time nor money for *Erholung."*[3] What Hitler was up to and why he refused to speak in public was the lingering mystery. "Hitler's apparent passivity is sowing confusion and unrest in the *völkisch* movement," noted a police intelligence report.

Only on Christmas Eve did Hitler return briefly to his familiar world—the home of Putzi and Helene Hanfstaengl. The wealthy couple had moved into a gracious villa in the leafy Herzog Park neighborhood. "You're back, Uncle Dolf!" said four-year-old Egon Hanfstaengl at the door. Putzi, pleased to show off his new home, led Hitler into the spacious main salon, dominated by a Blüthner grand piano. At the sight of the fine instrument, Hitler turned and said, "Hanfstaengl, please play me the 'Liebestod.'" He was requesting the tragic final moment in *Tristan und Isolde.* Within minutes, the two men had renewed their musical bond and Hitler was in a Wagnerian reverie.

Hitler's evening with the Hanfstaengls was a felicitous reentry into his Munich life. For little Egon, Hitler did his World War I artillery-sound imitations. During a late-evening discussion, he touched on politics. "Politics is not about proposals and programs, but about long, tough work until people are ready to equate some unknown person with a political idea. I think I've reached that point. And that's why the putsch was in some ways useful for our movement. No one can say I am unknown now, and that gives us a basis to start on again."[4]

Munich was tantalized by the reports of Hitler's coming book. Its conspicuous absence, almost as though planned by the sly Hitler, made it mysterious and intriguing. The naughty socialist *Münchener Post* in late January claimed that "Hitler's memoir, so pompously announced before the end of last year, about 'four years of fighting against cowardice, stupidity and criminality' has not been written and will never be written." Esser's *Nationalsozialist* took umbrage: "In view of this lying statement, we can report that Hitler's comprehensive book is with the Eher Verlag and is already set in type." The newspaper also ran an ad for the book with a brand-new title: *Mein Kampf*—the first appearance of the short, punchy, soon-to-be world-famous title in print.[5] Yet for all the uproar, Hitler's book was still delayed. It did not appear on bookstore shelves until July 18.

The pressure on Hitler to position himself in the swirling cauldron of *völkisch* politics was mounting. Hitler's indispensable first step was to have the bans lifted on the Nazi Party and its newspaper, the *Völkischer Beobachter*. Hitler went hat in hand for two meetings with Heinrich Held, the Bavarian governor. As only he could, Hitler presented himself as a prodigal son, remorseful of past sins and now convinced that violence and force had no part in politics. State authority had to be respected, he said. Above all, Hitler promised "not to stage a putsch." Held accepted Hitler's assurances and agreed to remove the bans on the party and the newspaper. "The wild beast is checked," said Held. "We can afford to loosen the chain."[6]

Hitler scheduled his resurrection for February 27, 1925. His choice of the Bürgerbräukeller was both predictable and effective.

Just as they had done on the night of Gustav Kahr's November 1923 speech that had ended in his temporary kidnapping by Hitler, the police had to close off the streets around the beer hall. Just as in 1923, anticipation and emotions were running high. But unlike the night of the putsch, this evening would not be marked by shots into the ceiling, hostage-taking, or proclamations of a deposed government. Instead, there would be a highly staged comeback.

Before the speech, Hitler made clear in a *Völkischer Beobachter* editorial that his first demand was instant peace among rival factions and unconditional obedience to him. Hitler's sense of mastery—of the movement and of the moment—was so complete that he would accept conditions from no one. Everyone had to rejoin the refounded party; no previous memberships would be carried over. It was to be a totally new beginning. There was no talk of shared leadership, joint decision-making, or special roles for special people. Hitler was to have absolute authority.

On the evening of the speech, however, it looked as though Hitler might have walked into a trap of his own making, raising expectations that he could not fulfill. General Ludendorff, Gregor Strasser, and Ernst Röhm weren't attending Hitler's grand show. Alfred Rosenberg also stayed away, dismissing the event as a "comedy" and anticipating the "brother-kissing" that Hitler would demand in such a setting. Hitler asked Drexler, as founder of the original German Workers' Party, to preside. But Drexler would agree only if Hitler first expelled the hated Hermann Esser, which Hitler refused to do. Finally, Hitler settled on Max Amann, a good businessman but no stem-winding speaker, to open the big evening.

Given the anticipation and adulation in the crowd, it probably wouldn't have mattered what Hitler said. He delivered in his usual style. Speaking for two hours, Hitler managed to whitewash all that had gone wrong over recent years. He also highlighted his belief that, in the fight with Jewish Marxism, there had been only two possibilities—"either the enemy walks over our dead bodies or we over theirs." The old Hitler was back, signaling that violence was still an option (and leading to the party's re-banning by Governor Held a few days later).

Hitler also issued a warning to rivals who might want to constrain him. "Anyone who thinks he can condition his joining the party with some stipulations doesn't know me very well," said Hitler to loud applause. "As long as I carry all the responsibility, I'm not willing to let others set conditions for me. And I take full responsibility for everything that happens in this movement!" Hitler finished to cheers and *"Heils!"* just as he had in years gone by. He could still whip up a crowd. Astonishingly, he even promised that if he had not fulfilled the members' expectations after one year, he would resign. Hitler had thrown down the gauntlet, daring anyone to pick it up.

Then came the coup de théâtre that was the real point of the evening. Demanding that feuding factions put aside their differences, Hitler called to the stage the sometimes bitter enemies who *had* showed up for the event. These included Gottfried Feder, Wilhelm Frick, and Rudolf Buttmann, the part of the *völkisch* movement that favored parliamentary participation; and Esser, Julius Streicher, and Artur Dinter, who opposed it. Various other players joined them on the stage. Hitler once again demanded the hearty handshakes and deep-in-the-eyes looks that he'd forced from his three hostages on this same stage fifteen months earlier, gestures of emotional and political commitment for the benefit of the crowd. The hack artist had composed a grand tableau of unity, with himself as the central figure, before thousands of witnesses. And, as on the evening of the putsch, the performance culminated with three thousand people singing *"Deutschland, Deutschland über alles."*

The rousing night in the Bürgerbräukeller was a triumphal return for Hitler. Despite its flaws — the absence of some top names, the soon-to-be-restored party ban — Hitler had used it as the springboard not only back to where he had been before, but to a level of leadership and control that was unprecedented. He had presented himself as god, and the believers had accepted. It would not mark the end of internal struggles — some would last up to the 1930s — but it signaled a relaunch of Hitler's *Führerpartei,* a leader-dominated party that would become his personal tool and vehicle for building a dictatorship. And the night of rhetoric and adoration signaled the end of Hitler's journey through exile, trial, and resurrection. Restored and reinvented, with his catastrophic putsch attempt far behind him, he had begun the long march to power.

EPILOGUE

What Finally Happened

*"If twelve or fifteen thousand Hebrew corrupters of the people
had been held under poison gas... the sacrifice of millions
at the front would not have been in vain."*
—ADOLF HITLER, *Mein Kampf*[1]

Seven months after his comeback speech, Hitler withdrew to his favorite place on earth, Berchtesgaden. There, in the Alps, he would continue writing his racist rancor, bombastic ideas, and histrionic plans for the world. Snug in a cottage rented from his friends, the Büchers, owners of the Platterhof Hotel (formerly Pension Moritz), Hitler composed volume two of *Mein Kampf.* This time, Hitler dictated his words to a secretary. As usual, Hitler was obsessing over Germany's defeat in World War I, the beginning of history in the Hitlerian bubble. Blaming Jewish back-stabbers and alleged profiteers for Germany's loss, he continued his habit of vitriolic and venomous comments about Jews. If twelve or fifteen thousand Jewish "scoundrels" had been "taken out at the right time," he claimed, "a

257

million worthwhile, proper German lives would have been saved."[2] These are the only lines in *Mein Kampf* suggesting that Hitler may have had visions of exterminating Jews by modern methods. Most historians, however, do not believe Hitler already planned massive death camps with gas chambers. Yet his statement clearly reveals a mind that could embrace mass annihilation.

Hitler's suggestion of gassing twelve or fifteen thousand Jews shrinks to a footnote in the annals of his actual crimes. His actions as dictator, warlord, and mass murderer bore out the hubristic plans he developed in Landsberg Prison and crystallized in *Mein Kampf.* The entire war in the West—what Americans think of as World War II—was in fact just *Rückendeckung,* or covering his rear, for Hitler's forward thrust to the East—just as he explained in *Mein Kampf.*[3] From the minute he left Landsberg until his final moment on earth, Hitler was obsessed with two things: capturing *Lebensraum* from Russia and ridding the world of Jews. Hitler had adopted *Lebensraum* as a concept while writing *Mein Kampf* in Landsberg; he had also concluded while in prison that he had to adopt "the harshest weapons"against Jews, as he revealed in his conversation with the Czech Nazi named Kugler. Twenty-one years later, in his final political testament composed on the day before he killed himself, Hitler exhorted the German people to "resist mercilessly the poisoner of all nations, international Jewry." Those were his last written words.

Hitler's year in Landsberg Prison soon became part of the growing Hitler myth. Like the failed putsch, his year behind bars was artfully blended into the legend of the future Führer's "years of struggle." After he took power in 1933, Hitler's "cell"—room number seven in the fortress building—was converted into a shrine and place of pilgrimage, with a large plaque over the door (ADOLF HITLER WAS IMPRISONED HERE) and a swastika flag on the table. An old upright typewriter—not the little portable on which Hitler had written *Mein Kampf*—was placed in the room for verisimilitude. Germans came by the thousands to stand for a few seconds before the open door to Hitler's room, turning Landsberg Prison into a tourist attraction. Special trains with up to two thousand passengers arrived on weekends; people stood in long queues to get behind the prison walls. Some worshipful followers even *walked* from North Germany to set foot on the hallowed ground where Hitler had lived for a year. In 1934, ten years after his imprisonment, Hitler himself paid the prison a visit, inspecting his old quarters and gazing, once again, through the barred windows of his cell. Signing the "Golden Book" for visitors, with his old prison mate Emil Maurice by his side, Hitler effectively consecrated the spot.

Landsberg, the town, thrived on the attention. In 1937 and 1938, Hitler Youth delegations marched 116 miles from Nuremberg to Landsberg following Nazi Party conventions. City fathers began marketing Landsberg as "the Hitler city" and "the birthplace of the National Socialist philosophy." In 1944, the city saw other new arrivals: Jewish prisoners driven from Auschwitz. More than twenty-three thousand captives were forced to live for months like half-blind animals in earthen huts and semi-underground barracks with clay roofs—cold, dark, damp, and overcrowded. An instant concentration camp of slave laborers had been created around Landsberg and the neighboring town of Kaufering for Hitler's last-ditch attempt to build the world's first jet fighter, the Messerschmitt 262. In ten frenzied months, at least six thousand of the enslaved Jews perished from overwork, hunger, executions, and typhus. Hundreds more died in a 1945 death march as U.S. forces approached Munich.

Following World War II, Landsberg willfully ignored its role in the persecution of the Jews, literally burying the past with bulldozers to build a commercial zone where many of the barracks once stood. "The barracks were seen as a stain on the city's history," said Manfred Deiler, a leader of Landsberg's European Holocaust Memorial Foundation. The organization is preserving the remaining barracks in remembrance of "genocide on our doorsteps" during the war's waning months. The civic activists' efforts have been rewarded with memorial headstones sent by the heads of ten European states from which the Jews had been taken—Václav Havel, Boris Yeltsin, and several others lent their names to the memorial. One section is becoming a visitors' site and documentation center. "These are the last relics in Germany of this kind of camp," said Deiler.

They are also the last remains of Landsberg's tortured involvement with Adolf Hitler.

From Hitler's stay in the prison, the most tangible legacy was *Mein Kampf.* The book went on to have a remarkable career, as its publishing trajectory has been called.[4] The 1925 press run of the first volume, 10,000 books, sold well, at least to the true believers. "Amann beginning to cash in on *Mein Kampf,*" noted Hanfstaengl in December, just as a second press run of 10,000 was begun.[5] Volume two, published in December 1926, sold more slowly. Both volumes were later consolidated into a single book, usually called the *Volksausgabe*—the "people's edition." Yet Hitler's turgid style and ideological obstinancy—along with the abject failure of his putsch— led political reviewers at the sophisticated publications to dismiss Hitler as "finished." "Adolf Hitler exhausted his whole arsenal in a single day," opined the oracular *Frankfurter Zeitung.*[6]

Interest in *Mein Kampf* picked up as Hitler's political fortunes soared in the early 1930s, with 240,000 books sold by the time he took office in January 1933.[7] Then the book leapt into the stratosphere, selling one million books by year's end, including a large number to Germany's public libraries.[8] By the time Hitler committed suicide in 1945, *Mein Kampf* had sold twelve million copies and had been translated into eighteen languages. And the book was not mere decoration or obligatory material in every German family's library. It was read. In a meticulous, 632-page study of the writing, publication, and reception of *Mein Kampf,* scholar Othmar Plöckinger refuted the long-standing myth that *Mein Kampf* was the biggest unread bestseller of all time. Through examination of German lending library records, for example, Plöckinger was able to show that the book enjoyed lively circulation numbers that belie the belief that people only owned the book for show or received it as a wedding gift. People read *Mein Kampf* by choice.[9]

The original manuscript for *Mein Kampf* is lost. Or rather, all the manuscripts (actually, typescripts) are lost, for the book is thought to have had numerous mutations as it was edited and re-edited by Hitler and various helpers before publication. Even at the time of Hitler's political triumphs, the manuscript was treated almost as a state secret. Though Hitler owned a copy, in 1940 he personally refused permission for the Nazi Party archivist to display any pages of it—or even photographs of the pages—in an exhibition celebrating the "Struggle for Germany's Greatness" at that year's party convention.[10] Helene Bechstein was reportedly given a copy by Hitler, which she either returned or lost to fire during the bombing of Berlin—though the story may be apocryphal. Almost all of Hitler's personal papers, in Berlin, Munich, and Berchtesgaden, were burned during the war's last week by his adjutant, Julius Schaub. Many original documents went up in smoke as Nazi archivists committed tons of their holdings to the furnaces in the final days of the war. Years later, as noted in chapter 9 ("Rearranging the World"), only the first five pages of the manuscript, plus Hitler's eighteen-page outline, were found.

Following World War II, *Mein Kampf* went into a strange limbo. American authorities had in 1945 seized Hitler's and the Nazi Party's remaining assets, including Max Amann's Eher Verlag publishing house. But the occupying power soon passed ownership to the revived Bavarian government. Hypersensitive to Munich's role as the breeding ground of the Nazi Party and as the "capital of the movement," as Hitler called it, the Bavarians immediately put *Mein Kampf* under wraps and kept it there for the next seven decades. With a seventy-year copyright in force, all discussion of republishing Hitler's book in German was thwarted by the Bavarian authorities, even though Germany's first postwar president, Theodor Heuss, recommended it as an object lesson for the young generation. Available only in the back rooms of antiquarian bookshops or in libraries for research purposes, *Mein Kampf* became both forbidden fruit and demonized detritus of the worst period of German history. The general public had a hard time finding it, but then almost nobody was looking. That changed, of course, with the arrival of the Internet, when the book was made available online, mainly by neo-Nazi groups. Yet even though it was there, only tiny numbers of right-wingers were interested in reading it. It is not known how many of them actually have made the long march through the tedious and pompous prose.

The Bavarian government's choke hold on *Mein Kampf* in German was scheduled to run out when the copyright expired on the last day of 2015. In 2009, Munich's Institute for Contemporary History (Institut für Zeitgeschichte), the leading center for Nazi-era research in Germany, began work on an annotated "critical edition" of Hitler's book—the first German-language version since World War II. The Institute had already produced for historical research a twelve-volume collection of Hitler's thousands of speeches, writings, and orders; a twenty-five-volume edition of Joseph Goebbels' diaries; and, in 1961, a newly discovered manuscript that Hitler had intended as the third volume of *Mein Kampf* (the work was issued as *Hitler's Second Book*). "It only made sense for us to close the gap by publishing the most important resource to Hitler's thinking, *Mein Kampf,*" said the Institute's project leader, Christian Hartmann.

With scholarly analysis and commentary appearing on almost every page of the two-volume, two-thousand-page edition, the new *Mein Kampf* would "demythologize" Hitler's hated and feared, but little-known work, said Hartmann. By publishing a version swaddled in scholarship from a modern perspective, the book was also intended to get a jump on popular publishers who might issue the book in its naked form. Israeli historian Dan Michman, head of international research at the Yad Vashem memorial museum, supported the Institute's republication project and noted that the new version of *Mein Kampf* would "look something like a Talmud."

Nonetheless, the publishing project soon hit snags and became an international controversy. Holocaust survivors' groups objected. Some feared the book could be used to stir up far-right politics and incite hatred. Yet researchers at the Institute plunged ahead, planning to issue their new version of the book in January 2016 with a drab, academic cover, not with Hitler's face and a big red slash on the jacket, as in the 1930s. *Mein Kampf* was expected to get new life, though an entirely different one from that of the 1920s and 1930s. Deconstructed and analyzed, Hitler's rambling, repetitive, sometimes dense text could be read for what it is—a political tract by an obsessed future dictator that is a "propaganda piece," as project leader Hartmann put it,[11] but also as an internally consistent and predictive "road map" to Hitler's future actions, as scholar Zehnpfennig has called it.[12] And, as President Heuss had suggested in 1959, *Mein Kampf* could finally be used as a history-teaching tool in German schools and universities.

Hitler's putsch, trial, and time in prison had brought together a murky swirl of characters and circumstances that would later play a role in the Third Reich. Hermann Göring, who was badly wounded in the putsch, would become number two in Hitler's homicidal regime and be sentenced to death at the Nuremberg trial; he cheated the hangman with a hidden cyanide pill. Heinrich Himmler, the bespectacled agronomist who carried Captain Ernst Röhm's flag on the night of the putsch, went on to head the SS, the most lethal part of the Hitlerian killing machine; he swallowed a poison pill shortly after his capture, cheating even the Nuremberg court. Röhm himself died much earlier; he was liquidated on Hitler's orders during the 1934 Night of the Long Knives.

Rudolf Hess, Hitler's most loyal and toadying acolyte, became deputy Führer of the Nazi Party and had a cabinet post. But the former Boswell of Landsberg Prison turned on his boss in 1941, flying a small plane to Scotland to make peace with the British. Regarded as unstable, he was immediately penned up, and at Nuremberg he received a life sentence. Hess spent the next forty-one years in Berlin's Spandau Prison, where he died by suicide in 1987.

Other putschists who rose high, then finally met their end on the Nuremberg gallows, were Alfred Rosenberg, the Baltic ideologue and writer who became Hitler's minister for the occupied eastern territories, including Ukraine; Wilhelm Frick, the former Munich police official who became Hitler's interior minister, drafting most of the Third Reich's laws against Jews; and Hans Frank, Hitler's personal legal adviser who had then served the Führer with great energy and brutality as governor-general of occupied Poland. While awaiting execution in a cell near the gymnasium where a gallows was to be built, Frank penned a one-thousand-page handwritten memoir that included insights from his frequent conversations and trips with Hitler. Frank's book was called, appropriately, *Im Angesicht des Galgens* (In the Shadow of the Gallows).

Otto Lurker, one of Hitler's Landsberg Prison guards, also

ended his life on the gallows. Moving from penitentiary work into Hitler's SS, Lurker was posted in the war to Austria, where he oversaw the executions of at least a thousand Slovenian prisoners in the Maribor concentration camp. In 1949, he was tried in Ljubljana and hanged.

A member of Hitler's 1923 inner circle who escaped both the Führer's wrath and a trial at Nuremberg was the gangly German-American Ernst Hanfstaengl. Hanfstaengl had wanted to have it both ways, riding Hitler's bandwagon to a high-profile position as his international press spokesman, while trying, occasionally, to moderate the excesses of Nazi rule after 1933. But by 1937, Hanfstaengl realized he had been targeted by his detractors, mainly Göring; he had to flee. He wrote that he was almost eliminated by being forced to parachute into the teeth of the Spanish Civil War before making his way to Switzerland and, finally, to Britain. He was interned as an enemy alien, later shipped to Canada, then to the United States, where he became a secret adviser to President Roosevelt's staff from imprisonment in a run-down plantation in Virginia. After the war, Hanfstaengl lived out his days near Munich, where he wrote his memoir. While predictably self-serving, Hanfstaengl's book nonetheless opened a useful window on Hitler's life in Munich leading up to the 1923 putsch. Hanfstaengl died in 1975 at age eighty-eight.

Some players in the events of 1923 and 1924 profited handsomely from their association with Hitler. Max Amann, the former army sergeant who took over the Eher publishing company, built a business empire on the soaring sales of *Mein Kampf* and the soaring circulation of the *Völkischer Beobachter*. Hitler appointed him head of the Reich Press Association and the Association of Newspaper Publishers, giving him enormous power over all publications in Germany, which he could force out of business if they did not toe the official line. Judge Georg Neithardt, the goateed jurist who had allowed Hitler the run of the proceedings at his treason trial and given him the cushy "honorary" sentence of "fortress imprisonment" (with parole in six months), also fared well when Hitler took power. Hitler rewarded Neithardt with the chief judgeship at the Bavarian Supreme Court. Upon the judge's death in 1941, Hitler personally had a large wreath laid in the Führer's name at the funeral.

The man who most insistently opposed Hitler and his ambitions during his treason trial, Gustav von Kahr, suffered a brutal fate. During the 1934 Night of the Long Knives, the former commissioner general—now a retired civil servant—was dragged from his apartment, tortured by members of the SS, and, finally, killed. Kahr's mutilated body was found in a swamp near the Dachau concentration camp. Hitler's co-conspirator and co-defendant in the trial, General Erich Ludendorff, rapidly fell from Hitler's favor and moved into a mystical brand of politics that slammed Christians as much as Jews, turning himself into a political eccentric. He and Hitler became estranged and even enemies. Ludendorff died in 1937.

The Bürgerbräukeller beer hall that was trashed by Hitler's men on the night of his putsch profited mightily from its association with the Nazis. By the time Hitler took power in 1933, the failed putsch had become heroic legend. Its Nazi victims were officially treated as revered martyrs, memorialized by a large plaque and a perpetual honor guard at Odeon Square. The sixteen killed were entombed nearby in a Greek-style "temple of honor." Each year on the anniversary of the putsch—November 8—Hitler led a ritual march from Odeon Square to the Bürgerbräukeller, where he gave a speech.

But the regularity of this ceremonial pomp nearly brought Hitler down. In 1939, just two months after Hitler had invaded Poland to start World War II, the Bürgerbräukeller became the scene of an assassination attempt that nearly ended the Hitler nightmare. Over a two-month period, working at night after the beer hall was closed, a clever carpenter named Georg Elser, who wanted to "improve the conditions of the workers and avoid a war," had installed a time-delayed explosive into a support column right behind the Bürgerbräukeller speaker's podium. Elser knew that Hitler always spoke for at least one hour, beginning at 8:30 p.m. The bombmaker set his device to detonate at 9:20 p.m. But, because the Munich airport that night was socked in by fog, Hitler began his speech early, at 8 p.m. After speaking for an hour and seven minutes, he left the Bürgerbräukeller at 9:07 p.m. to catch a train back to Berlin. Thirteen minutes later, Elser's bomb ripped through the beer hall, killing eight people and wounding sixty. The spot where Hitler had been standing thirteen minutes earlier was devastated. "Those thirteen minutes were the most costly in the history of the twentieth century," wrote German author Claus Christian Malzahn.[13] The Bürgerbräukeller is now gone, a victim of wartime bombing, neglect, and urban development. All that remains is a plaque on the spot where the support column stood, commemorating Georg Elser.

Today, Landsberg Prison remains a Bavarian state penal institution, housing more than five hundred inmates. Hitler's room, along with all the other "cells" in the fortress building, was demolished following World War II. The internal walls were removed and the large, open room reverted to the function it had when the prison first opened—a space for small prison industries. But the outer walls of the building still stand. Unchanged are the high windows with their slightly corroded bars—the same ones Hitler looked through every day that he was in Landsberg Prison. When, in 2015, the author climbed the stairs to the second floor and approached Hitler's windows, he could see through those rough bars the same simple green landscape that extended daily across Hitler's vision. Standing where Hitler lived, slept, and worked conveyed an eerie feeling of being in Hitler's space, on the very spot where many of the future dictator's distorted and diabolical ideas were committed to paper. Hitler had been gone for ninety years, but his spirit somehow lingered in the old fortress building, then 106 years old. From this place, and from that man, had emanated the single greatest human-made disaster in history. Much of it had been conceived in this small room.

There was nothing grand about the gallows. It was a plain wooden box with a stair leading up one side and a closed-in room below, so that the dangling body would not be visible. This was no execution stage like the great public hangings in seventeenth- and eighteenth-century London or the tumbrels and guillotines on the Place de la Concorde in Paris. This was an ignoble ending. The condemned man was always dressed in plain clothes, as though going to work in a factory. He always looked grim. His hands were tied. He was walked silently up the stairs. At the top stood a man in a suit holding a noose. There was also a priest, fully draped in the tradition of Catholic Bavaria, with a lace-fringed white surplice and the full sleeves of his calling, holding a black book. At the corners of the gallows stood the men whose uniforms gave away the proceedings: U.S. Army soldiers, wearing their dress helmets with military-police markings.

Landsberg Prison, the Bavarian penitentiary where Hitler had been held for a year, had been turned into U.S. Army War Criminal Prison No. 1. Its purpose was meting out punishment to some of the worst malefactors of World War II. One of its jobs was ending the lives of Germans convicted of crimes against humanity—usually mass murder in concentration camps—during the war. From 1946 through 1951, 259 men were hanged on the simple gallows built

only fifty feet from the fortress building where Hitler and his followers had lived (another twenty-seven men were executed by firing
squad). The men who climbed the gallows on these drab German
mornings were paying the final price for the evil project Hitler had
set in motion two decades earlier in cell number seven. Launching
the long drama had taken months of effort—Hitler's twenty-five-
day treason trial, his long weeks of writing, his lectures to his fellow
prisoners, his thirteen months behind bars. But for these men who
had followed his path into the abyss, it took only seconds: a sentence
read, a benediction spoken, a black hood over the head, then the
noose. For them the war ended right where it had begun, as visions
of grandeur in the mind of the man who unleashed his vision of
racial purity and territorial conquest on the world.

Acknowledgments

The special joy of writing a research-based book lies in contact with the impressive scholars who have devoted much of their professional lives to the subject. Again and again, I was the lucky recipient of generous advice and guidance from Othmar Plöckinger in Salzburg; Paul Hoser and Christian Hartmann in Munich; Jeffrey Herf in Maryland; and Alan E. Steinweis in both Vermont and Munich. At the same time, I benefited from the contribution to my understanding of German politics and history over many years from Robert Gerald Livingston, Jackson Janes, and Jeremiah Riemer. Other scholars and experts who willingly gave of their time and experience were Roman Töppel, Reinhard Weber, David Clay Large, Christoph Safferling, Dan Michman, and Jakob Zollmann.

Laurence Latourette and Jonathan M. Weisgall, exceptionally thoughtful men with writerly minds, read my manuscript and were more than generous with counsel and encouragement.

Underlying it all are my rich friendships with some of Germany's best writers and journalists: Claus Christian Malzahn, Gabor Steingart, Clemens Wergin, Gregor Peter Schmitz, and Henryk Broder. Thanks to Schmitz, I also had the benefit of research talent at *Der Spiegel* in the hot pursuit of elusive documents, including

Hauke Janssen and Conny Neumann. Munich photographer Wolfgang Weber added useful details to the sought-after story.

A special case among these supportive colleagues is Michael S. Cullen, an American author in Berlin who is uniquely qualified to guide anyone writing about Germany. Cullen writes serious history and essays in German, and has been my close friend for nearly fifty years.

Every researcher is existentially dependent on archivists and librarians. This book benefited from the guiding and sometimes warning hand of Klaus Lankheit, a deep reservoir of knowledge of Hitler and the Third Reich and chief archivist at Munich's indispensible Institut für Zeitgeschichte (Institute for Contemporary History) — where Simone Paulmichl facilitated my access to scholars and resources. I also received timely support from David Morris, Mark Dimunation, and Amber Paranick at the Library of Congress; from Holly Reed and Sharon Culley at the U.S. National Archives; from Evi Hartmann at Washington's German Historical Institute; from Sylvia Krauss, Johann Pörnbacher, and Josef Anker at the Bayerisches Hauptstaatsarchiv; from Christoph Bachmann and his crack crew at the Staatsarchiv München; from Peter Fleischmann at the Staatsarchiv Nürnberg; from numerous staffers at Munich's huge and deeply endowed Bayerische Staatsbibliothek (BSB). Special thanks to Angelika Betz in the amazing photo archive of the BSB.

My work in these institutions was made far more efficient by the outstanding research assistance of Courtney Marie Burrell, a gifted graduate student at Munich's Ludwig-Maximilians-Universität.

To Harald Eichinger, along with prison director Monika Gross, I am indebted for a revealing tour of Landsberg Prison and the spot where Hitler lived, worked, and slept. Thanks also go to Daniella Philippi, spokesperson of Bavarian governor Horst Seehofer, for making the visit possible, and to retired prison historian Klaus Weichert for responding willingly to my queries.

But one Landsberger deserves special gratitude. Manfred Deiler is a leader of the brave, sometimes isolated association of citizen activists and historians who have gradually uncovered Landsberg's role in mistreating Jewish slave laborers near the end of World War II. Deiler and his colleagues have for two decades worked to preserve the remains of the degrading earthen barracks that housed the doomed prisoners. In the process, Deiler has become a repository of data and documents about Hitler's stay in Landsberg Prison and its conversion into a shrine after Hitler took power. Deiler welcomed me into his home, guided me through the thicket of his holdings, and repeatedly responded to my requests for clarification. He does righteous labor and it is all plain to see at http://www.buergervereinigung-landsberg.org.

Writers need writers as friends and supporters in the sometimes daunting business of opening a new window on difficult subject matter. My indispensable circle of support includes James Reston Jr., Laurence Leamer, Roger M. Williams, Erla Zwingle, Mark Olshaker, Ann Blackman, Michael Putzel, Mark Perry, Joel Swerdlow, and Dan Moldea.

Books arise in numerous ways. This one began with an essay in the *New York Times,* and I am grateful to op-ed editor Clay Risen for his help in shaping and running the piece. Nothing goes anywhere in publishing without good agents and editors, and I had both in Gail Ross and Dara Kaye, at Ross Yoon Agency, and John Parsley and Jean Garnett, at Little, Brown—all masters at guiding a writer toward the finish line.

Finally, my efforts would still be somewhere between wishful and flailing if it were not for the steady, editorially incisive and devoted support of my wife, Linda Harris. As always, I owe the greatest debt to her.

Notes

Prologue. The Unfathomable Ascent

1. Richard Hanser, *Putsch! How Hitler Made Revolution* (New York: David McKay Co., 1970), 389.
2. Karl Sommer, *Beiträge zur bayerischen und deutschen Geschichte in der Zeit von 1910–1933* (Bayreuth: Hopf, 1991), 197.
3. Hans Frank, *Im Angesicht des Galgens* (Munich: Alfred Beck Verlag, 1953), 46–47.
4. Hanser, *Putsch!*, 396.
5. Heinrich August Winkler, *Germany: The Long Road West, Volume I: 1789–1933* (New York: Oxford University Press), 2006–2007, 2.
6. Frank, *Im Angesicht*, 25.
7. Robin Flick, "Fascism in Germany," 1975, https://www.marxists.org/subject/fascism/blick/ch13.htm.

Chapter 1. Discovering the Mission

1. Ian Kershaw, *Hitler: 1889–1936: Hubris* (New York: W. W. Norton & Company, 1998), 73.
2. Ernst Deuerlein, "Der Hitler-Putsch: Bayerische Dokumente zum 8./9. November 1923 (Sonderdruck aus Band 9)," 79.
3. Wilhelm Hoegner (anon.), *Hitler und Kahr: Die bayerischen Napoleonsgrössen von 1923: Ein im Untersuchungsausschuss des Bayerischen Landtags aufgedeckter Justizskandal,* parts 1 and 2 (Munich, 1928), 53.
4. *Hitler-Prozess* (trial transcript), part 1, 49.
5. Hans Mommsen, *Aufstieg und Untergang der Republik von Weimar 1918–1933* (Berlin: Ullstein Taschenbuch, 1989–2009), 645–47.

6. Reinhard Sturm, "Weimarer Republik Informationen zur politischen Bildung," 261 (2011), Bundeszentrale für politische Bildung: Bonn (ISSN 0046-9408).

7. David Clay Large, *Where Ghosts Walked: Munich's Road to the Third Reich* (London: W. W. Norton, 1997), 159.

8. Kershaw, *Hitler: 1889–1936*, 170–71.

9. David Jablonsky, *The Nazi Party in Dissolution: Hitler and the Verbotzeit 1923–1925* (London: Routledge, 1989), 7.

10. Eugene Davidson, *The Making of Adolf Hitler: The Birth and Rise of Nazism* (New York: Macmillan, 1977), 186, citing Otto Gessler, *Reichswehrpolitik in der Weimarer Zeit* (Stuttgart: Deutsche Verlags-Anstalt, 1958), 248.

11. Gordon A. Craig, *Germany: 1866–1945* (New York: Oxford University Press, 1978), 434.

12. *Hitler-Prozess* (trial transcript), part 1, 61.

13. Brigitte Hamann, *Hitler's Vienna: A Dictator's Apprenticeship* (New York: Oxford University Press, 1999), 164; Kershaw, *Hitler: 1889–1936*, 54–56.

14. Volker Ullrich, *Adolf Hitler: Biographie: Band I: Die Jahre des Aufstiegs 1889–1939* (S. Fischer; Frankfurt am Main, 2013), 52, with footnote to his letter to the magistrate of Linz, January 21, 1914; Kershaw, *Hitler: 1889–1936*, 52.

15. Adolf Hitler, *Mein Kampf: Zwei Bände in einem Band, Ungekürzte Ausgabe,* 851st–855th. (Munich: Zentralverlag der NSDAP, Frz. Eher Nachf., 1943), 137.

16. Hitler, *Mein Kampf,* 13.

17. Hitler, *Mein Kampf,* 83–86.

18. Hitler's outline for *Mein Kampf,* Blatt 10, Florian Beierl and Othmar Plöckinger, "Neue Dokumente zu Hitlers Buch *Mein Kampf.*" *Vierteljahrshefte für Zeitgeschichte* 57, no. 2 (2009): 310. For copyright reasons, the eighteen original pages can been seen only in the print edition of the journal, not in the online version

19. Hitler, *Mein Kampf,* 44–45.

20. Hitler, *Mein Kampf,* 59.

21. Kershaw, *Hitler: 1889–1936*, 61–62. Other historians argue that Hitler's anti-Semitism did not appear until years later, following World War I, in Munich. See Sven Felix Kellerhoff, "Adolf Hitler wurde spät zum Antisemiten," *Die Welt,* March 3, 2009.

22. Interview with the author, February 2, 2015.

23. Hitler, *Mein Kampf,* 139.

24. Hitler, *Mein Kampf,* 138.

25. Ullrich, *Adolf Hitler,* 63.

26. Milan Hauner, *Hitler: A Chronology of His Life and Time* (New York: Milan Hauner, 1983), 12.

27. Heinrich Hoffmann's crowd shot. "Hitler—wie ich ihn sah," part 1, ZDF History, https://www.youtube.com/watch?v=vw356iha8so, 20–47 seconds, television documentary.

28. Hitler's outline for *Mein Kampf,* Blatt 9, Beierl and Plöckinger, "Neue Dokumente," 304.

29. Kershaw, *Hitler: 1889–1936,* 73.

30. Frank, *Im Angesicht,* 46; Thomas Weber, *Hitler's First War: Adolf Hitler, the Men of the List Regiment, and the First World War* (New York: Oxford University Press, 2010), 140.

31. Weber, *Hitler's First War,* 139.

32. Kershaw, *Hitler: 1889–1936,* Illustration 8, 162–63.

33. Gerhard L. Weinberg, ed., *Hitler's Table Talk 1941–1944: His Private Conversations* (New York: Enigma Books, 2000–2008), 177.

34. Weber, *Hitler's First War,* 139–41, from U.S. interrogators.

35. Weber, *Hitler's First War,* 142–43.

36. Weber, *Hitler's First War,* 53.

37. Hitler, *Mein Kampf,* 223.

38. Hitler, *Mein Kampf,* 64.

39. Hitler, *Mein Kampf,* 224.

40. Hauner, *Hitler,* 16.

41. Winifried Nerdinger, Hans Günter Hockerts, Marita Krauss, Peter Longerich, Mirjana Grdanjski, and Markus Eisen, eds., *Munich and National Socialism: Catalogue of the Munich Documentation Center for the History of National Socialism* (Munich: C. H. Beck, 2015), 52.

42. Kershaw, *Hitler: 1889–1936,* 124.

43. Kershaw, *Hitler: 1889–1936,* 123; Ernst Deuerlein, "Hitlers Eintritt in die Politik und die Reichswehr: Dokumentation," *Vierteljahrshefte für Zeitgeschichte,* 7, no. 2 (1959): 179–84; Karl Alexander von Müller, *Mars und Venus: Erinnerungen 1914–1919* (Stuttgart, 1954), 338. Müller, a respected academic, was a problematic character who became a Nazi "fellow traveler" during the Third Reich; he joined the Nazi Party, trained some key anti-Semitic scholars, and lent his professional standing to the regime. Yet he refrained from any scurrilous writings of his own. Despite these strong nationalistic leanings and support of Hitler's regime in the 1930s, historians seem to have found no reason to discount Müller's credibility as an eyewitness observer of the events that he experienced during Hitler's rise in the 1920s.

44. Hitler, *Mein Kampf,* 235.

45. Deuerlein, "Hitlers Eintritt," 200.

46. Hitler, *Mein Kampf,* 3.

47. August Kubizek, *The Young Hitler I Knew* (London: Greenhill Books, 2006), 37; Kershaw, *Hitler: 1889–1936,* 21.

48. Kershaw, *Hitler: 1889–1936,* 132.

49. Albrecht Tryell, *Führer befiehl…Selbstzeugnisse aus der "Kampfzeit" der NSDAP* (Düsseldorf, 1969), 20. Drexler, in a letter covering "Mein Politisches Erwachen," says he still works at the *Schraubstock.*

50. Hauner, *Hitler,* 17–18.
51. Hitler, *Mein Kampf,* 237–38.
52. Hitler, *Mein Kampf,* 238.
53. Mommsen, *Aufstieg und Untergang,* 205–6.
54. Ernst Hanfstaengl, *Hitler: The Memoir of a Nazi Insider Who Turned Against the Führer* (New York: Arcade Publishing, 1957), 2011, 39.
55. Hitler, *Mein Kampf,* 239.
56. Kershaw, *Hitler: 1889–1936,* 126.
57. Konrad Heiden, *Adolf Hitler: Das Zeitalter der Verantwortungslosigkeit,* vol. 1 (Zurich: Europaverlag, 1936), 76–77.
58. Hoegner, *Hitler und Kahr,* part 2, 102.

Chapter 2. The Charmed Circle

1. Joachim C. Fest, *Hitler* (New York: Harcourt Brace Jovanovich, 1973), 165.
2. Raoul de Roussy de Sales, ed., *Adolf Hitler: My New Order* (New York: Reynal and Hitchcock, 1941), 6.
3. Reginald H. Phelps, "Hitler als Parteiführer im Jahre 1920," *Vierteljahrshefte für Zeitgeschichte* 11, no 3 (1963): 295, from police report.
4. Hitler, *Mein Kampf,* 527.
5. Hitler, *Mein Kampf,* 524.
6. Kershaw, *Hitler: 1889–1936,* 152.
7. Hitler speech of April 12, 1922, in Roussy de Sales, *Adolf Hitler,* 22.
8. Hanfstaengl, *Hitler,* 51 and 89.
9. Hermann Esser, documents (interviews), Institut für Zeitgeschichte, ED 561/5–3.
10. The Württemberg envoy, Mommsen, *Aufstieg und Untergang,* 209.
11. Hitler, *Mein Kampf,* 556.
12. Hitler, *Mein Kampf,* 542.
13. Hagen Schulze, *Freikorps und Republik 1918–1920* (Boppard am Rhein: H. Boldt, 1969); Robert Gerwarth and John Horne, *War in Peace: Paramilitary Violence in Europe After the Great War* (Oxford: Oxford University Press, 2012), 70.
14. Trevor-Roper, *Hitler's Secret Conversations, 1941–1944* (New York: Farrar, Straus and Young, 1953), 126.
15. Othmar Plöckinger, *Geschichte eines Buches: Adolf Hitlers "Mein Kampf" 1922-1945: Eine Veröffentlichung des Instituts für Zeitgeschichte* (Munich: R. Olden-bourg Verlag, 2006), 52.
16. Frank, *Im Angesicht,* 31.
17. Plöckinger, *Geschichte,* 13.
18. Kershaw, *Hitler: 1889–1936,* 158.
19. Truman Smith, *Berlin Alert: The Memoirs and Reports of Truman Smith* (Stanford: Hoover Institution Press, 1984), 46.

20. Hanfstaengl, *Hitler,* 36–37.
21. Hanfstaengl, *Hitler,* 47–51.
22. Kershaw, *Hitler: 1889–1936,* 189.
23. Hanfstaengl, *Hitler,* 42.
24. Adolf Hitler, *Monologe im Führerhauptquartier 1941–1944: Die Aufzeichnungen Heinrich Heims,* ed. Werner Jochmann (Hamburg: Albrecht Knaus, 1980), 43.
25. Historisches Lexikon Bayerns, http://www.historisches-lexikon-bayerns.de/artikel/artikel_44472.
26. Fest, *Hitler,* 165.
27. Eberhard Jäckel and Axel Kuhn, eds., *Hitler: Sämtliche Aufzeichnungen, 1905-1924* (Stuttgart: Deutsche Verlagsanstalt, 1980), 728.

Chapter 3. The Mounting Pressure

1. Hanser, *Putsch!,* 319.
2. Ullrich, *Adolf Hitler: Biographie,* 156.
3. Kershaw, *Hitler: 1889–1936,* 193.
4. http://en.wikipedia.org/wiki/Reichswehr.
5. Davidson, *The Making of Adolf Hitler,* 189.
6. Hanfstaengl, *Hitler,* 86.
7. Hauner, *Hitler,* 39; Hanfstaengl, *Hitler,* 85–86.
8. Phelps, "Hitler als Parteiführer," 274–97.
9. Hanfstaengl, *Hitler,* 52.
10. Tryell, *Führer befiehl,* 48.
11. Heinrich Hoffmann, *Hitler Was My Friend: The Memoirs of Hitler's Photographer* (London: Frontline Books, 1955, 2011), 45.
12. Hanfstaengl, *Hitler,* 34.
13. Hanfstaengl, *Hitler,* 70.
14. Ernst Deuerlein, *Hitler: Eine politische Biographie* (Munich: List Verlag, 1959), 165–66.
15. J. Noakes and G. Pridham, eds. *Nazism: A History in Documents and Eyewitness Accounts 1919–1945, Vol. 1: The Nazi Party, State and Society 1919–1939* (New York: Schocken Books, 1983), 25–26.
16. Roussy de Sales, *Adolf Hitler,* xiii. During 1933–1936, Hitler found time to give six hundred speeches even while running Germany.
17. Phelps, "Hitler als Parteiführer," 286.
18. Sven Felix Kellerhoff, *Mein Kampf: Die Karriere eines deutschen Buches* (Stuttgart: Klett-Cotta, 2015), 211.
19. Kellerhoff, *Mein Kampf: Die Karriere,* 76.
20. Jeffrey Herf, *The Jewish Enemy: Nazi Propaganda During World War II and the Holocaust* (Cambridge, MA: Harvard University Press, 2006), viii.
21. George Sylvester Viereck, "Hitler: The German Explosive," *The American Monthly,* October 1, 1923.

22. Plöckinger, *Geschichte,* 13.
23. Hanfstaengl, *Hitler,* 80.
24. Ernst "Putzi" Hanfstaengl, "I Was Hitler's Closest Friend," *Cosmopolitan,* March, 1943, 43.
25. Lothar Gruchmann, "Hitlers Denkschrift an die Bayerische Justiz vom 16. Mai 1923," *Vierteljahrshefte für Zeitgeschichte,* 39, no. 2 (1991): 324.
26. George Sylvester Viereck, "Hitler: The German Explosive," *The American Monthly,* October 1, 1923; Hauner, *Hitler,* 42.
27. Konrad Heiden, *The Führer: Hitler's Rise to Power* (New York: Carroll & Graf, 1999), 224.
28. Rudolf Hess, *Briefe 1908–1933: Herausgegeben von Wolf Rüdiger Hess* (Munich: Georg Müller Verlag, 1987), 299.
29. Hanfstaengl, *Hitler,* 83.

Chapter 4. A Hot Autumn

1. Mommsen, Hans, *Aufstieg und Untergang,* 212.
2. *New York Times,* September 3, 1923; Read, *The Devil's Disciples: Hitler's Inner Circle* (New York: W. W. Norton, 2003), 86.
3. Anthony Read, *The Devil's Disciples: Hitler's Inner Circle* (New York: W. W. Norton, 2003), 86, by police estimates.
4. Hauner, *Hitler,* 42, reference to *New York Times,* September 3, 1923.
5. Hauner, *Hitler,* 42; Read, *The Devil's Disciples,* 87.
6. Large, *Where Ghosts Walked,* 172; Reiner Pommerin, "Die Ausweisung von 'Ostjuden' aus Bayern 1923," *Vierteljahrshefte für Zeitgeschichte,* 34, no. 3 (1986): 311.
7. In his 1924 treason trial Hitler said he'd learned that Seeckt's wife was not in fact Jewish, and a retraction by the *Völkischer Beobachter* was planned but overtaken by events and never printed. *Hitler-Prozess* (trial transcript), 39.
8. Wilhelm Hoegner, *Die Verratene Republik: Deutsche Geschichte, 1919–1933* (Munich: Nymphenburger Verlagshandlung, 1979), 171.
9. Hoegner, *Die Verratene Republik,* 171.
10. Hanns Hubert Hofmann, *Der Hitlerputsch: Krisenjahre deutscher Geschichte 1920–1924* (Munich: Nymphenburger Verlagshandlung, 1961), 124.
11. Hofmann, *Der Hitlerputsch,* 128, based on Friedrich von Rabenau, Seeckt: *Aus seinem Leben 1918–1936* (Leipzig: Hase & Koehler, 1940), 370.
12. Hoegner, *Hitler und Kahr,* 85.
13. Hoegner, *Hitler und Kahr,* 13.
14. Read, *The Devil's Disciples,* 91; Hoegner, *Die Verratene Republik,* 176.
15. Hofmann, *Der Hitlerputsch,* 284–94.
16. *Hitler-Prozess* (trial transcript), 162.
17. Hoegner, *Hitler und Kahr,* 114–15.
18. Hoegner, *Hitler und Kahr,* 114–15.

19. In trial testimony as reported by *Berliner Tageblatt,* Seisser says both statements were "untrue and freely invented," "Die Verfassungsverstösse," *Berliner Tageblatt,* March 12, 1924.

20. *Hitler-Prozess* (trial transcript), 1005.

21. Jäckel and Kuhn, *Hitler: Sämtliche Aufzeichnungen,* 1032.

22. Otto Freiherr von Berchem, in Gritschneder *Nachlass (Papers), Bayerisches Hauptstaatsarchiv,* 238–58, author's notes. Also Hoegner, *Hitler und Kahr,* 116–17.

23. *Hitler-Prozess* (trial transcript), 791.

24. Hoegner, *Hitler und Kahr,* 80.

25. Hoegner, *Hitler und Kahr,* 79–80. Yet in the trial he claimed flatly in this context that "for Lossow, Seisser, and me, there was no question of any military action or something like that against Berlin." *Hitler-Prozess* (trial transcript), 792.

26. Hoegner, *Hitler und Kahr,* 80.

27. Hanfstaengl, *Hitler,* 88–89.

28. Robert Schauffler, "Munich—A City of Good Nature," *Century,* 56 (1909), 71.

29. Hoegner, *Hitler und Kahr,* 53.

30. Hoegner, *Hitler und Kahr,* 53.

31. Hoegner, *Hitler und Kahr,* 52.

32. "Wir müssen diese Leute hineinkompromettieren." Hanfstaengl, *Hitler,* 88.

33. Hoegner, *Hitler und Kahr,* 81.

34. Hofmann, *Der Hitlerputsch,* 143.

35. Hoegner, *Hitler und Kahr,* 127.

36. Hoegner, *Hitler und Kahr,* 121.

37. Hoegner, *Hitler und Kahr,* 136–38.

38. Hoegner, *Hitler und Kahr,* 136–37.

39. Hoegner wrote: "In recent years it had become a habitual sport of the Bavarian government to sharply deny frequently occurring putsch rumors…with an acid bath of mockery." Hoegner, *Hitler und Kahr,* 136.

Chapter 5. The Putsch

1. Karl Sommer, *Beiträge zur bayerischen* (author's files), 197.

2. "Eindrücke eines Augenzeugen," *Münchener Zeitung,* November 9, 1923 (front page).

3. H. Francis Freniere, Lucie Karcic, Philip Fandek (translators), *The Hitler Trial before the People's Court in Munich* (Arlington, VA: University Publications of America, 1976), 65.

4. *Hitler-Prozess* (trial transcript), part 1, 50.

5. *Hitler-Prozess* (trial transcript), part 1, 309.

6. *Hitler-Prozess* (trial transcript), part 1, 50.

7. Hofmann, *Der Hitlerputsch,* 162.

8. Hanfstaengl, *Hitler,* 36.

9. "Die Ereignisse des gestrigen Abends," *Münchener Zeitung,* November 9, 1923.
10. John Toland, *Adolf Hitler,* vol. 1 (New York: WHS Distributors, 1976), 166.
11. Hofmann, *Der Hitlerputsch,* 164–65.
12. Historians believe the evidence shows that Ludendorff knew exactly what was up. Ludendorff's own stepson said the wily general later told him he had intentionally stayed away from the Bürgerbräukeller—at first. Hoegner, *Hitler und Kahr,* 196. What the old general may have been telling the triumvirate was: I don't like this any more than you do, and for a simple reason: Ludendorff wanted the top job—chief dictator, not chief of the army—for himself. He said as much to a visitor only two days before the putsch. Hoegner, *Hitler und Kahr,* 112.
13. Hofmann, *Der Hitlerputsch,* 166.
14. Freniere, *The Hitler Trial,* 67.
15. Otto Gritschneder, *Der Hitler-Prozess und sein Richter Georg Neithardt* (Munich: C. H. Beck, 2001), 23; *Münchener Zeitung,* front page, November 9, 1923.
16. Hoegner, *Hitler und Kahr,* 168.
17. Hans Kallenbach, *Mit Adolf Hitler auf Festung Landsberg* (Munich: Verlag Kress & Hornung, 1939), 28.
18. Kallenbach, *Mit Adolf Hitler,* 27.
19. Kershaw, *Hitler: 1889–1936,* 174.
20. Harold J. Gordon. Jr., *Hitler and the Beer Hall Putsch* (Princeton: Princeton University Press, 1972), 271–73.
21. Hoegner, *Hitler und Kahr,* 149.
22. Hoegner, *Hitler und Kahr,* 149.
23. Frank, *Im Angesicht,* 61.
24. The Bürgerbräukeller later presented the Nazi Party with a never-paid bill for "beer, sausage, food, coffee, broken furniture, shattered beer mugs, music stands and 148 sets of stolen cutlery" and a special bill to Hitler for his eggs, tea, and meat loaf. Gritschneder, *Der Hitler-Prozess,* 140.
25. Ernst Hanfstaengl, *15 Jahre mit Hitler. Zwischen Weissem und Braunem Haus* (München: Piper, 1980), 141.
26. Gritschneder Nachlass, Box 239, document from printing house. "Because their unit was so strong, it was impossible for us to resist. They took 290,000 fifty-billion mark bills equaling 14,500 trillion marks and 105,000 billion-mark bills equaling 105 trillion marks. All we could achieve was that a supervisor oversaw the delivery and had receipts given for the amount."
27. *Hitler-Prozess* (trial transcript), 62.
28. *Hitler-Prozess* (trial transcript), 57.
29. Gordon, *Hitler and the Beer Hall Putsch,* 353.
30. Hoegner, *Die Verratene Republik,* 186.
31. Indictment against "Joseph Berchthold and comrades" in "little Hitler trial," People's Court Munich 1, May 29, 1924, reprinted in Kallenbach, *Mit Hitler,* 29.

32. Gordon, *Hitler and the Beer Hall Putsch,* 353.
33. *Hitler-Prozess* (trial transcript), 62.
34. Gordon, *Hitler and the Beer Hall Putsch,* 358.
35. Freniere, *The Hitler Trial,* 70.
36. Ullrich, *Adolf Hitler: Biographie,* 180, from Detlev Clemens, *Herr Hitler in Germany* (Göttingen: Vandenhoek and Ruprecht, 1996), 80.
37. "Der vierte Tag des Hitlerprozesses," *Süddeutsche Zeitung,* February 29, 1924.
38. Gordon, *Hitler and the Beer Hall Putsch,* 360.
39. *Hitler-Prozess* (trial transcript), part 3, 1177.
40. Esser, documents.
41. Ullrich, *Adolf Hitler: Biographie,* 178.
42. Hanfstaengl, *Hitler,* 27–29.
43. Hanfstaengl, *15 Jahre,* 61.
44. Hanfstaengl, *Hitler,* 106–9.
45. Jablonsky, *The Nazi Party,* 43.
46. Hanfstaengl, *Hitler,* 108.

Chapter 6. Hitting Bottom

1. Alois Maria Ott, "Aber plötzlich sprang Hitler auf…," *Bayern Kurier,* November 3, 1973.
2. Prison history, "100 Jahre JVA Landsberg am Lech," 30; Heinz A. Heinz, *Germany's Hitler* (London: Hurst and Blackett Ltd., 1934), 170.
3. Franz Hemmrich, "Adolf Hitler in der Festung Landsberg," handwritten, Institut für Zeitgeschichte, ED 153; Archiv Manfred Deiler, 4.
4. Otto Lurker (SS-Sturmführer), *Hitler hinter Festungsmaurern: Ein Bild aus trüben Tagen* (Berlin: E. S. Mittler & Sohn, 1933), 14. Ironically, the "fortress" in 2015 was again being used for small prison industries, such as packaging solid state boards and lipstick. Author's visit, February 10, 2015.
5. Professor George Sigerson, M.D., "Custodia Honesta for Political Prisoners: Custom in Foreign Nations," *Votes for Women,* April 26, 1912.
6. Kallenbach, *Mit Adolf Hitler,* 50.
7. Klaus Weichert, prison historian, letter to the author, July 13, 2015.
8. Hemmrich, "Adolf Hitler," 3.
9. By mutual request, Landsberg's two famous prisoners never met. Arco-Valley was a passionate opponent of Hitler's. From prison history, "100 Jahre JVA Landsberg am Lech," 30.
10. Hemmrich, "Adolf Hitler," 14.
11. Trevor-Roper, *Hitler's Secret Conversations,* 281.
12. Kallenbach, *Mit Adolf Hitler,* photograph, 112b.
13. Hemmrich, "Adolf Hitler," 5–6.

14. Gritschneder, *Der Hitler-Prozess*, Fritz Wiedemann, *Der Mann, der Feldherr werden wollte* (Vellberg und Kettwig: Verlag S. Kappe, 1964), 55.

15. Bavaria's governor Eugen von Knilling to the envoy of neighboring Baden-Württemberg, in Plöckinger, *Geschichte*, 21.

16. Hemmrich, "Adolf Hitler," 11.

17. Ullrich, *Adolf Hitler: Biographie*, 180.

18. Hemmrich, "Adolf Hitler," 18.

19. Esser, documents.

20. Toland, *Adolf Hitler*, vol. 1, 190.

21. Ernst Deuerlein, *Der Aufstieg der NSDAP in Augenzeugenberichten* (Munich: Deutscher Taschenbuch Verlag, 1989), 202.

22. Plöckinger, *Geschichte*, 29.

23. Deuerlein, *Aufstieg*, 202.

24. Plöckinger, *Geschichte*, 21.

25. Hemmrich, "Adolf Hitler," 13.

26. Alois Maria Ott, letter to Werner Maser, December 12, 1973, from Institut für Zeitgeschichte, ED 699/42.

27. Ott, letter to Werner Maser, ED 699/42.

28. This entire section comes from Alois Maria Ott, "Aber plötzlich sprang Hitler auf...," *Bayerischer Kurier*, November 3, 1973; "Von guter Selbstzucht und Beherrschung," *Der Spiegel* 16 (1989): 61.

29. Hanfstaengl, *Hitler*, 113.

30. Hemmrich, "Adolf Hitler," 15.

31. Plöckinger, *Geschichte*, 32.

32. Nachlass Gritschneder (Papers), Bayerisches Hauptstaatsarchiv, Boxes 238–58.

33. His *Foundations of the Nineteenth Century*, written originally in German *(Grundlagen des neunzehnten Jahrhunderts)*, was the preeminent racist tract of the early twentieth century, establishing the extremist notion that Aryans and especially Nordic peoples were the natural lords of the universe.

34. Brigitte Hamann, *Winifred Wagner: A Life at the Heart of Hitler's Bayreuth* (New York: Harcourt, 2002, 2005), 70–71.

35. Ehard immediately afterward wrote a detailed reconstruction of the entire conversation. Bayerisches Hauptstaatsarchiv, Nachlass Ehard (Ehard Papers), no. 94; *Hitler-Prozess* (trial transcript), appendix 5, part 1, 299–307.

36. Nachlass Ehard (Ehard Papers), 710.

37. *Hitler-Prozess* (trial transcript), 301.

38. Otto Gritschneder, *Bewährungsfrist für den Terroristen Adolf H.: Der Hitler-Putsch und die bayerische Justiz* (Munich: C. H. Beck, 1990), 42.

39. The senders called them *Liebesgaben*.

40. Plöckinger, *Geschichte*, 33, footnote to Paula Schlier, *Petras Aufzeichnungen*, (Innsbruck: Brenner-Verlag, 1926), 136.

41. Hemmrich, "Adolf Hitler," 16.
42. Facsimile of letter in Toland, *Adolf Hitler,* 224–25.
43. Hess, *Briefe,* 332.
44. Hemmrich, "Adolf Hitler," 12.
45. Lurker, *Hitler hinter,* 8. Details on Wrede in Jablonsky, *Dissolution,* 181.
46. Lurker, *Hitler hinter,* 8.
47. Hemmrich, "Adolf Hitler," 12.
48. Prison files in Staatsarchiv München, JVA 12417.
49. Plöckinger, *Geschichte,* 14–15.
50. Gordon, *Hitler and the Beer Hall Putsch,* 474.
51. Wikipedia, https://en.wikipedia.org/wiki/Dietrich_Eckart.
52. Jäckel und Kuhn, *Hitler: Sämtliche Aufzeichnungen,* 1038.
53. Hemmrich, "Adolf Hitler," 25.
54. Hemmrich, "Adolf Hitler," 22–23.
55. *Hitler-Prozess* (trial transcript), 308.
56. Kubizek, *The Young Hitler,* 179–80.
57. Kubizek, *The Young Hitler,* 179–80.
58. Alan E. Steinweis, *Studying the Jew: Scholarly Antisemitism in Nazi Germany* (Cambridge, MA: Harvard University Press, 2006), 25.
59. Frank, *Im Angesicht,* 46.
60. Timothy W. Ryback, *Hitler's Private Library: The Books that Shaped His Life* (New York: Knopf, 2008), frontispiece.
61. Hamann, *Hitler's Vienna,* 74–75.
62. Kellerhoff, *Mein Kampf,* 67.
63. Hitler, *Mein Kampf,* 36–38.
64. Frank, *Im Angesicht,* 47.
65. Plöckinger, *Geschichte,* 20. The memorandum has never been found, but it was strongly referenced during Hitler's trial.
66. Plöckinger, *Geschichte,* 21.

Chapter 7. A Trial for Treason

1. Gritschneder, *Der Hitler-Prozess und sein Richter Georg Neithardt,* 13.
2. Before becoming the Reichswehr's Infantry School, the building had been the training academy for the old Bavarian Army. Over its entrance were inscribed the words, "War School" (*Kriegsschule*). See photo, Gritschneder, *Der Hitler-Prozess,* 124.
3. Thomas R. Ybarra, "Lossow Admits Fooling Plotters," *New York Times,* March 11, 1924.
4. "Ludendorff Cool as Trial Begins," *New York Times,* February 27, 1924.
5. *Münchener Zeitung,* February 28, 1924.
6. Freniere, *The Hitler Trial,* xxix.
7. Gordon, *Hitler and the Beer Hall Putsch,* 457.

8. Hanfstaengl, *Hitler,* 113.

9. *Süddeutsche Zeitung,* February 26, 1924.

10. *Münchener Post,* February 29, 1924.

11. "Der vierte Tag des Hitler-Prozesses," *Süddeutsche Zeitung,* February 30 [marked on clipping but must mean February 29], 1924.

12. Dr. Carl Misch, *Vossische Zeitung,* February 26, 1924.

13. "Der vierte Tag des Hitler-Prozesses," *Süddeutsche Zeitung,* February 30 [marked on clipping but must mean 29], 1924.

14. *Hitler-Prozess* (trial transcript), illustration 1, sketch 12a.

15. Dr. Carl Misch, "Gerichtstag," *Vossische Zeitung,* February 26, 1924.

16. *Münchener Zeitung,* February 29, 1924.

17. "Die Sitzung ist eröffnet," *Vossische Zeitung,* February 26, 1924.

18. *Neues Münchener Tagblatt,* March 12, 1924.

19. Dr. Carl Misch, "Gerichtstag," *Vossische Zeitung,* February 26, 1924.

20. Deuerlein, *Aufstieg,* 205.

21. Gritschneder, *Bewährungsfrist,* 63.

22. Gritschneder, *Der Hitler-Prozess,* 54.

23. *Hitler-Prozess* (trial transcript), 17.

24. Gritschneder, *Der Hitler-Prozess,* 43.

25. *Hitler-Prozess* (trial transcript), 1223.

26. Gritschneder, *Der Hitler-Prozess,* 65.

27. The *London Times* says "nearly four hours" in "Munich Treason Trial," *London Times,* February 27, 1924. So does the *Vossische Zeitung* in "Zweiter Tag im Hitler-Prozess," February 28, 1924. Likewise the record of a meeting of the Bavaria Council of Ministers on March 4 in Deuerlein, *Aufstieg,* 215–16. However, the trial transcript suggests it lasted about three hours.

28. "Es sei unmöglich den Redestrom Hitlers zu hemmen." Comment by Gürtner in cabinet meeting. Deuerlein, *Aufstieg,* 16.

29. Kershaw, *Hitler: 1889–1936,* 23–54.

30. *Hitler-Prozess* (trial transcript), 20. Hitler would later use almost exactly the same opener in *Mein Kampf.*

31. Deuerlein, *Hitler,* 71.

32. *Berliner Tageblatt,* Nr. 97, Abend-Ausgabe, February 26, 1924.

33. This and all other quotes from Hitler's opening speech come from *Hitler-Prozess* (trial transcript), 20–65.

34. Freniere, *Hitler Trial,* 70.

35. "Hitlers Verteidigungsrede," *Frankfurter Zeitung,* February 26, 1924.

36. "En allemagne, Le procès Hitler-Ludendorff," *Le Temps,* March 1, 1924.

37. Gritschneder, *Der Hitler-Prozess,* 56–57.

38. "Das neue Mekka," *Vossische Zeitung,* February 27, 1924.

39. Deuerlein, *Aufstieg,* 205.

NOTES

Chapter 8. The Judgment of History

1. *Hitler-Prozess* (trial transcript), 161.
2. "Public Excluded at Munich," *London Times,* February 29, 1924.
3. *Hitler-Prozess* (trial transcript), 195.
4. *Hitler-Prozess* (trial transcript), part 1, 39.
5. *Hitler-Prozess* (trial transcript), 194–200.
6. "Münchner Eindrücke—Aus dem Gerichtssaal von unserem besonderen Vertreter," *Pressebüro Krauss,* March 23, 1924.
7. "Munich Trial: General Ludendorff's Story," *London Times,* March 1, 1924.
8. *Hitler-Prozess* (trial transcript), 252–85.
9. *Hitler-Prozess* (trial transcript), 277–78.
10. Frank, *Im Angesicht,* 51.
11. T. R. Ybarra, "Ludendorff's Talk at Treason Trial Dismays His Party," *New York Times,* March 2, 1924.
12. *Hitler-Prozess* (trial transcript), 203–5.
13. "Antwort des Zentrums an Ludendorff," *Berliner Tageblatt,* March 2, 1924.
14. Gritschneder, *Der Hitler-Prozess,* 113.
15. "Knallerbsen," *Münchener Post,* March 4, 1924 (dateline; no appearance date available).
16. *Hitler-Prozess* (trial transcript), 447.
17. "En Allemagne, Le procès Hitler-Ludendorff," *Le Temps,* March 1, 1924.
18. Thomas R. Ybarra, "Prosecutor Drops Ludendorff Case," *New York Times,* March 7, 1924.
19. Deuerlein, *Augstieg,* 215–16.
20. "Das Mass ist voll," *Vossische Zeitung,* March 6, 1924.
21. Names in Gritschneder, *Der Hitler-Prozess,* 113.
22. Thomas R. Ybarra, "Prosecutor Drops Ludendorff Case," *New York Times,* March 7, 1924.
23. Nachlass Ehard (Ehard Papers) 99, Bayerisches Hauptstaatsarchiv, 40–41.
24. "Konnte Dr. Ehard den Aufstieg Hitlers verhindern?" *Süddeutsche Zeitung,* June 1949, in Ehard Nachlass (Ehard Papers), 98, Bayerisches Hauptstaatsarchiv.
25. Deutsche Wetterzentrale. http://www.wetterzentrale.de/cgi-bin/webbbs/wzconfig1.pl?read=93.
26. "Entweder bedingungslose Unterwerfung oder Kampf," *Deutsche Presse,* March 12, 1924.
27. "Der Hochverratsprozess in München," *Berliner Tageblatt,* March 10, 1924.
28. "Ermittlungsverfahren gegen Kahr-Lossow," *Vossische Zeitung,* March 11, 1924.
29. *"Räuberunwesen"* in *"Der seltsame Prozess,"* by Dr. Ernst Feder, *Berliner Tageblatt,* March 15, 1924.
30. *Hitler-Prozess* (trial transcript), part 2, 737.

31. "Die Aussage Lossows," *Neues Münchener Tagblatt,* March 12, 1924.

32. *München-Augsburger Abendzeitung,* March 12, 1924.

33. "Seisser," *Süddeutsche Zeitung,* March 13, 1924.

34. Mommsen, *Aufstieg und Untergang,* 212.

35. "The Munich Trial: Von Kahr Cross-examined," *London Times,* March 13, 1924.

36. *Hitler-Prozess* (trial transcript), 964–65.

37. "Kahr," *Deutsche Presse,* March 13, 1924.

38. Weinberg, *Hitler's Table Talk,* 170.

39. "Moralität und Legalität," *Völkischer Kurier,* March 15, 1924.

40. "Moralität und Legalität," *Vossische Zeitung,* March 15, 1924.

41. "Moralität und Legalität," *Völkischer Kurier,* March 15, 1924.

42. *Hitler-Prozess* (trial transcript), 1034.

43. "Der Vorhang fällt," *Münchener Post,* March 28, 1924.

44. Deuerlein, *Augstieg,* 221.

45. "Das Schlusswort im Prozess," *Allgemeine Zeitung,* March 31, 1924.

46. Thomas R. Ybarra, "Ludendorff Exalts Himself with Gods," *New York Times,* March 28, 1924.

47. Thomas R. Ybarra, "Ludendorff Exalts Himself with Gods," *New York Times,* March 28, 1924.

48. "Trommeln," *Vossische Zeitung,* March 28, 1924.

49. "Der Vorhang fällt," *Münchener Post,* March 28, 1924.

50. "Höhnische Verherrlichung des Hochverrats," *Münchener Post,* March 27, 1924.

51. Thomas R. Ybarra, "Munich in Ferment, Awaiting Verdict," *New York Times,* March 29, 1924.

52. Author's notes from Staatsarchiv München.

53. Thomas R. Ybarra, "Munich in Ferment, Awaiting Verdict," *New York Times,* March 29, 1924.

54. Thomas R. Ybarra, "Munich in Ferment, Awaiting Verdict," *New York Times,* March 29, 1924.

55. Thomas R. Ybarra, "Munich in Ferment, Awaiting Verdict," *New York Times,* March 29, 1924.

56. "Kahr, Lossow, Seisser zur 'Erholung' in Italien," *Allgemeine Zeitung,* March 29, 1924.

57. "Der scharzweissrote Wimpel," *Vossische Zeitung,* April 1, 1924.

58. Double chins from Otto Strasser, *Hitler and I* (trans. from *Hitler et moi*), 1940, http://mailstar.net/otto-strasser-hitler.html.

59. "Ludendorff est acquitté," *Le Petit Parisien,* front page, April 2, 1924.

60. *Hitler-Prozess* (trial transcript), 297.

61. *Hitler-Prozess* (trial transcript), 364.

62. Gritschneder, *Der Hitler-Prozess,* 55.

63. Quoted in *Frankfurter Zeitung,* April 5, 1924.
64. "Judicial Bankruptcy," by Ernst Feder, *Berliner Tageblatt,* April 1, 1924.
65. "Verdict Called April Fool Joke," *New York Times,* April 2, 1924.
66. Gritschneder, *Der Hitler-Prozess,* 15.
67. "Deutschlands Justizschande" *Vorwärts,* April 2, 1924.
68. Toby Thacker, *Joseph Goebbels: Life and Death, 2009* (New York: Palgrave Macmillan, 2009), 33–34.

Chapter 9. Rearranging the World
1. Hemmrich, "Adolf Hitler," 25.
2. Hess, *Briefe,* 323.
3. Photo, U.S. Holocaust Memorial Museum, http://www.ushmm.org/propaganda/archive/hitler landsberg/.
4. Plöckinger, *Geschichte,* 33.
5. Hemmrich, "Adolf Hitler," 41.
6. Werner Maser, *Adolf Hitler,* Mein Kampf: *der Fahrplan eines Welteroberers: Geschichte, Auszüge, Kommentare* (Esslingen: Bechtle, 1974), title page.
7. Jäckel and Kuhn, *Hitler: Sämtliche Aufzeichnungen,* 1216.
8. Jäckel and Kuhn, *Hitler: Sämtliche Aufzeichnungen,* 1216–27.
9. Plöckinger, *Geschichte,* 34, footnote to "Mitteilung vom 27.9.1951 in: IfZ-Archiv, Munich, ZS 137."
10. Hess, *Briefe,* 273.
11. Beierl and Plöckinger, "Neue Dokumente," 261–79.
12. Plöckinger, *Geschichte,* 42.
13. Plöckinger, *Geschichte,* 40.
14. Plöckinger, *Geschichte,* 34, and Beierl and Plöckinger, 273, footnote to *Volksruf* (Salzburg), May 17, 1924.
15. Archiv Manfred Deiler, http://www.buergervereinigung-landsberg.de/festungshaft/DokumenteHItlerFestungshaft.pdf.
16. "Abschrift. Besuche für den Gefangenen Adolf Hitler," Staatsarchiv München, No. 14344.
17. Hemmrich, "Adolf Hitler," 44.
18. Photo, Anna Maria Sigmund, *Des Führers bester Freund* (Munich: Wilhelm Heyne Verlag, 2005), 81.
19. Beierl and Plöckinger, "Neue Dokumente," 268.
20. Hess, *Briefe,* 349.
21. Hemmrich, "Adolf Hitler," 35–36.
22. Plöckinger, *Geschichte,* 406, footnote, *Völkisches Echo,* July 11, 1924.

Chapter 10. The Boss
1. Kallenbach, *Mit Adolf Hitler,* 52–53.
2. Kallenbach, *Mit Adolf Hitler,* 51.

3. Anna Maria Sigmund, *Des Führers,* 57–58.
4. Lurker, *Hitler hinter,* 23.
5. Hess, *Briefe,* 324.
6. Kallenbach, *Mit Adolf Hitler,* 61.
7. Kallenbach, *Mit Adolf Hitler,* 47–48.
8. Hemmrich, "Adolf Hitler," 58.
9. Hess, *Briefe,* 349.
10. Kallenbach, *Mit Adolf Hitler,* 96.
11. Kallenbach, *Mit Adolf Hitler,* 97.
12. Hemmrich, "Adolf Hitler," 41.
13. Hemmrich, "Adolf Hitler," 92–93.
14. Lurker, *Hitler hinter,* Illustration 17, 66–67.
15. Hemmrich, "Adolf Hitler," 33.
16. Kallenbach, *Mit Adolf Hitler,* 78.
17. Dr. Brinsteiner Landsberg Prison medical report, April 2, 1924, in Lurker, *Hitler hinter,* 68.
18. Hanfstaengl, *Hitler,* 114.
19. Kallenbach, *Mit Adolf Hitler,* 79.
20. Lurker, *Hitler hinter,* 41.

Chapter 11. The Holy Book

1. Weinberg, *Hitler's Table Talk,* 218.
2. Werner Jochmann, *Nationalsozialismus und Revolution: Ursprung und Geschichte der NSDAP in Hamburg 1922–1933* (Frankfurt, 1963), 77–78.
3. Jäckel and Kuhn, *Hitler: Sämtliche Aufzeichnungen,* 1247, from *Völkischer Kurier,* July 7, 1924.
4. Hess, *Briefe,* 349.
5. Jochmann, *Nationalsozialismus,* 91.
6. Hitler, *Mein Kampf,* xxvii.
7. H. R. Trevor-Roper, "The Mind of Adolf Hitler," *Hitler's Table Talk 1941–1944: His Private Conversations,* London, 2000–2008, xlii.
8. Weinberg, *Hitler's Table Talk,* xxii.
9. Beierl and Plöckinger, "Neue Dokumente," 294.
10. Kershaw, *Hitler: 1889–1936,* 240.
11. Hitler, *Mein Kampf,* 64–65.
12. Hitler, *Mein Kampf,* 42.
13. Kershaw, *Hitler: 1889–1936,* and Hamann, 74.
14. Hitler, *Mein Kampf,* 177.
15. Barbara Zehnpfenning, "Nationalsozialismus als Anti-Marxismus? Hitlers programmatisches Selbstverständnis in 'Mein Kampf,'" *Die weltanschaulichen Grundlagen des NS-Regimes: Ursprünge, Gegenentwürfe, Nachwirkungen.* Tagungsband der XXIII. Königswinterer Tagung im Februar 2010, 79–99.

16. Hitler, *Mein Kampf,* 116.

17. Fest, *Hitler,* 214.

18. Otto Strasser in Kershaw, *Hitler: 1889–1936,* 242.

19. Kershaw, *Hitler: 1889–1936,* 241.

20. Eberhard Jäckel, *Hitlers Weltanschauung* (Stuttgart: Deutsche Verlags-Anstalt, 1981), 7.

21. Fritz Stern, *The Politics of Cultural Depair: A Study in the Rise of the German Ideology* (Berkeley: University of California Press, 1961, 1974), xi.

22. Zehnpfenning, "Nationalsozialismus," 82.

23. Hitler, *Mein Kampf,* 358.

24. Hitler, *Mein Kampf,* 313.

25. Hitler, *Mein Kampf,* 70.

26. Barbara Zehnpfennig, *Adolf Hitler: Mein Kampf: Weltanschauung und Programm: Studienkommentar* (Munich: Wilhelm Fink, 2011), 247.

27. Plöckinger, *Geschichte,* 50, footnote to Bundesarchiv Bern (Switzerland), Nachlass Hess (Hess Papers), 1.211–1989/148, 33.

28. Letter from Ilse Hess to Werner Maser, December 28, 1952. "Fahrplan eines Welteroberers: Adolf Hitlers 'Mein Kampf,'" von Werner Maser, *Der Spiegel,* Nr. 32, August 1, 1966, p. 38.

29. Hanfstaengl, *Hitler,* 115.

30. Hanfstaengl, *Hitler,* 115.

31. Hess, *Briefe,* 346.

32. Barbara Zehnpfenning, "Nationalsozialismus," 79–99.

33. Hitler, *Mein Kampf,* 149.

34. Hitler, *Monologe,* 58.

35. Hess, *Briefe,* 341–43.

36. Weber, *Hitler's First War,* 28ff.

37. Hess, *Briefe,* 324.

38. Hess, *Briefe,* 330.

39. Hemmrich, "Adolf Hitler," 44.

40. Edmund A. Walsh, S. J., "The Mystery of Haushofer," *Life,* September 16, 1946, 107.

41. Frank, *Im Angesicht,* 46.

42. Hess, *Briefe,* 322.

43. Toland, *Adolf Hitler,* vol. 1, 208, footnote to testimony at Nuremberg, Oct. 7, 1945, 7.

44. Hess, *Briefe,* 345.

45. Jäckel, *Weltanschauung,* 38; Jäckel and Kuhn, *Hitler: Sämtliche Aufzeichnungen,* 96.

46. Plöckinger, *Geschichte,* 52.

47. Hitler, *Mein Kampf,* 334–337.

48. Hitler, *Mein Kampf,* 333.

49. Deuerlein, *Aufstieg,* 236.

50. Plöckinger, *Geschichte,* 53.

51. Hess, *Briefe,* 347.

52. Plöckinger, *Geschichte,* 55.

53. Plöckinger, *Geschichte,* 54.

54. Hitler, *Mein Kampf,* 229.

55. Hitler, *Monologe,* 262.

56. Beierl and Plöckinger, "Neue Dokumente," 293.

57. Beierl and Plöckinger, "Neue Dokumente," 294.

58. Hitler, *Mein Kampf,* 317.

59. Hitler, *Mein Kampf,* 324.

60. Kellerhoff, *Mein Kampf,* 86.

61. Jäckel and Kuhn, *Hitler: Sämtliche Aufzeichnungen,* 1242.

62. Noakes and Pridham, eds., *Nazism: A History,* 37.

63. Kurt G. W. Ludecke, *I Knew Hitler: The Lost Testimony by a Survivor from the Night of the Long Knives* (Barnesly: Pen & Sword, 2011 [orig. 1938]), 175.

64. Ludecke, *I Knew Hitler,* 179.

65. Jochmann, *Nationalsozialismus,* 91.

66. Hitler, *Mein Kampf,* 379.

67. Hitler, *Mein Kampf,* 376.

68. Kallenbach, *Mit Hitler,* 150.

69. Hess, *Briefe,* 338.

70. Staatsarchiv München, JVA 12437.

71. Hess, *Briefe,* 347.

Chapter 12. A Second Chance

1. Hitler, *Mein Kampf,* 256.

2. Weinberg, *Hitler's Table Talk,* 216.

3. Kershaw, *Hitler: 1889–1936,* 237.

4. Gritschneder, *Bewährungsfrist,* 116–17.

5. Plöckinger, *Geschichte,* 61, footnote, *Das Buch der Deutschen,* 3ff.

6. Plöckinger, *Geschichte,* 56.

7. Hess, *Briefe,* 353.

8. Gritschneder, *Bewährungsfrist,* 126.

9. Gritschneder, *Bewährungsfrist,* 129.

10. Gritschneder, *Bewährungsfrist,* 130.

11. Hitler, *Monologe,* 259–60.

12. Plöckinger, *Geschichte,* 62; Hess, *Briefe,* 359.

13. Plöckinger, *Geschichte,* 62.

14. Weinberg, *Hitler's Table Talk,* 217.

Chapter 13. Starting Over

1. Hanfstaengl, *Hitler*, 125.
2. Weinberg, *Hitler's Table Talk*, 217.
3. Plöckinger, *Geschichte*, 63.
4. Hanfstaengl, *Hitler*, 125.
5. Plöckinger, *Geschichte*, 67–68.
6. Large, *Where Ghosts Walked*, 203.

Epilogue. What Finally Happened

1. Hitler, *Mein Kampf,* 772.
2. Hitler, *Mein Kampf,* 772.
3. Hitler, *Mein Kampf,* 741.
4. Kellerhoff, *Mein Kampf,* title page.
5. Plöckinger, *Geschichte*, 175.
6. "Erledigung Hitlers," *Frankfurter Zeitung und Handelsblatt (Erstes Morgenblatt),* 70, no. 841 (November 11, 1925).
7. Plöckinger, *Geschichte*, 183.
8. Plöckinger, *Geschichte*, 184–86.
9. Plöckinger, *Geschichte*, 419ff.
10. Plöckinger, *Geschichte*, 154–55.
11. Interview with the author, June 12, 2014.
12. Sven Felix Kellerhoff, "'Mein Kampf'zeigt Hitler als systematischen Denker," *Die Welt* (interview with Barbara Zehnpfennig), January 17, 2012. http://www.welt.de/kultur/history/article13819610.
13. Claus Christian Malzahn, *Deutschland, Deutschland: Kurze Geschichte einer geteilten Nation* (Munich: Deutscher Taschenbuch Verlag, 2005), 7.

Bibliography

Abel, Theodore. *Why Hitler Came Into Power.* Cambridge, MA: Harvard University Press, 1938.

Arendt, Hannah. *Eichmann in Jerusalem: A Report on the Banality of Evil.* New York: Penguin, 1964.

Baynes, N. H., ed. *Speeches of Adolf Hitler: Early Speeches, 1922–1924, and Other Selections.* New York: Howard Fertig, 2006.

Beierl, Florian, and Othmar Plöckinger. "Neue Dokumente zu Hitlers Buch *Mein Kampf.*" *Vierteljahrshefte für Zeitgeschichte* 57, no. 2 (2009): 261–279.

Berchem, Otto Freiherr von, in Gritschneder Nachlass, 238–258, Bayerisches Hauptstaatsarchiv, author's notes.

Bessel, Richard. *Germany After the First World War.* Oxford: Clarendon Press, 1993.

Bonn, M. J. *Wandering Scholar.* London: Cohen and West, 1949.

Boone, J. C. *Hitler at the Obersalzberg.* Self-published, 2008.

Bullock, Alan. *Hitler: A Study in Tyranny.* 1952. Rev. ed., New York: Konecky and Konecky, 1962.

Bytwerk, Randall L., ed. *Landmark Speeches of National Socialism.* College Station: TX: A&M University Press, 2008.

Chamberlain, Houston Stewart. *Die Grundlagen des neunzehnten Jahrhunderts* (The Foundations of the Nineteenth Century). 1899. Translated by John Lees. 1911. Reprinted facsimile of 1899 edition, Chestnut Hill, MA: Adamant Media Corporation, 2003.

Craig, Gordon A. "Engagement and Neutrality in Weimar Germany." *Journal of Contemporary History* 2, no. 2 (Literature and Society) (1967): 49–63.

Craig, Gordon A. *The Germans.* New York: Meridian, 1983.

Craig, Gordon A. *Germany 1866–1945.* Oxford: Oxford University Press, 1978.

Cullen, Michael S. *Der Reichstag*. Berlin: Bebra Verlag, 1999.

Davidson, Eugene. *The Making of Adolf Hitler: The Birth and Rise of Nazism*. New York: Macmillan, 1977.

Deiler, Manfred. Archiv Manfred Deieler.

De Jonge, Alex. *The Weimar Chronicle: Prelude to Hitler*. New York: New American Library, 1978.

Deuerlein, Ernst. *Hitler: Eine politische Biographie*. Munich: List Verlag, 1959.

Deuerlein, Ernst. *Der Hitler-Putsch: Bayerische Dokumente zum 8./9. November 1923* (Sonderdruck aus Band 9). Stuttgart: Deutsche Verlags-Anstalt, 1962.

Deuerlein, Ernst. "Hitlers Eintritt in die Politik und die Reichswehr: Dokumentation." *Vierteljahrshefte für Zeitgeschichte* 7, no. 2 (1959).

Dietrich, Otto. *The Hitler I Knew: Memoirs of the Third Reich's Press Chief*. New York: Skyhorse Publishing, 2010.

Domarus, Max. *The Essential Hitler: Speeches and Commentary*, ed. Patrick Romane. Mundelein, IL: Bolchazy-Carducci, 2007.

Ehard, Hans. Nachlass (Ehard Papers), Bayerisches Hauptstaatsarchiv no. 94.

"Eindrücke eines Augenzeugen," *Münchener Zeitung*, front page, November 9, 1923.

Esser, Hermann documents (postwar interviews), Institut für Zeitgeschichte, ED 561/5-3.

Evans, Richard J. *The Coming of the Third Reich*. New York: Penguin, 2004.

Fest, Joachim C. *The Face of the Third Reich: Portraits of the Nazi Leadership*. 1970. Reprint, New York: Da Capo Press, 1999.

Fest, Joachim C. *Hitler*. New York: Harcourt Brace Jovanovich, 1973.

Fest, Joachim C. *Plotting Hitler's Death: The Story of the German Resistance*. Translated by Bruce Little. New York: Henry Holt, 1996.

Fleming, Gerald. *Hitler and the Final Solution*. Berkeley: University of California Press, 1982.

Forever in the Shadow of Hitler? Original documents of the Historikerstreit, the controversy concerning the singularity of the Holocaust. Translated by James Knowlton and Truett Cates. New Jersey: Humanities Press, 1993.

Fraenkel, Heinrich. *The German People Versus Hitler*. New York: Routledge, 1940.

Frank, Hans. *Im Angesicht des Galgens: Deutung Hitlers und seiner Zeit auf Grund eigener Erlebnisse und Erkenntnisse. Geschrieben im Nürnberger Justizgefängnis*. Munich: Friedrich Alfred Beck Verlag, 1953.

Frey, Alexander Moritz. *The Cross Bearers*. New York: Viking, 1930.

Friedrich, Otto. *Before the Deluge: A Portrait of Berlin in the 1920s*. New York: Harper and Row, 1972.

Gassert, Philipp, and Daniel S. Mattern. *The Hitler Library: A Bibliography*. Westport, CT: Greenwood Press, 2001.

Gay, Peter. *My German Question: Growing Up in Nazi Berlin*. New Haven: Yale University Press, 1998.

Gerlich, Fritz. *Ein Publizist gegen Hitler: Briefe und Akten 1930–1934*. Paderborn: Ferdinand Schöningh, 2010.

Gilbert, G. M. *Nuremberg Diary*. New York: Signet, 1947.

Goldensohn, Leon, ed. *Nuremberg Interviews: An American Psychiatrist's Conversations with the Defendants and Witnesses*. New York: Knopf, 2004.

Gordon, Harold, J. Jr. *Hitler and the Beer Hall Putsch*. Princeton: Princeton University Press, 1972.

Görtemaker, Heike B. *Eva Braun: Life with Hitler*. Translated by Damion Searls. New York: Knopf, 2011.

Gregor, Neil. *How to Read Hitler*. London: W. W. Norton and Company, 2005.

Gritschneder, Otto. *Bewährungsfrist für den Terroristen Adolf H.: Der Hitler-Putsch und die bayerische Justiz*. Munich: Verlag C. H. Beck, 1990.

Gritschneder, Otto. *Der Hitler-Prozess und sein Richter Georg Neithardt: Skandalurteil von 1924 ebnet Hitler den Weg*. Munich: Verlag C. H. Beck, 2001.

Gritschneder Nachlass, Bayerisches Hauptstaatsarchiv, Boxes 238–258.

Gruchmann, Lothar. "Hitlers Denkschrift an die Bayerische Justiz vom 16. Mai 1923," *Vierteljahrshefte für Zeitgeschichte* 39, no. 2 (1991).

Gruchmann, Lothar, and Reinhard Weber, eds., assisted by Otto Gritschneder. *Der Hitler-Prozess* (trial transcript): *Wortlaut der Hauptverhandlung vor dem Volksgericht München* 1, part 1–4. Munich: K. G. Saur, 1997 [cited in endnotes as *Hitler-Prozess* (trial transcript)].

Haffner, Sebastian. *Defying Hitler: A Memoir*. Translated by Oliver Pretzel. New York: Farrar, Straus and Giroux, 2000.

Haffner, Sebastian. *The Meaning of Hitler*. Cambridge, MA: Harvard University Press, 1983.

Hamann, Brigitte. *Hitler's Vienna: A Dictator's Apprenticeship*, New York: Oxford University Press, 1999.

Hamann, Brigitte. *Winifred Wagner: A Life at the Heart of Hitler's Bayreuth*. New York: Harcourt, 2005.

Hanfstaengl, Ernst. *15 Jahre mit Hitler: Zwischen Weissem und Braunem Haus*. 1970. Reprint, Munich: R. Piper & Co. Verlag, 1980.

Hanfstaengl, Ernst. *Hitler: The Memoir of a Nazi Insider Who Turned Against the Führer*. 1957. Reprint, New York: Arcade, 2011.

Hanfstaengl, Ernst. "I Was Hitler's Closest Friend," *Cosmopolitan*, March 1943, p. 43.

Hanser, Richard. *Putsch! How Hitler Made Revolution*. New York: Peter H. Wyden, 1970.

Hant, Claus. *Young Hitler*. London: Quartet, 2010.

Harris, Robert. *Selling Hitler: The Extraordinary Story of the Con Job of the Century — The Faking of the Hitler "Diaries."* New York: Pantheon Books, 1986.

Hauner, Milan. *Hitler: A Chronology of His Life and Time*. New York: St. Martin's, 1983.

Hayman, Ronald. *Hitler and Geli.* New York: Bloomsbury, 1997.

Heiden, Konrad. *The Führer.* Edison: Castle Books, 2002 (from editions of 1934–1939).

Heiden, Konrad. *Hitler-Biographie.* Vol. 1, *Adolf Hitler: Das Zeitalter der Verantwortungslosigkeit.* Zürich: Europaverlag, 1936.

Heinz, Heinz A. *Germany's Hitler.* London: Hurst and Blackett, 1934.

Hemmrich, Franz. "Adolf Hitler in der Festung Landsberg," handwritten, Institut für Zeitgeschichte, ED 153; Archiv Manfred Deiler.

Herf, Jeffrey. *The Jewish Enemy: Nazi Propaganda During World War II and the Holocaust.* Cambridge, MA: Harvard University Press, 2006.

Herf, Jeffrey. *Nazi Propaganda for the Arab World.* New Haven: Yale University Press, 2009.

Herf, Jeffrey. *Reactionary Modernism: Technology, Culture, and Politics in Weimar and the Third Reich.* New York: Cambridge University Press, 1984.

Hess, Rudolf. *Briefe 1908–1933: Herausgegeben von Wolf Rüdiger Hess.* Munich: Georg Müller Verlag, 1987.

Historisches Lexikon Bayerns, http://www.historisches-lexikon-bayerns.de/artikel/artikel_44472.

Hitler, Adolf. *Mein Kampf.* Translated by Ralph Manheim. Introduction by Konrad Heiden. 1943. Reprint, Boston: Houghton Mifflin, 1971.

Hitler, Adolf. *Mein Kampf: Zwei Bände in einem Band. Ungekürzte Ausgabe.* 851st–855th printing. Munich: Zentralverlag der NSDAP, Frz. Eher Nachf., 1943.

Hitler, Adolf. *Monologe im Führerhauptquartier 1941–1944: Die Aufzeichnungen Heinrich Heims,* ed. Werner Jochmann. Hamburg: Albrecht Knaus, 1980.

Hitler, Adolf. "Warum musste ein 8. November kommen?" *Deutschlands Erneuerung,* April 1924.

"Hitler-Ludendorff Prozess," Akten, Auswärtiges Amt, Presse-Abteilung, Politisches Archiv des Auswärtigen Amts, Bd. 1, R 122415.

Hitler: Reden, Schriften, Anordnungen, Institut für Zeitgeschichte, Munich. 14 vols. (thus far). Munich.

Hitler's Secret Conversations, 1941–1944. Introduction by H. R. Trevor-Roper. New York: Farrar, Straus and Young, 1953.

Hoegner, Wilhelm (pseud). *Hitler und Kahr: Die bayerischen Napoleonsgrössen von 1923: Ein im Untersuchungsausschuss des Bayerischen Landtags aufgedeckter Justizskandal,* parts 1 and 2. Munich: Landesausschuss der S.P.D. in Bayern, 1928.

Hoegner, Wilhelm. *Die Verratene Republik: Deutsche Geschichte, 1919–1933.* 1958. Reprinted, Munich: Nymphenburger Verlagshandlung, 1979.

Hoffmann, Heinrich. *Hitler Was My Friend: The Memoirs of Hitler's Photographer.* 1955. Reprint, London: Frontline Books, 2011.

Hofmann, Hanns Hubert. *Der Hitlerputsch: Krisenjahre deutscher Geschichte 1920–1924.* Munich: Nymphenburger Verlagshandlung, 1961.

Horn, Wolfgang, "Ein unbekannter Aufsatz Hitlers aus dem Frühjahr 1924." *Vierteljahrshefte für Zeitgeschichte* 16, no. 3 (1968): 280–94.

Hoser, Paul. *Die politischen, wirtschaftlichen und sozialen Hintergründe der Münchner Tagespresse zwischen 1914 und 1934* 2 (series 3, *Europäische Hochschulschriften*, vol. 447). Frankfurt am Main: 1990 (diss. University of Munich, 1988).

Hoser, Paul. "Die Rosenbaum–Krawalle von 1921 in Memmingen." In *Geschichte und Kultur der Juden in Schwaben III. Zwischen Nähe, Distanz und Fremdheit*, edited by Peter Fassl, 95–110. Augsburg, 2007.

Jablonsky, David. *The Nazi Party in Dissolution: Hitler and the Verbotzeit 1923– 1925*. London: Frank Cass, 1989.

Jäckel, Eberhard. *Hitlers Weltanschauung: Entwurf einer Herrschaft*. 1969. Rev. ed., Stuttgart: Deutsche Verlags-Anstalt, 1981.

Jäckel, Eberhard, and Axel Kuhn, eds. *Hitler: Sämtliche Aufzeichnungen, 1905– 1924*. Stuttgart: Deutsche Verlagsanstalt, 1980.

Jetzinger, Franz. *Hitler's Youth*. Westport, CT: Greenwood Press, 1976.

Jochmann, Werner. *Nationalsozialismus und Revolution: Ursprung und Geschichte der NSDAP in Hamburg, 1922–1933: Dokumente*. (Veröffentlichungen der Forschungsstelle für die Geschichte des Nationalsozialismus in Hamburg, Bd. III). Frankfurt a. M.: Europäische Verlagsanstalt, 1963.

Junge, Traudl. *Until the Final Hour: Hitler's Last Secretary*. London: Weidenfeld and Nicolson, 2003.

Kaes, Anton, Martin Jay, and Edward Dimendberg, eds. *The Weimar Republic Sourcebook*. Berkeley: University of California Press, 1994.

Kallenbach, Hans. *Mit Adolf Hitler auf Festung Landsberg*. Munich: Verlag Kress & Hornung, 1939.

Kellerhoff, Sven Felix. "Adolf Hitler wurde spät zum Antisemiten." *Die Welt,* March 3, 2009.

Kellerhoff, Sven Felix. *'Mein Kampf': Die Karriere eines Buches*. Stuttgart: Klett-Cotta, 2015.

Kellerhoff, Sven Felix. "*Mein Kampf* zeigt Hitler als systematischen Denker." *Die Welt* (interview with Barbara Zehnpfennig), January 17, 2012.

Kempe, Frederick. *Father/Land: A Personal Search for the New Germany*. Bloomington: Indiana University Press, 1999.

Kempka, Erich. *I Was Hitler's Chauffeur: The Memoirs of Erich Kempka*. London: Frontline Books, 2010.

Kershaw, Ian. *Hitler: 1889–1936: Hubris*. London, New York: W. W. Norton, 1998.

Kershaw, Ian. *Hitler: 1936–1945: Nemesis*. London, New York: W. W. Norton, 2000.

Klemperer, Victor. *I Will Bear Witness 1933–1941: A Diary of the Nazi Years*. Translated by Martin Chalmers. New York: Modern Library, 1999.

Korn, Salomon. *Geteilte Erinnerung.* Berlin: Philo, 1999.

Kubizek, August. *The Young Hitler I Knew.* London: Greenhill Books, 2006.

Lambert, Angela. *The Lost Life of Eva Braun.* New York: St. Martin's, 2006.

"Landsberg im 20. Jahrhundert." Bürgervereinigung zur Erforschung der Landsberger Zeitgeschichte. (Citizens' Association to Research Landsberg's Contemporary History). http://www.buergervereinigung-landsberg.de/gedenkstaette/landsberg.htm.

Laqueur, Walter. *Weimar: A Cultural History. 1918–1933.* New York: Putnam, 1974.

Large, David Clay. *Where Ghosts Walked: Munich's Road to the Third Reich.* New York, London: W. W. Norton, 1997.

Larson, Erik. *In the Garden of Beasts: Love, Terror, and an American Family in Hitler's Berlin.* New York: Crown Publishers, 2011.

Linge, Heinz. *With Hitler to the End: The Memoirs of Adolf Hitler's Valet.* London: Frontline Books, 2009.

Lipstadt, Deborah E. *The Eichmann Trial.* New York: Schocken Books, 2011.

Ludecke [Lüdecke], Kurt G. W. *I Knew Hitler: The Lost Testimony of a Survivor from the Night of the Long Knives.* 1938. Reprint, Barnsley, South Yorkshire: Pen & Word, 2013.

Lurker, Otto (SS-Sturmführer). *Hitler hinter Festungsmauern: Ein Bild aus trüben Tagen.* Berlin: E. S. Mittler & Sohn, 1933.

Maier, Charles S. *The Unmasterable Past: History, Holocaust, and German National Identity.* Cambridge, MA: Harvard University Press, 1997.

Malzahn, Claus Christian. *Deutschland, Deutschland: Kurze Geschichte einer geteilten Nation.* Munich: Deutscher Taschenbuch Verlag, 2005.

Maser, Werner. *Adolf Hitler, Mein Kampf: der Fahrplan eines Welteroberers: Geschichte, Auszüge, Kommentare.* Esslingen: Bechtle, 1974.

Maser, Werner. *Hitlers* Mein Kampf: *Entstehung, Aufbau, Stil, Änderungen, Quellen, Quellenwert, kommentierte Auszüge.* Munich: Bechtle Verlag, 1966.

Maser, Werner. *Der Sturm auf die Republik: Frühgeschichte der NSDAP.* Stuttgart: Deutsche Verlags-Anstalt, 1973.

Maser, Werner, ed. *Hitler's Letters and Notes.* New York: Bantam, 1976.

Mommsen, Hans. *Aufstieg und Untergang der Republik von Weimar 1918–1933.* Berlin: Ullstein, 1989–2009.

Mommsen, Hans. *The Rise and Fall of Weimar Democracy.* Chapel Hill: University of North Carolina Press, 1989.

Moorhouse, Roger. *Killing Hitler: The Plots, the Assassins, and the Dictator Who Cheated Death.* New York: Bantam Dell, 2006.

Müller, Karl Alexander von. *Im Wandel einer Welt, Erinnerungen, 1919–1932.* Munich: Süddeutscher Verlag, 1966.

Müller, Karl Alexander von. *Mars und Venus: Erinnerungen 1914–1919.* Stuttgart: Verlag Gustav Klippert, 1954.

Nagorski, Andrew. *Hitlerland: American Eyewitnesses to the Nazi Rise to Power.* New York: Simon and Schuster, 2012.

Nerdinger, Winifried, Hans Günter Hockerts, Marita Krauss, Peter Longerich, Mirjana Grdanjski, and Markus Eisen, eds. *Munich and National Socialism: Catalogue of the Munich Documentation Center for the History of National Socialism.* Munich: C. H. Beck, 2015.

Nicholls, A. J. *Weimar and the Rise of Hitler,* 4th ed. New York: St. Martin's, 2000.

Noakes, J., and G. Pridham, eds. *Nazism: A History in Documents and Eyewitness Accounts 1919–1945. Vol. 1, The Nazi Party, State and Society 1919–1939.* New York: Schocken Books, 1983.

O'Donnell, James P. *The Bunker: Hitler's Last Days and Suicide.* New York: Bantam Books, 1979.

Ott, Alois Marie. "Aber plötzlich sprang Hitler auf…" *Bayern Kurier,* November 3, 1973.

Persico, Joseph E. *Nuremberg: Infamy on Trial.* New York: Penguin, 1994.

Phelps, Reginald H. "Hitler als Parteiführer im Jahre 1920," *Vierteljahrshefte für Zeitgeschichte* 11, no. 3 (1963).

Plöckinger, Othmar. *Geschichte eines Buches: Adolf Hitlers "Mein Kampf" 1922–1945: Eine Veröffentlichung des Instituts für Zeitgeschichte.* Munich: R. Oldenbourg Verlag, 2006.

Plöckinger, Othmar. *Unter Soldaten und Agitatoren: Hitlers prägende Jahre im deutschen Militär, 1918–1920.* Paderborn: Ferdinand Schöningh, 2013.

Pommerin, Reiner. "Die Ausweisung von 'Ostjuden' aus Bayern 1923," *Vierteljahrshefte für Zeitgeschichte* 34, no. 3 (1986).

Rabenau, Friedrich von Seeckt. *Aus seinem Leben 1918–1936.* Leipzig: Hase, 1941.

Rauschning, Hermann. *Hitler Speaks: A Series of Political Conversations with Adolf Hitler on His Real Aims.* London: Thornton Butterworth, 1939.

Read, Anthony. *The Devil's Disciples: Hitler's Inner Circle.* New York, London, 2003.

Remak, Joachim, ed. *The Nazi Years: A Documentary History.* New York: Simon and Schuster, 1969.

Reuth, Ralf Georg. *Goebbels.* Translated by Krishna Winston. New York: Harcourt Brace, 1993.

Rhodes, Richard. *Masters of Death: The SS-Einsatzgruppen and the Invention of the Holocaust.* New York: Knopf, 2002.

Rosenbaum, Ron. *Explaining Hitler: The Search for the Origins of His Evil.* New York: Harper Perennial, 1999.

Rosenbaum, Ron, ed. *Those Who Forget the Past: The Question of Anti-Semitism.* New York: Random House, 2004.

Rosenberg, Alfred. *Memoirs of Alfred Rosenberg, with commentaries by Serge Lang and Eric Posselt.* Chicago: Ziff-Davis, 1949.

Rosenberg, Alfred. *The Myth of the Twentieth Century: An Evaluation of the Spiritual-Intellectual Confrontations of our Age.* 1930. Reprint, Torrance, CA: Noontide Press, 1982.

Ryback, Timothy W. *Hitler's Private Library: The Books that Shaped His Life.* New York: Knopf, 2008.

Sales, Raoul de Roussy de, ed. *Adolf Hitler: My New Order.* New York: Reynal and Hitchcock, 1941.

Schroeder, Christa. *He Was My Chief: The Memoirs of Adolf Hitler's Secretary.* London: Frontline Books, 2009.

Sherratt, Yvonne. *Hitler's Philosophers.* New Haven: Yale University Press, 2013.

Shirer, William L. *Berlin Diary. The Journal of a Foreign Correspondent 1934–1941.* New York: Knopf, 1941.

Shirer, William L. *The Rise and Fall of the Third Reich: A History of Nazi Germany.* New York: Simon and Schuster, 1960.

Sigmund, Anna Maria. *Des Führers bester Freund: Hitler, seine Nichte Geli Raubal und der "Ehrenarier" Emil Maurice—eine Dreiecksbeziehung.* Munich: Wilhelm Heyne Verlag, 2005.

Sigmund, Anna Maria. *Women of the Third Reich.* Richmond Hill, ON: NDE Publishing, 2000.

Smith, Truman. *Berlin Alert: The Memoirs and Reports of Truman Smith.* Stanford, CA: Hoover Institution Press, 1984.

Snyder, Louis L. *Encyclopedia of the Third Reich.* New York: Paragon House, 1989.

Snyder, Timothy. *Bloodlands: Europe Between Hitler and Stalin.* New York: Basic Books, 2010.

Sommer, Karl. *Beiträge zur bayerischen und deutschen Geschichte in der Zeit von 1910–1933.* Munich: Selbstverlag der Erben, 1981 (Bayerische Staatsbibliothek).

Speer, Albert. *Erinnerungen.* Berlin: Propyläen Verlag, 1969.

Steger, Bernd, "Der Hitlerprozess und Bayerns Verhältnis zum Reich 1923/24." *Vierteljahrshefte für Zeitgeschichte* 25, no. 4 (1977): 44–66.

Steinweis, Alan E. *Studying the Jew: Scholarly Antisemitism in Nazi Germany.* Cambridge, MA: Harvard University Press, 2006.

Stern, Fritz. *The Politics of Cultural Despair: A Study in the Rise of the Germanic Ideology.* Berkeley: University of California Press, 1961.

Sturm, Reinhard. "Weimarer Republik. Informationen zur politisichen Bildung." Vol. 261. Bonn: Bundeszentrale für politische Bildung (2011). ISSN 0046-9408.

Toland, John. *Adolf Hitler.* Vols. 1 and 2. New York: Doubleday, 1976.

Toland, John. *Hitler: The Pictorial Documentary of His Life.* New York: Ballantine Books, 1976.

Trevor-Roper, H. R. *The Last Days of Hitler.* New York: Macmillan, 1947.

Tyrell, Albrecht. *Führer befiehl... Selbstzeugnisse aus der "Kampfzeit" der NSDAP.* Düsseldorf: Droste Verlag, 1969.

Tyrell, Albrecht. *Vom 'Trommler' zum 'Führer': Der Wandel von Hitlers Selbstverständnis zwischen 1919 und 1924 und die Entwicklung der NSDAP.* Munich: Fink, 1975.

Ullrich, Volker. *Adolf Hitler: Biographie:* Vol. 1, *Die Jahre des Aufstiegs 1889–1939.* Frankfurt am Main: S. Fischer Verlag, 2013.

Viereck, George Sylvester. "Hitler: The German Explosive." *American Monthly,* October 1, 1923.

Von Below, Nicolaus. *At Hitler's Side: The Memoirs of Hitler's Luftwaffe Adjutant 1937–1945.* Translated by Geoffrey Brooks. London: The Military Book Club, 2001.

"Von guter Selbstzucht und Beherrschung." *Der Spiegel,* April 17, 1989, p. 61.

Waite, Robert G. L. *The Psychopathic God: Adolf Hitler.* New York: Basic Books, 1977.

Weber, Thomas. *Hitler's First War: Adolf Hitler, the Men of the List Regiment, and the First World War.* Oxford: Oxford University Press, 2010.

Wehler, Hans-Ulrich. *Scheidewege der deutschen Geschichte.* Munich: Beck, 1995.

Weinberg, Gerhard, L., ed. *Hitler's Second Book: The Unpublished Sequel to* Mein Kampf *by Adolf Hitler.* New York: Enigma Books, 2003.

Weinberg, Gerhard L., ed. *Hitler's Table Talk 1941–1944: His Private Conversations.* London: Enigma Books, 2000–2008.

Winkler, Heinrich August. *Germany: The Long Road West.* Vol. I, *1789–1933.* Translated by Alexander J. Sager. Oxford: Oxford University Press, 2006–2007.

Wucher, Albert. *Die Fahne hoch: Das Ende der Republik and Hitlers Machtübernahme.* Munich: Süddeutscher Verlag, 1963.

Zehnpfennig, Barbara. *Adolf Hitler: Mein Kampf: Weltanschauung und Programm: Studienkommentar.* Paderborn: Wilhelm Fink, 2011.

Zehnpfennig, Barbara. "Ein Buch mit Geschichte, ein Buch der Geschichte: Hitler's 'Mein Kampf,'" *Aus Politik und Zeitgeschichte,* Bundeszentrale für politische Bildung, 2015.

Zentner, Christian. *Adolf Hitlers* Mein Kampf: *Eine kommentierte Auswahl.* Munich: Paul List Verlag, 1974.

German Newspapers and Magazines Reviewed (During Hitler's Trial, 1924)

Allgemeine Rundschau
Allgemeine Zeitung
Augsburger Postzeitung
Bayerischer Kurier

Berliner Tageblatt
Darmstädter Tagblatt
Das Bayerische Vaterland
Der Bund (Bern)
Der Oberbayer
Deutsche Presse
Frankfurter Zeitung
Grossdeutsche Zeitung
Hamburger Fremdenblatt
München-Augsburger-Abendzeitung
Münchener Zeitung
Münchner Neueste Nachrichten
Münchener Post
Neue Freie Presse (Vienna)
Neue Freie Volkszeitung
Neues Münchener Tagblatt
Saarbrücker Zeitung
Süddeutsche Zeitung
Völkischer Beobachter
Völkischer Kurier
Vorwärts
Vossische Zeitung

Satirical Publications

Simplicissimus
Fliegende Blätter
Ulk
Lachen Links
Kladderadatsch

Others

New York Times
The Times (London)
Le Temps (Paris)
Le Petit Parisien (Paris)

Index

About the Author

PETER ROSS RANGE is a world-traveled journalist who has covered war, politics, and international affairs. A specialist on Germany, he has written extensively for *Time,* the *New York Times, National Geographic,* the London *Sunday Times Magazine, Playboy,* and *U.S. News & World Report,* where he was a national and White House correspondent. He has also been an Institute of Politics Fellow at Harvard's Kennedy School of Government, a guest scholar at the Woodrow Wilson International Center for Scholars in Washington, and a Distinguished International Visiting Fellow at the University of North Carolina Journalism School. He lives in Washington, DC.